George Smith

Short history of Christian missions from Abraham and Paul to Carey,

Livingstone, and Duff

George Smith

Short history of Christian missions from Abraham and Paul to Carey, Livingstone, and Duff

ISBN/EAN: 9783337263386

Printed in Europe, USA, Canada, Australia, Japan

Cover: Foto ©ninafisch / pixelio.de

More available books at **www.hansebooks.com**

Handbooks for Bible Classes and Private Students.

EDITED BY
REV. MARCUS DODS, D.D.,
AND
REV. ALEXANDER WHYTE, D.D.

IN PREPARATION.

THE BOOK OF PSALMS. By Rev. Professor BINNIE, D.D., Aberdeen.

THE GOSPEL ACCORDING TO ST. JOHN. By Rev. GEORGE REITH, M.A., Glasgow.

THE BOOK OF ACTS. By Rev. GEORGE WEBSTER THOMSON, M.A., Aberdeen.

THE FIRST EPISTLE TO THE CORINTHIANS. By Rev. MARCUS DODS, D.D., Glasgow.

THE EPISTLE TO THE PHILIPPIANS. By Rev. JAMES MELLIS, M.A., Southport.

THE EPISTLE TO THE COLOSSIANS. By Rev. SIMEON R. MACPHAIL, M.A., Liverpool.

CHURCH AND STATE. By A. TAYLOR INNES, Esq., Advocate, Edinburgh.

CHRISTIAN ETHICS. By Rev. Professor LINDSAY, D.D., Glasgow.

A LIFE OF ST. PAUL. By Rev. JAMES STALKER, M.A., Kirkcaldy.
[*Shortly.*

THE WORK OF THE SPIRIT. By Rev. Professor CANDLISH, D.D.

APOLOGETICS. By Rev. JAMES IVERACH, M.A., Aberdeen.

PALESTINE. By Rev. ARCH. HENDERSON, M.A., Crieff.

THE BOOK OF EXODUS. By JAMES MACGREGOR, D.D., late of New College, Edinburgh.

[*For Volumes already issued see next page.*

HANDBOOKS FOR BIBLE CLASSES.

NOW READY.

THE EPISTLE TO THE GALATIANS. By JAMES MACGREGOR, D.D., late of New College, Edinburgh. *Price* 1s. 6d.

THE POST-EXILIAN PROPHETS. With Introductions and Notes. By Rev. MARCUS DODS, D.D., Glasgow. *Price* 2s.

A LIFE OF CHRIST. By Rev. JAMES STALKER, M.A., Kirkcaldy. *Price* 1s. 6d.

THE SACRAMENTS. By Rev. Professor CANDLISH, D.D., Glasgow. *Price* 1s. 6d.

THE BOOKS OF CHRONICLES. By Rev. Professor MURPHY, LL.D., Belfast. *Price* 1s. 6d.

THE CONFESSION OF FAITH. By Rev. JOHN MACPHERSON, M.A., Findhorn. *Price* 2s.

THE BOOK OF JUDGES. By Rev. Principal DOUGLAS, D.D., Glasgow. *Price* 1s. 3d.

THE BOOK OF JOSHUA. By Rev. Principal DOUGLAS, D.D., Glasgow. *Price* 1s. 6d.

THE EPISTLE TO THE HEBREWS. By Rev. Professor DAVIDSON. D.D., Edinburgh. *Price* 2s. 6d.

SCOTTISH CHURCH HISTORY. By Rev. N. L. WALKER, Dysart. *Price* 1s. 6d.

THE CHURCH. By Rev. Professor BINNIE, D.D., Aberdeen. *Price* 1s. 6d.

THE REFORMATION. By Rev. Professor LINDSAY, D.D., Glasgow. *Price* 2s.

THE BOOK OF GENESIS. By Rev. MARCUS DODS, D.D., Glasgow. *Price* 2s.

THE EPISTLE TO THE ROMANS. By Rev. Principal BROWN, D.D., Aberdeen. *Price* 2s.

PRESBYTERIANISM. By Rev. JOHN MACPHERSON, M.A., Findhorn. *Price* 1s. 6d.

LESSONS ON THE LIFE OF CHRIST. By Rev. WM. SCRYMGEOUR, Glasgow. *Price* 2s. 6d.

THE SHORTER CATECHISM. By Rev. ALEXANDER WHYTE, D.D., Edinburgh. *Price* 2s. 6d.

THE GOSPEL ACCORDING TO ST. MARK. By Rev. Professor LINDSAY, D.D., Glasgow. *Price* 2s. 6d.

A SHORT HISTORY OF CHRISTIAN MISSIONS. By GEORGE SMITH, LL.D., F.R.G.S. *Price* 2s. 6d.

HANDBOOKS

FOR

BIBLE CLASSES

AND PRIVATE STUDENTS.

EDITED BY

REV. MARCUS DODS, D.D.,

AND

REV. ALEXANDER WHYTE, D.D.

A SHORT HISTORY OF CHRISTIAN MISSIONS.
BY GEORGE SMITH, LL.D., F.R.G.S.

EDINBURGH:
T. & T. CLARK, 38 GEORGE STREET.
1884.

PRINTED BY MORRISON AND GIBB,

FOR

T. & T. CLARK, EDINBURGH.

LONDON,	HAMILTON, ADAMS, AND CO.
DUBLIN,	GEORGE HERBERT.
NEW YORK,	SCRIBNER AND WELFORD.

SHORT HISTORY

OF

CHRISTIAN MISSIONS

FROM

ABRAHAM AND PAUL

TO

CAREY, LIVINGSTONE, AND DUFF

BY

GEORGE SMITH, LL.D., F.R.G.S.
COMPANION OF THE ORDER OF THE INDIAN EMPIRE
AUTHOR OF THE
'LIFE OF DR. WILSON,' 'DR. DUFF,' ETC.

EDINBURGH
T. & T. CLARK, 38 GEORGE STREET
1884

NOTE.

ALL quotations from *The New Testament of our Lord and Saviour Jesus Christ* are made from what is commonly called the Revised Version, 1881.

Facts regarding Modern Missions have been brought down to the latest date possible.

SERAMPORE HOUSE, MERCHISTON,
   EDINBURGH, 28*th April* 1884.

TABLE OF CONTENTS.

INTRODUCTION.

WHAT IS A MISSIONARY?

	PAGE
The word Missionary,	1
The word Evangelist,	2
The Theology of Missions,	4
The Historical Development of Missions,	6

PART I.

JUDAIC PREPARATION, B.C. 2000 TO A.D. 70.

CHAPTER I.

THE MISSIONARY COVENANT—FOUNDATION OF THE CITY OF GOD IN HISTORY.

Abraham the First Missionary,	7
Palestine the First Missionary Centre,	9
Melchizedek,	10
The Missionary Covenant,	11
The City of God founded,	13
The First Missionary at Work,	13
Heathenism the Prodigal Son,	14

CHAPTER II.

JUDAISM THE FIRST MISSIONARY RELIGION.

The Jewish Theocracy,	15
Relation to the Heathen of the Theocratic Revelation,	15
Jonah,	16

The Angel of Jehovah, ... 17
The Holy Spirit in the Theocracy, ... 17
Prophecy, in Seer and Psalmist, ... 17
Missionary or Messianic Psalms, ... 19
Solomon, ... 19
Isaiah, ... 20
Daniel's Two Visions of the Four Empires, ... 20
The Written Word, ... 21

CHAPTER III.

CHRIST THE KING OF THE MISSIONARY HOST—THE MISSIONARY CHARGE.

The Fulness of the Time, ... 23
The Jesus of History, ... 25
Relation of Christ to Jews and Gentiles, ... 25
Christ's Missionary Methods, ... 27
Missionary Charge to and Prayer for every Disciple, . . 28
The Kingdom of Christ, ... 30
The Parables of the Kingdom, ... 31

CHAPTER IV.

THE HOLY SPIRIT THE LEADER OF THE MISSIONARY HOST.

Christian Missions the Work of the Spirit, ... 32
The First Christian Missionaries, ... 33
Stephen, "The Crown," 34
Paul, the Apostle of the Nations, ... 35
Christianity conquering the Cities, ... 36
The Name Christian, ... 37
Paul's Three Mission Tours from Antioch, ... 38
John the Divine, ... 42
The Missionary Apocalypse, ... 43

PART II.

LATIN PREPARATION, A.D. 70 TO 1784.

CHAPTER V.

THE ROMAN EMPIRE SUBDUED BY THE CITY OF GOD.

Christianity after the Fall of Jerusalem, ... 47
Christianity and the Empire, ... 48

	PAGE
The Ten Persecutions,	49
The First Missionary Triumph,	50
The Destruction of Paganism,	51
The Conversion of the Empire,	52
The Four Patriarchates of the East,	53
Alexandria as a Missionary Centre,	54
Pantænus and the Catechumens' School,	55
Cosmas, the Merchant-Missionary,	56
Constantine,	57
Constantine's Christian Legislation,	57
Council of Nicæa,	58
Theodosius,	58

CHAPTER VI.

THE CONVERSION OF THE SCOTS AND ENGLISH.

Britain from the first a Missionary Land,	59
The Romano-British Church,	59
Gildas the Wise,	60
The Scots of Ireland,	61
Sukkat or Patricius,	62
Colum or Columba,	65
The Culdees,	67
The Man Columba,	68
The Columban Church,	70
The Romano-English Church,	71
Gregory the Great,	71
St. Augustin,	72
Absorption of the British by the Papal Church,	73
Hild or Hilda,	75
Cuthbert,	76
Theodore,	76

CHAPTER VII.

THE CONVERSION OF THE GOTHS AND THE FRANKS.

The Gothic Nation,	77
Arianism a Compromise with Heathenism,	77
Ulfila, the Apostle of the Goths,	78
Chrysostom,	80
Valentinus,	80
Jerome,	80
The Franks,	81
Martin of Tours,	81
The Anti-Arian Baptism of Clovis,	82
Honoratus, Germanus, Lupus, Cæsarius,	83
Columbanus, Gallus, Kilian, Tradpert,	84

CHAPTER VIII.

THE CONVERSION OF THE TEUTONS AND THE NORTHMEN.

	PAGE
Scots and Anglo-Romish Missionaries contrasted,	85
Winfrith or Bonifacius,	86
Walpurga,	89
Bæda,	89
Alcuin,	89
King Ælfred,	90
The Northmen,	91
Anskar	91
Norway,	93
Conversion of Western Europe,	94

CHAPTER IX.

MISSIONS TO SLAVS, MOHAMMEDANS, AND JEWS.

The Slavs,	96
Cyrillus and Methodius,	96
Adalbert of Prussia,	97
Otto of Bamberg,	98
Vladimir of Russia's Baptism,	99
The Saracens and the Crusades,	100
Francis of Assisi,	101
Marco Polo and Franciscan Missions,	102
Raimundus Lullius,	102
The First Missionary to the Mohammedans,	103
Monte Corvino,	108
Intolerant Missions,	109

CHAPTER X.

THE REFORMATION ONLY INDIRECTLY MISSIONARY.

The Reformation a Home Mission,	110
The Discovery of America and the Opening up of India,	111
John Wiclif,	112
Martin Luther,	113
Melancthon,	114
Erasmus,	114
The Missionary Treatise of Erasmus,	115
Coligny and Calvin,	119
Gustavus Vasa of Sweden,	119
Oxenstierna,	120

CHAPTER XI.

THE DAWN OF MODERN MISSIONS—THE DANISH-HALLE AND MORAVIAN MISSIONS.

	PAGE
Two Reformation Principles of Missions,	121
Grotius and Walæus,	122
Lutheran Orthodoxy and Missionary Pietism,	123
Baron von Welz,	123
Leibniz,	124
Danish-Halle Mission to India,	124
Hans Egéde,	127
Missions of the Unitas Fratrum,	127
Count von Zinzendorf,	128
Growth of the Moravian Missions,	129
Franke's and Zinzendorf's Work,	131

CHAPTER XII.

THE DAWN OF MODERN MISSIONS—THE ENGLISH IN NORTH AMERICA AND IN INDIA.

The Open Door and the Open Eye,	132
Scotland,	132
England,	133
The Pilgrim Fathers,	134
The First Protestant Missionary Corporation,	135
Cromwell,	135
John Eliot,	136
The Mayhews and Brainerds,	137
The Wesleys,	138
The East India Company,	138
Schwartz,	141
Kiernander,	142
The Real Missionary Influence of the East India Company,	144

CHAPTER XIII.

THE MISSIONARY COMPROMISE OF THE LATIN CHURCH WITH HEATHENISM.

Monachism and Missions,	145
The Counter-Reformation,	146
Francis Xavier,	146
Xavier's Missionary Principles,	147
Xavier's Missionary Methods,	148
Propaganda Institutions,	149

	PAGE
India—Results,	150
The Madura Mission,	150
Goa and the Present Organization of Indo-Romish Missions,	151
Japan, China, and the Philippine Islands,	151
Africa,	153
Results,	154

PART III.
ENGLISH-SPEAKING UNIVERSAL EVANGELIZATION, 1784–1884.

CHAPTER XIV.
FOUNDATION OF ENGLISH MISSIONS—WILLIAM CAREY THE FIRST ENGLISH MISSIONARY, 1761–1834.

Prayer the Origin of Modern Missions,	155
William Carey the First Englishman who was a Foreign Missionary,	157
Foundation of the Baptist Society,	159
Carey's Six Years of Preparation in Dinajpore,	160
Abraham and Carey,	161
Carey, Marshman, and Ward in Serampore—Financial,	162
Carey, Marshman, and Ward in Serampore—Spiritual,	163
Results of the Serampore Mission,	164
Death and Burial of William Carey,	165
Progress of the Baptist Missionary Society,	165

CHAPTER XV.
THE GREAT MISSIONARY AND BIBLE SOCIETIES, 1792.

England and Scotland—

The London Missionary Society,	166
The Scottish Missionary Society,	168
The Glasgow Missionary Society,	169
Robert Haldane's Proposed India Mission,	170
The Church Missionary Society,	171
Bible and Pure Literature Societies,	172
Christian Missions to the Jews by Societies,	174
The Wesleyan Methodist Missionary Society,	175
The Society for the Propagation of the Gospel in Foreign Parts,	175
The Society of Friends,	176
Medical Missions,	176
Women's Missions,	177

The United States of America—

The Board of Commissioners for Foreign Missions,	177
The Baptist Missionary Union,	178
The Methodist Episcopal Society,	179
The American Bible and Tract Societies,	179

The Continent of Europe—

The Netherlands Missionary Society,	180
The German Protestant Missionary Societies,	181
The Paris Society for Evangelical Missions,	182
The Norwegian, Swedish, and Swiss Societies,	182

CHAPTER XVI.

THE CHURCHES BECOME MISSIONARY, 1830.

Scotland, Ireland, and England—

The Church v. a Society as a Missionary Organization,	183
Alexander Duff,	184
The Free Church of Scotland's Foreign Missions,	185
The Established Church of Scotland,	188
The United Presbyterian Church of Scotland,	188
The Presbyterian Church of Ireland,	189
The Presbyterian Church of England,	189
The Presbyterian Churches of the Colonies, Canada, Australasia, South Africa,	190

The United States of America—

The Presbyterian Church, North and South,	191
The Protestant Episcopal Church,	191
The United Presbyterian Church,	191
The Reformed (Dutch) Church and the Reformed Presbyterian Church,	192
The Evangelical Lutheran Church,	192
General Results of Foreign Missionary Churches and Societies,	192

CHAPTER XVII.

EVANGELICAL MISSIONS AND MANKIND.

Christians and Non-Christians in 1884,	194
Native Christians (Reformed) in 1884,	196
Communicants,	196

CONTENTS.

Asia— PAGE

British Asia,	199
India and Burma,	200
Ceylon, Straits Settlements, Mauritius,	200
Russian Asia,	201
Portuguese Asia,	202
French Asia	202
Dutch Asia,	202
China,	202
Corea,	203
Japan,	204
Siam,	205
Turkey,	205
Persia,	207
Arabia,	207

Australasia and South Seas—

Australasia,	208
New Zealand,	208
South Sea Islands,	208

The Two Americas—

Greenland and Labrador,	208
Red Indians in Canada and United States,	208
West Indies,	208
Central and South America,	208

Africa and Madagascar—

Egypt,	209
West Africa,	210
South Africa,	210
East and Central Africa,	210
Madagascar and Other Islands,	210
The Position,	210
The Future,	211

CHAPTER XVIII.

SHORT BIBLIOGRAPHY OF MISSIONS.

General,	213
India,	214
China and Japan,	215
Australasia and South Seas,	215
America,	215
Africa and Madagascar,	216
General Missionary Conferences,	216
English Periodicals,	217
Christianity the Reason of History,	218

INDEX,	219

SHORT HISTORY OF CHRISTIAN MISSIONS.

INTRODUCTION.

WHAT IS A MISSIONARY?

The word Missionary—The word Evangelist—The Theology of Missions—Augustine, Milton, Duff, Jonathan Edwards, Leighton—The Historical Development of Christian Missions.

The word Missionary, from the Latin, is the same as the word apostle, from the Greek, meaning one sent or sent forth. Besides being the special title of the Galilæans and of Paul, whom Jesus Christ personally selected, trained, and supernaturally endowed to be the first distinctively Christian missionaries of the Holy Spirit, the word apostles is applied to others in the New Testament, where it is translated "messengers" or missionaries. To the Corinthian church Paul described the brethren who had been appointed by the churches to travel with him, as "the messengers of the churches, the glory of Christ" (2 Cor. viii. 23). To the saints in Christ Jesus at Philippi, Paul wrote of Epaphroditus, whom he was sending to them, as "my brother and fellow-worker and fellow-soldier, and your messenger" or apostle (Phil. ii. 25). The missionary, then and now, is one called by God, obedient to the command of the Risen Lord, endowed with the Spirit of Christ, and sent forth from Christendom to non-Christian peoples. He is sent by the whole body of believers forming any one of its Churches, or by a society of believers acting in place of or independently of an organized church, to make disciples of all nations, baptizing them in the name of the Father, and of the Son, and of the Holy Ghost. The *subject* of the mission is Christ's death and resurrection for repentance and remission of sins, as described by the Risen Lord (Luke xxiv. 46, 47). It behoved "that the Christ should suffer and rise again from the dead the third day; and that repentance and remission of sins should be preached in His name among all the nations, beginning from Jerusalem: ye are witnesses of these things." The *methods* of the mission are stated in Matthew's report (xxviii. 19, 20) of the farewell commandments which Jesus on earth gave "through the Holy Ghost," as teaching or discipling; by Mark (xvi. 15-20), as preaching or heralding, accompanied by powers of healing, speaking with new tongues, and casting out devils; by Luke, as witnessing unto Christ unto the uttermost part of the earth; by John, on the Risen Lord's third appearance (xxi. 15-17), as feeding and tending His lambs and His sheep. The subject is one unchangeable truth, historical fact, gracious revelation centred in the person of Christ as God; the methods through which the life-giving truth may be presented are varied as the needs, the circumstances, the culture of the nations among whom the missions are placed. The *persons* who may be sent are all members of the Church of Christ, both men and women, represented by the first Christians to whom Christ entrusted the commission as He ascended; even sons and daughters, young men and handmaidens, who were among the "all" filled with the Holy Spirit on the day of Pentecost (Acts ii. 4-21), according to the word of the prophet Joel. For each member of the body of Christ a missionary place may be found now, as it was in the experience of the Apostolic Church. The many who are not called to go themselves, are bound to send substitutes for the service,—sons, daughters, offerings,—and to pray without ceasing to the Lord of the harvest. As a matter of order and historical adaptation to the conditions of non-Christian peoples, missionaries are ordained to preach, trained to teach, certificated to heal, and skilled to win savage races from lawlessness by the industrial arts. But every method is evangelistic, being subordinated to the one message to sinful men (Rom. iii. 25, 26), "Christ Jesus, whom God set forth a propitiation, through faith, by His blood, to show His righteousness, because of the passing over of the sins done aforetime, in the forbearance of God, . . . that He might Himself be just and the justifier of him that hath faith in Jesus."

The word Evangelist, meaning the publisher of glad tidings, was applied to an order which, like the apostles proper, passed away with the Apostolic Church. But it best describes the ideal and the work of the missionary to non-Christians, as distinguished from the minister, or pastor, or teacher, settled over a fixed Christian congregation or community. The ascending Lord "gave some to be apostles; and some, prophets; and some, evangelists; and some, pastors and teachers." There the missionary stands midway between the apostles and prophets on the one hand, and the pastors and teachers on the other. He is the evangelist whose work it is to found churches, not to be fixed as the pastor or teacher of any one church. If the twelve apostles had successors, these were the evangelists, the missionaries. All missionary methods, apostolic and modern, have for their immediate and highest object the foundation of indigenous congregations of a Native Church. When such congregations have been fostered into living, expanding, aggressive units, the time comes for the foreign missionary overseer, whether he be Presbyterian, Congregational, or Episcopalian in his polity, to push on to unevangelized districts, encouraging or allowing the Native Church to rise to "the full measure of its duties and responsibilities, until it possesses an organic independent existence of its own." This is common sense, and it was apostolic practice. Paul, the model of all missionaries, spoke the gospel of God, now "with much contention," "not in word only, but also in power, and in the Holy Ghost, and in much assurance" (1 Thess. i. 5); and again "even as a nurse cherisheth her children" (1 Thess. ii. 7). Not a few Gentiles "turned from idols to serve the living and true God." These, as brethren, disciples, saints, were then formed into a society or *ecclesia*, in every city, under elders and deacons appointed with the consent of the congregation. Each church was organized not only for its own spiritual growth, but on a system of charity towards the more needy saints and of missionary development all around it. But outside both of the apostles who were to pass away, and of the presbyters and deacons who were congregational, there was the evangelist. Philip, one of the first seven deacons of the church at Jerusalem, became "the evangelist," who, through the chamberlain of Candace, brought Ethiopia to Christ; who, from the Roman and Eastern splendour of Cæsarea, seems to have done more than even James to win Syria to the Cross. Timothy, who was Paul's vicar-apostolic at Ephesus, was thus counselled: "Do the work of an evangelist, make full proof of thy ministry. For I am now ready to be offered, and the time of my departure is at hand." The apostles apart, Stephen,

Philip, and Timothy were the first missionaries; they held the office of which every true missionary has been prouder than of all other positions or callings, ecclesiastical or secular.

The Theology of Missions is carried back by Augustine in his great missionary treatise, *De Civitate Dei*, to the difference (*diversitas*) that arose among the angels. In that his fine spiritual instinct finds the beginnings of the kingdom of God, if the new federation of fallen principalities and powers, of the world-rulers of this darkness, and the spiritual hosts of wickedness in the heavenly places (Eph. vi. 12), were not to be allowed to corrupt the human race. Milton has followed this method throughout his two poems, which form one grand missionary epic.[1] The whole angelology of Milton, from the Father's declaration of His decree that to the Son every knee shall bow, through the devil's temporary triumph in the fall of man, to his tremendous defeat after the temptation in the wilderness, is based on and splendidly illustrated by the missionary progress:—

> "Hail, Son of the Most High, heir of both worlds,
> Queller of Satan, on Thy glorious work
> Now enter, and begin to save mankind."

Throughout, therefore, Milton sees in the idolatry of successive ages the personalities of evil incarnated to mislead mankind—

> "And devils to adore for deities."

The most fervid expounder of missions, as well as most devoted missionary worker in modern times, Dr. Duff, went farther back still, finding the root of missions, their supreme importance and unearthly grandeur, in the decrees of God. "The purpose from all eternity to create the universe, visible and invisible, for the manifestation of the divine glory, the permission of the fall of man, in order that, through the assumption of human nature by the everlasting Son of the Father and the sacrificial shedding of His precious blood, myriads of the fallen and guilty might be redeemed and exalted to a higher position than that from which they fell, and all this in a way so marvellous that the glory of the attributes and perfections of the Supreme God might shine forth more brightly therein than in all the works of creation besides; the immeasurable antiquity as regards conception and purpose, the

---

[1] The *Paradise Lost* and *Paradise Regained* should be read in this light, along with the poet's Latin *Treatise on Christian Doctrine*, discovered only sixty years ago, and translated by Bishop Sumner.

elevation and unearthly grandeur of the missionary enterprise when thus viewed in its true scriptural light, as the divinely-appointed means of carrying forward the great scheme of redemption to its glorious consummation;"—such was Duff's description to his students of the lofty design of missions, which inspired him to be what he became.

The first Evangel-message, as it has been called, is that of Gen. iii. 15, in which the Messianic hope bursts forth, in the declaration that the contest with evil to which the human race became exposed by the Fall, shall issue in ultimate victory, though not without injury. Jonathan Edwards, in his *History of the Work of Redemption*, began with the Fall of Man. Theologically his work should be read, but it was written at a time when modern missions had hardly come to the birth, at the spiritually most barren period of the Church's life.

The time has come for scholars to study the methods and results of the missionary enterprise, and from these to generalize new chapters in both Apologetic and Homiletic Theology. The idea which Edwards expressed when, in 1739, he entitled his history of the work of redemption, *Outlines of a Body of Divinity in a Method entirely new*, can be realized only now when the Church has entered and is rejoicing in its first missionary epoch worthy of the name.

Concerning the salvation which some five thousand Protestant foreign missionaries, and some thirty thousand native missionaries of all kinds, are now preaching in almost every heathen land, and to at least half the whole number of Mohammedans, the Apostle Peter represents the prophets as "searching what time or what manner of time the Spirit of Christ which was in them did point unto, when it testified beforehand the sufferings of Christ and the glories that should follow them; . . . which things angels desire to look into" (1 Pet. i. 11, 12). Leighton, writing about 1650, thus comments on this passage, in language which Coleridge pronounces to be the most beautiful allegory he had anywhere read:—

"This sweet stream of their doctrine did, as a river, make its own banks fertile and pleasant as it ran by, and flowed still forward to after ages, and by the confluence of more such prophecies, grew greater as it went, till it fell in with the main current of the gospel in the New Testament, both acted and preached by the Great Prophet Himself whom they foretold to come, and recorded by His apostles and evangelists, and thus united into one river, clear as crystal. This doctrine of salvation in the Scriptures hath still refreshed the City of God, His Church under the gospel, and still will do so till it empty itself into the ocean of eternity. . . . The agreement of the predictions of the prophets with the things themselves, and the preaching of the apostles following, make up one organ or great instrument, tuned by the same hand and sounding by the same breath of the Spirit of God. . . . For this end He sent His Son out of His bosom, and for this end He sends forth His messengers to divulge that salvation which His Son hath wrought, and sends down His Spirit upon them that they may be fitted for so high a service. . . .

"The cherubim wonder how guilty man escapes their flaming swords and re-enters Paradise. The angels see that their companions who fell are not restored, but behold their room filled up with the spirits of just men, and they envy it not. . . . The angels look upon what they have already seen with delight and admiration, and what remains, namely, the full accomplishment of this great work in the end of time, they look upon with desire to see it finished,—that mystery of godliness, God manifested in the flesh, and, it is added, seen of angels (1 Tim. iii. 16).

"We see here excellent company, and examples not only of the best of men that have been,—we have them for fellow-servants and fellow-students, —but if that can persuade us, we can all study the same lesson with the very angels, and have the same thoughts with them. This the soul doth which often entertains itself with the delightful admiration of Jesus Christ and the redemption He hath wrought for us."

The Historical Development of Christian Missions is the subject with which we have to deal. That begins with Abraham as a preparation; it culminates in the conversion of the Roman Empire; it is continued in the conversion of the peoples of Europe to the Reformation of the sixteenth century, and in the Peace of 1783 which recognised the independence of the American Republic. This *Præparatio Evangelica* then passes into the organized and truly catholic attempts to evangelize all nations, for which Great Britain's possession of India and many Colonies, and America's marvellous extension, have made the past century remarkable, though, at the best and in the light of the future, this is still the day of small things.

Part I. Judaic Preparation, 2000 B.C. to 70 A.D.

Part II. Latin Preparation, 70 to 1784 A.D.

Part III. English-speaking Universal Evangelization—One Century, 1784 to 1884 A.D.

PART I.

JUDAIC PREPARATION, B.C. 2000 TO A.D. 70.

CHAPTER I.

THE MISSIONARY COVENANT—FOUNDATION OF THE CITY OF GOD IN HISTORY.

Abraham the First Missionary—Palestine the First Missionary Centre—Melchizedek—The Missionary Covenant—The City of God founded—The First Missionary at Work—Heathenism the Prodigal Son.

Abraham ("father of a multitude") opens the long procession of missionaries, inspired and uninspired, who cover the period of the last four thousand years which the birth of Christ divides into two equal portions. The Eternal Son of the Father, who declared, "Verily, verily, I say unto you, Before Abraham was, I am," linked the patriarch on to Himself and His own kingdom in the significant words, "Abraham rejoiced to see my day, and he saw it and was glad" (John viii. 56). Abraham was the first man whom God sent forth as a missionary; the first in whom He adopted the policy of separating the Church from the world, believers from idolators, that the Church might be strong to evangelize the world; the first individual whom He admitted to covenant-making with Himself. Abraham was the founder at once of the catholic Church in all ages, of the circumcised Jewish race who became the custodiers of the first missionary religion, of the human family from whom Christ came in the flesh, and of the Arab race whom Mohammedanism has converted into the most aggressive foes of Christ. The Epistles to the Romans, Galatians, and Hebrews show, dogmatically, that Abraham was at once a type of Christ and the Old Testament precursor of Paul, who, two thousand years after, applied to the Gentiles Abraham's universal doctrines of faith, forgiveness, and righteousness, historically consummated in the death, the resurrection, and the mediatorial reign which form the "day" of Christ.

Four hundred years after the Flood, the Shemite or Semitic family of Terach was settled among the Hamitic tribes of the coast of the Persian Gulf, where the Euphrates unites with the Tigris river. Idolatry had so spread that even this Shemitic family had become infected. The traditions of the Talmud and Koran alike represent Terach as a maker and seller of idols, like the teraphim which his descendant Laban used in Jacob's time. The same legends picture the young Abraham as an early protester against idolatry and the worship of the sun, moon, and fire. The place was Ur or Hur, now Mugheir, then known for its Chaldæan temple to the Moon-god. The time was about 2000 B.C., when there appeared to Abraham, what the first Christian martyr Stephen described as "the God of glory," and said unto him, "Get thee out of thy land and from thy kindred, and come unto the land which I shall show thee." It was the first missionary call, often repeated since to prophet and apostle by the Angel of the covenant, by the Lord of glory in the flesh, by the Lord in glory especially to Paul,—repeated not less really though in the still small voice, in dream and vision, or in startling providence, to the modern missionary. The call has been always the same, to "get out" from home, to "come" to the land of God's choosing, to "go" to the people who cry for help, to "leave" kindred and all things "for My sake and the gospel's."

The family consisted of the father Terach, the ninth in descent from Shem after the Flood, and three boys, Abram ("father of elevation") as he was first called, Nahor, and Haran. Nahor remained behind (Gen. xi. 31), at least for a time, and Haran had died, leaving a son, Lot. With the intention of reaching the far-distant and fertile Syrian coast of the Mediterranean at Canaan, Abram set out, with Sarah ("princess") his wife and half-sister, Terach his father, and Lot his nephew. They followed the river up its fertile valley for four hundred miles to a camping ground on the little Belik tributary, at a spot fifty miles to the east of the Euphrates, on the edge of the desert. They named the settlement Haran, in memory of the dead son and brother. There Terach died during the long halt, while Abraham was being ripened in years and faith and the wisdom of the highest civilisation of that day, for the next step; Haran became his college. We have the original clay tablets of the time, and the later Assyrian translations, found in the very spots; and the book of Genesis itself tells us of the "signet" of Judah in the third generation after. So wondrously has the personality of Abraham marked history at its earliest source, that the Talmud, Josephus, and the Koran represent Abraham as introducing into Egypt the knowledge of astronomy and arithmetic; the Parsees see in him their Zoroaster or Zarathustra; and all the traditions unite in attributing to him the authorship of certain books. In Haran, however, no more than in Hur, was he separate from idolatry. The last traces of the old life passed away with his father Terach. The desert had to be placed between the infant Church and the universal heathenism; he crossed it by "the way of holiness" familiar to his descendants, and used by the magi on their way to Bethlehem. The missionary Abraham was seventy-five years of age, and had yet a hundred years before him, when, after a short halt at Damascus, where the Arabs still profess to show his habitation, he symbolically took possession of "the promised land" by building an altar first at Shechem, then near Bethel, and then at Hebron, on the way to Egypt. The divine call, which had silently drawn him at Hur, and had audibly spoken at Haran of "a land that I will show thee," and of "a great nation that I will make thee," declared at these three central spots, "All the land which thou seest, to thee will I give it; . . . and I will make thy seed as the dust of the earth" for number.

Palestine thus became the first, the greatest Missionary Centre of the race, for the two thousand years from Abraham to Christ. In itself emphatically the shepherd-land of antiquity, with a soil and a climate which God Himself made the theme of prophet and of poet, in geographical position it is without a rival. In Asia this portion of Syria touches Africa on the one side, and Europe on the other. It is the chief gate between East and West, South and North. Flanked by the only other centres of world-wide empire which the history of civilisation commemorates, Alexandria and Constantinople, it commands them both. What Western Syria was to the earliest civilisation, standing between the Euphrates and the Nile on one side, and the Bosphorus on the other, it is still, notwithstanding the barren hoof of the Muslim. Close to Hebron, its southern hollow is the object of the ambition of the world-powers of the present day, and is still the greatest missionary and military and commercial route to the far East from which Abraham came. Its northern valleys are prevented only by Turkish misrule from becoming the line of "the world's highway" connecting the railway systems of Europe and British India. The future of missionary triumphs, even more than the past of history, is with this Syrian shore, with Hebron and Calvary. Abraham came to spend nearly a century among a people of the "lowlands," or Canaan, who had borrowed the primitive Accadian belief from which he had migrated, the foul worship of the Sun-god in the male form of Baal, represented by manifold Baalim, and of the female form of Ashtoreth in a thousand Ashtaroth. He came to a land of human sacrifices, the devotion ignorantly expressed by which God sanctified to the covenanting family, first typically by the substitution of a ram for Isaac, and nationally by circumcision.

If Hur, and Haran, and Egypt, which stress of famine led Abraham to visit, were already so given over to idol and nature worship that a later prophet described Chaldea as "the land of graven images, and they are mad upon their idols" (Jer. l. 38), much more was **Canaan.** The cruelty of Moloch and the impurity of Ashtoreth were filling the cup of iniquity which sank the people to a depth of horror probably unmatched in the history of the race. Wandering about among the fathers of those whom his three millions of descendants were afterwards to exterminate, Abraham represented and practised the faith and the worship of Adam and Enoch and Noah; this was the one personal, righteous, "most high God, possessor of heaven and earth," whose promise to Adam and Noah had been confirmed in his own call, that neither flaming sword nor drowning flood shall destroy man, but in himself "shall all families of the earth be blessed." With Abraham as with Adam and his first-born, the only sanctuary was the altar under the vault of heaven, and on it the firstlings of the flock; the only home a nomadic tent, which was moved south from Ebal and Gerizzim to Egypt and back to Hebron. But as the scholar finds in ancient paganism, and the modern missionary in the conscience and traditions of heathenism, traces of the knowledge of the one true God, to which witness a successful appeal may be made, so was it with Abraham, at a time not five centuries removed from the early deposit of divine truth in Noah and Shem.

Melchizedek stands out for a moment, clear and yet mysterious, from the mist which the secular writer calls prehistoric, but which Holy Scripture irradiates with peculiar light. He at least of all his age and race, without outward call or recorded consecration like Abraham's, appears as greater than Abraham, who paid him tithes, and received, in the bread and wine, his kingly, priestly blessing (Gen. xiv. 18–20). He was historically the leader of one of those Shemite migrations such as had led Abraham's family as far south as the Persian Gulf. Melchizedek's family had never fallen away into idolatry as Terach's seems to have done. King of Salem, most probably the Jerusalem of after times, and "priest of the most high God," Melchizedek is employed by David (Ps. cx. 4), with the approval of our Lord (Matt. xxii. 41–45), as a higher type of Christ than Abraham was even when about to sacrifice Isaac on Mount Moriah. But both agree in their superiority, as catholic representatives or missionaries of the God of all the families of the earth, to the narrow and temporary uses of Judaism and its Levitical priesthood. Paul, in the Epistle to the Romans (iv.), puts Abraham in his right place as the heir of the world through the righteousness of faith, before circumcision. The Epistle to the Hebrews, while exalting the faith of Abraham as the missionary founder of the city of God upon earth (xi. 10), makes Melchizedek's position and history an argument for the inferior and temporary character of that secondary portion of the work of Abraham, as the circumcised father of the Jews, through whose Levitical priesthood "perfection" or completeness could not be obtained. Thus early were peace and righteousness, the forgiveness of sins and the doing of God's will, proclaimed by a priest-king whom the Messiah accepted as His type, as faith and obedience were declared by Abraham, who saw the "day" of Christ and was glad.

The Missionary Covenant was now made with Abraham. After ten years' wanderings, during which God had said to him, "This is the land," but had not made similarly plain where the seed was to come from, even Abraham's faith cried for fruit: "What wilt Thou give me, seeing I go childless?" So his faithful descendants of all missionary races in all ages since have often cried, and the Lord Himself has pointed them to the husbandman who hath long patience, till the seed becomes precious fruit. The answer to Abraham was God's offer of Himself: "Fear not, I am thy shield and thy exceeding great reward." God is better than all or anything that His servants desire, even, as they think, for the good of His kingdom. Sons, in the flesh or in the faith, will come in troops, at the right time, to the man who has as his shield and reward the most high God, possessor of heaven and earth. So God gave Himself to Abraham, as He had never done to man before, in a covenant, made not with the race as in Noah's time to save the bodies of men, but with the spiritual father of all who should believe. Next to the gift of His own Son, in the incarnation and its messages to the virgin mother and the watching shepherds, there is no such example of God's grace to sinful man as the first of all covenants, the conditioned pledge to Abraham, and through him to the race. For thirty hours, from sun-down on one day to dark night on the next, the first missionary, at the very midtime of his life, sat in watchful meditation or lay in wrapt vision (Gen. xv.) beside the five sacrificial animals which he had divided, so that God might visibly pass between them. Against the midnight horror of great darkness, the man saw God as a pillar of fire enwrapped in smoke, ratifying the covenant graciously but awfully after the manner of men. His own personal life, his heirs' and that of his descendants after the flesh for the next four centuries, were revealed to him.

But before and far above that came the word of the Lord who had placed him under the nightly vault of the Syrian sky: "Look now toward heaven and tell the stars, if thou be able to number them; so shall thy seed be." "And he believed in the Lord, and He counted it to him for righteousness." Paul, the apostolic missionary to the non-Jewish world, most plainly applies the universal covenant with Abraham, "the father of all that believe," in his Epistle to the Romans (iv.), and still more in detail in that to the Galatians (iii. 8–29). "The Scripture, foreseeing that God would justify the nations by faith, preached the gospel beforehand unto Abraham, saying, In thee shall all the nations be blessed. . . . There can be neither Jew nor Greek, there can be neither bond nor free, there can be no male and female; for ye are all one man in Christ Jesus. And if ye are Christ's, then are ye Abraham's seed, heirs according to promise." The fulfilling of that covenant, apparently now slow, now by leaps, but always according to what has been called God's leisure and God's haste, is the History of Missions. Abraham made a mistake about Ishmael; he was ready to sacrifice Isaac; he possessed when he died only the cave at Hebron where the Mohammedans guard the tomb of him whom they call El Khaleel, the Friend of God. But every Christian who is a son of faithful Abraham knows of a surety that he will yet be glad in the sight of the "day of Christ," as this covenant made Abraham. Every missionary, who has faith to identify himself with Abraham, fears no danger, and has no distrust beside that voice, "I am thy shield;" spares no sacrifice even to the death when he realizes that pledge, "I am thy exceeding great reward."

The symbol of the universal missionary covenant is the living, life-giving fire of God's presence, veiled by the protecting, guiding cloud of His grace,—the bush burning but not consumed, viewed from the human, the Christ's side. The principle of the covenant is that each man and woman who enters into it, of every time and race and degree of culture, and all combined in one Universal Church, is appointed to preserve and to propagate, under divine power and guidance, the true knowledge of the incarnate God, "till we all attain unto the unity of the faith and of the knowledge of the Son of God unto a full-grown man, unto the measure of the stature of the fulness of Christ" (Eph. iv. 13).

The City of God was thus founded in the history of men who were building their Babylon, typical of all godlessness, on idolatries, by the "sojourner in the land of promise," the "dweller in tents" who had faith to look for "the city which hath the foundations, whose Builder and Maker is God" (Heb. xi. 10). We shall see the foundations extending, and the walls rising all through the ages; while as Babylon in all its empire-forms becomes a ruin,—fit throne for the prince of this world,—the hearts of the faithful are comforted, and their energies are stimulated by the closing vision of the last of the apostles, "the Holy City, the New Jerusalem, coming down out of heaven from God" (Rev. xxi. 2).

The First Missionary at Work.—The book of Genesis shows us Abraham not only as a missionary wanderer, as a passive example, and as a type of the Highest, but as discharging active missionary functions with a love, a zeal, and a boldness second only to those of Christ Himself. To him sitting in the tent-door in the heat of the day on the plains of Mamre, there came a Theophany, Jehovah represented by three angels. "And the Lord said, Shall I hide from Abraham the thing which I do, seeing that Abraham shall surely become a great and mighty nation, and all the nations of the earth shall be blessed in him?" (xviii. 18). The time had come for the destruction of the impenitent heathen of the vale of Siddim. Not because the nephew Lot was there, a merely passive protester against the very grievous sin of Sodom, not from purely human pity, but as divinely-called missionary, as divinely-invited intercessor, as divinely-encouraged mediator, as covenanter for the salvation of all, of every race who should believe, and specially charged with the land of which Siddim was then the fairest portion, Abraham appealed personally to the covenant God for mercy that the worst of all heathen might repent, if only fifty, or forty-five, or forty, or thirty, or twenty, or ten righteous were found in Sodom. Failing ten, even yet Abraham did not abandon hope, for he "gat up early in the morning to the place where he stood before the Lord, and he looked, . . . and, lo, the smoke of the country went up as the smoke of a furnace," and God remembered Abraham by sparing only Lot. The History of Missions begins well with the sixfold wrestling of Abraham for the vilest and most hopeless sinners to whom missionaries have ever been sent. The Dead Sea remains to tell us still that man, in his freedom, may himself place a limit to God's long-suffering, but also to assure us that God Himself counts the prayer and the labour of His Church even for peoples among whom not ten can be found righteous enough to show the work of the law written in their hearts (Rom. ii. 15). Abraham twice worked for the worst heathen, for the most hopeless race outside of the particular covenant of the Jews, but included in the universal missionary covenant,—as a conqueror, when he rescued the kings of the five cities of Siddim (Gen. xiv. 1–16) from the vengeance of Chedorlaomer, king of his own ancestral land at the head of the Persian Gulf; and as a missionary, when he mediated for them with God Himself.

Heathenism is the Prodigal Son among the swine of lust and idolatry, of self and the world, with a conscience nevertheless which repels the sin he follows, and a craving for God—a feeling after Him, if haply he may find Him—which is at once the relic of a primeval religion and the anticipation of a truth yet to be revealed to him. To recall the conscience and arouse the craving, the missionary is sent, going with a courage like Abraham's and a love like Christ's, because sure that the Judge of all the earth does right, and that it is that Judge who sends him, as He invited the mediation of His friend Abraham.

CHAPTER II.

JUDAISM THE FIRST MISSIONARY RELIGION.

The Jewish Theocracy—The Relation to the Heathen of the Theocratic Revelation—Jonah—The Angel of Jehovah—The Holy Spirit in the Theocracy—Prophecy in Seer and Psalmist—The Missionary or Messianic Psalms—Solomon—Isaiah—Daniel's two Visions—The Written Word.

The Jewish Theocracy—word first used by Josephus—formed, particularly, for the next two thousand years, the first stage of the development of the universal missionary covenant in which all the families of the earth are to bless themselves. As Creator and Lord, Jehovah is the God of all nations, but Israel was the mediatory till the Messiah came. "Ye shall be a peculiar treasure unto me above all people, for all the earth is mine; and ye shall be unto me a kingdom of priests and an holy nation" (Ex. xix. 5). The Old Testament history is a record of Israel's apostasy. The chosen nation did not always testify for the true God before the heathen, but against Him. He cast them out of the Holy Land, and scattered them among the heathen powers which ruled the very centres of Hur or Babylon, where Abraham received his first call, and Haran or Nineveh, where he heard the voice, "Get thee out." But these powers of the world, while fulfilling the counsels of God, exalted themselves against Him, so that they were destroyed, and a new generation of the covenant people returned to the covenant land with supplications. There, after the exile, the worship of the one God was carefully maintained, and the succession of the prophets culminated in the coming of the Messiah. Judaism, as a preparatory missionary system, fulfilled its purpose in the cry from the Cross, "It is finished," and entered its second and final historical judgment, which continues to this day, in the destruction of Jerusalem.

The Relation to the Heathen of the Theocratic Revelation is regulated by the gracious design of God in the universal covenant with Abraham as the first, the father, of all believers, underrunning the particular privilege of the chosen Jews. Both the Jews and the heathen suffered judgments, in their measure, because of their opposition to the purposes of the kingdom of God. But the older prophets saw that kingdom enlarged by the extension of the theocracy to heathen nations, as under David and Solomon (Amos ix. 11). The later prophets saw it enlarged not only, as then, by the sword of the theocratic king, but by the word of God, so as to include even the Ammonites and Moabites, whom the law of Deuteronomy (xxiii. 4) excluded for hiring Balaam to curse Israel. Both psalmists and prophets rejoice in the transfer of the theocratic relation to all mankind, and in the bringing in of all the precious things of the Gentiles to the glory of the divine kingdom. Such is the vision of Haggai (ii. 6, 9), who saw, as the result of the Lord's shaking of heaven and earth and of all nations, the coming of what our English Version translates as " the desire of all nations," of what Luther rendered " the consolation of all the heathen " (*aller Heiden Trost*), and of what some read literally as " the precious things of all the nations of the world." Even heathen powers are to be so turned that Egypt and Assyria shall be missionary peoples. " Israel shall be the third with Egypt and with Assyria, even a blessing in the midst of the land : whom the Lord of hosts shall bless, saying, Blessed be Egypt my people, and Assyria the work of my hands, and Israel mine inheritance " (Isa. xix. 24). The last of the prophets (Mal. i. 11) told the Jews who dishonoured God by their impure offerings, in words quoted by missionaries from Augustine to the present time, " From the rising of the sun unto the going down of the same, my name shall be great among the Gentiles, and in every place incense shall be offered unto my name, and a pure offering." The predictions of the restoration of the Jews to the covenant land, and their alliance with the Gentiles, so that these are to assist in completing the restoration (Isa. xi. 10, lxvi. 18, 21 ; Zeph. iii. 10), find their highest confirmation and interpretation in the inspired words of the Jewish missionary to the Gentiles (Rom. xi. 25, 26): "A hardening in part hath befallen Israel, until the fulness of the Gentiles be come in ; and so all Israel shall be saved : even as it is written." In the Scriptures, of which these are specimens, missions to Jews, Mohammedans, and heathen find the same historical root, the same spiritual warrant, the same divine pledge of success.

Jonah (B.C. 862) is an instance of the proud particularism of the Jews, which reached its height in the Pharisees of our Lord's time and the fall of the holy city. The book of Jonah is a no less noteworthy proof of the pity, for the heathen, of Jehovah who sent forth the reluctant missionary, and the patience of God, meant to lead them to repentance (iv. 10, 11).

The Angel of Jehovah (*Maleach*, Heb.) also watched over the development of the missionary covenant. Eleven times, from Abraham to David, did One appear, described as angel, and three times as man, but on every occasion speaking of Himself as Jehovah or God, so that we must believe each of these appearances at least to have been a true Theophany. The angel of the Lord who in the New Testament announced the coming incarnation, never speaks as God, but only as a messenger, as also at the resurrection and in the Acts of the Apostles. The Maleach Jehovah of the Old Testament is the being in whom God makes His presence known to man in a manner which the senses of man can bear, and only to develope the missionary covenant, universal or particular, by such active interposition. Until that development had reached, in history, the incarnation of God in the Son of Man and King of glory, the angel of Jehovah was typical of the incarnation.

The Holy Spirit in the Theocracy worked as the peculiar prerogative of its leaders, like Moses (Isa. lxiii. 11), of its holy men and women, and especially of the prophets and psalmists. The Spirit was an extraordinary influence which guided with wisdom in difficulty, or inspired for revelation, not an outpouring on all, nor an indwelling in every believer, as the divine gift became on and after the Pentecostal effusion. The possession of this indwelling is that which, more than any other gift, marks the Church of the new covenant off from that of the old. The prophets of the theocracy, while themselves under the supernatural influence only on extraordinary occasions, promised this outpouring and indwelling to every true member of the Church: " All thy children shall be taught of the Lord " (Isa. liv. 13); " They shall all know me, from the least of them unto the greatest of them, saith the Lord" (Jer. xxxi. 34); " I will pour out my Spirit upon all flesh " (Joel ii. 28).

Prophecy, in Seer and Psalmist, was the great missionary agency of Judaism, the chief of those creative forces which culminated in Christ. As Abraham rejoiced to see Christ's day, Isaac was led, against his personal and natural desire, to transmit the covenant blessing to Jacob; and **Jacob**, in his dying charge, to hand it on to **Judah.** The same divine sovereignty which called Abraham, as it calls men and women openly now, preferred Isaac to Ishmael, and Jacob to Esau, and Judah to his eleven brethren. That sovereignty placed women originally heathen, like **Rahab** and **Ruth**, in the covenant line of whom Christ came, as if to mark its everlasting universality as well as temporary particularism. To **Moses** the covenant vision of fire and smoke, glory veiled by grace and reached by suffering, was repeated in the burning bush. He became at once the prophet who typified the Christ, the mediator by whom the law was given, the saviour of the Judaic Church when it seemed to be almost lost amid the idolatries and the bondage of Egypt, the maker of the Abrahamic family into the Jewish nation, and its leader back to the promised land. Of that land **Joshua**, guided by One who declared Himself to be the Captain of the Lord's host, took formal possession for the twelve tribes. **David**, chosen as Isaac and Jacob had been, completed the actual possession of the whole covenant territory granted by God to Abraham, and became, in his house and his songs of prophecy, the direct founder of the stricter Messianic idea. The last words of "the man who was raised up on high, the anointed of the God of Jacob, and the sweet Psalmist of Israel," form an instructive contrast to the missionary covenant with Abraham a thousand years before, as they picture the ideal of righteous government and identify its realization with that new covenant which Christ ordered and made sure in all things (2 Sam. xxiii. 2, 3): "The Spirit of the Lord spake by me, and His word was in my tongue; the God of Israel said, the Rock of Israel spake to me, He that ruleth over men must be just, ruling in the fear of God. And he shall be as the light of the morning when the sun riseth, even a morning without clouds, as the tender grass springing out of the earth by clear shining after rain." From this time, for the next thousand years, the Messiah, the Redeemer, is expected as King, and the expectation is spread by the captive tribes and by the Dispersion, after the Restoration, until it is shared by Greek thinker and Roman emperor. While the earliest prophets, like Elijah, Joel, and Amos, are silent regarding the King and His Kingdom, the later, like Micah and Isaiah, from the middle of the eighth century, are full of Messianic prophecies, directly missionary like Zechariah's, and indirectly, like those which had their immediate fulfilment in the contemporary kings.[1]

[1] *The Post-Exilian Prophets*, by Marcus Dods, D.D., 1879.

The **Missionary or Messianic Psalms**, ii., xlv., lxxii., and cx., find their key in that last song of David, sadly confessing the failure of his own house to realize the fruitful reign of righteousness. His vision is filled by the Spirit with the completion of the theocratic kingship, and its merging into the universal power and glory of the universal kingship in One who was at once his Son and Lord. The occasion which led to the composition of Ps. xlv. may have been "the marriage of an Israelite king, perhaps Solomon, with the daughter of the Egyptian king;" but the older Jewish theology and the Church ever since have adopted the allegorical interpretation, and have found in the Messianic references the noblest strain of liturgical worship. The missionary character of the psalm is still more pronounced, for it is an ode which triumphs over the introduction of the heathen into the kingdom of God. So, too, the originally harvest pæan, Ps. lxvii. Psalm ii. roots the missionary covenant in the decree of the Father and the heirship of the whole earth by the Son. Ps. lxxii. prays for His coming as the Prince of peace, the righteous defender of the poor, and the King to whom all kings and peoples shall do homage. It quotes (verse 17) the very words of the missionary covenant, "Men shall be blessed in Him; all nations shall call Him blessed;" and concludes with a doxology which, in evangelic richness, might have closed the Apocalypse of John, "Blessed be His glorious name for ever, and let the whole earth be filled with His glory. Amen, and Amen." Psalm cx. celebrates the final subjugation of heathenism by Christ the King, and ascribes to Him the everlasting priesthood foreshadowed by Melchizedek, a union so new that its announcement is confirmed by the oath of Jehovah.

Solomon, coming midway between Abraham and Christ, in two ways advanced the development of the missionary covenant. He brought some heathen peoples under Jewish rule, and more under Judaic influence, representing to the old world of Asia the prosperity and the prestige secured by the favour of the Messiah, very much as Great Britain does now in the East. His name is thus stamped on literature and legend, mountain and river, to the present day. And he built the first temple on the Moriah summit, where Abraham offered up Isaac, but enlarged by those vast foundations which are still a marvel. This work of seven years, the hewn stones of which reproduced the tabernacle proportions just doubled, while essentially Jewish in symbol and ritual, was a visible protest and a proof to all of the unity and the power of the personal Jehovah. The prayer and sacrifice by which the typical king, in all his glory, dedicated the building, recognised the universal character of the covenant on which that of the Jews rested, in the requests on behalf of "a stranger that is not of Thy people Israel, but cometh out of a far country for Thy name's sake" (1 Kings viii. 41); "Hear Thou in heaven Thy dwelling-place, and do according to all that the stranger calleth to Thee for; that all people of the earth may know Thy name, to fear Thee." "I have heard thy prayer and thy supplication which thou hast made before me," was the divine answer.

Isaiah, of the later prophets of Judah and Israel, most fully developes the idea of the Messiah, justifying the ways of God to the apostate Jews amid the catastrophes which scattered them for a time. The last twenty-seven chapters (xl.–lxvi.) picture in detail the mission of the Servant of Jehovah to all the human race. There is nothing in inspired literature so consoling to the missionary Church and the faithful solitary missionary, as this message, which bursts forth, "Comfort ye, comfort ye, my people, saith your Lord," and at once leaps over seven hundred years to the voice of him that crieth in the wilderness: "O Jerusalem, that bringest good tidings, lift up thy voice with strength: lift it up, be not afraid; say unto the cities of Judah, Behold your God" (xl. 10). It was on the reference to Abraham, "I called him alone, and blessed him, and increased him" (li. 2), that Carey used to stay himself before he had a convert. The central figure of the prophecy is "My Servant," with marred visage and form, sprinkling many nations, cut off out of the land of the living for the transgression of "My people," an offering for sin, but justifying many, dividing the spoil with the strong. The prayer of Solomon for the sons of the stranger becomes amplified with evangelical fulness: "Even them will I bring to my holy mountain, and make them joyful in my house of prayer; . . . for mine house shall be called an house of prayer for all nations" (lvi. 7). Thus is introduced the New Jerusalem, the City of God.

Daniel's Two Visions of the Four Empires, if less rich, are more particular, and almost historical in their details (ii. and vii.). A colossal image, signifying the unity of heathenism in its opposition to God, is composed of four kingdoms; and four great beasts rise successively out of the sea, tossed by the four winds of heaven, as the heathen world is storm-tossed. They are destroyed by the kingdom of God, as a Little Stone not made with hands, growing greater till it fills the earth; yea, in the second vision, by the Son of Man Himself, whom Daniel beheld as He "came with the clouds of heaven, and came to the Ancient of days. And they brought Him near before Him; and there was given Him dominion, and glory, and a kingdom, that all people, nations, and languages should serve Him: His dominion is an everlasting dominion, which shall not pass away, and His kingdom that which shall not be destroyed" (vii. 13). The older critics immediately interpret the four kingdoms as the Chaldæan, Medo-Persian, Grecian, and Roman; the successive empires of gold, of silver, of brass, and of iron, which have preceded the missionary kingdom of Christ. A full History of Missions would trace the working out of God's purpose through them all. It is significant that we find the latest and, by general acknowledgment, the first authority on Roman Britain writing thus, as the closing passage of his secular history[1]: "This land of Britain, which has a wondrous history and holds so high a place among the nations of the earth, shows in every part traces of the fourth great empire—the Iron—which was to precede the coming of a better and kindlier dominion, the Little Stone cut out of the mountain without hands, which grew great and filled the earth. We have distinct traces in every part of this island how that great Iron Empire sought to fix itself firmly, and to mingle with the seed of men, but did not prevail. It failed because it was based upon an unsound principle, that of force and conquest rather than of justice and truth; but we have also seen how it prepared the way for a better kingdom, which has taken root and filled the land, and has substituted truth and justice, tempered with mercy, for despotic military rule." The Jews of the Captivity and the Dispersion, headed by the royal Daniel himself, the Belteshazzar or head of the colleges of Chaldæa, became true theistic missionaries to the East, to Greece, to Italy, and to Egypt, down to the days of the Parsee magi who were guided by the star of Jesus to the cradle at Bethlehem.

The Written Word, which plays so important a part in the Reformation and Modern Missions, came slowly to Judaism; but the very formalism and sectarianism of its followers made them the more careful custodians of the life-giving oracles of God. Oral tradition, in an age of long lives, handed down the Word of God. The three lives of Abraham, Isaac, and Jacob covered 315 years.

[1] Scarth's *Roman Britain*, 1883.

Even if Abraham did not, as supposed, take with him to Syria and Egypt the art to which we owe the clay tablets of Chaldæa in his day, Jacob's son Joseph, like Moses after him, was learned in all the wisdom of the Egyptians. The Ten Commandments which formed the legal beginning of the Kingdom of God in Israel, were written on stone tablets, and the "book of the law" (Deut. xxxi. 24) was from that time a series of contemporary annals. For the age in which they lived, the Jewish nation were at all times better supplied with literature than any other people, inspired or uninspired. But as a missionary system Judaism made little use of what it possessed in its relation to the surrounding heathenism, from which it attracted comparatively few proselytes. Grace and truth came by Jesus Christ not only to the Gentile, but to the Jew, whose restoration to the universal kingdom of God will form part of the restitution of all things.

CHAPTER III.

CHRIST THE KING OF THE MISSIONARY HOST—THE MISSIONARY CHARGE.

The Fulness of the Time—The Jesus of History, the Son of God and the Son of Man—The Relation of Christ to Jews and Gentiles — Christ's Missionary Methods — The Missionary Charge and Prayer for every Disciple—The Kingdom of Christ—The Parables of the Kingdom.

The Fulness of the Time came 1888 years ago,—or four years before the current chronology introduced by the monk Dionysius in the sixth century,—in the year 749 of the foundation of Rome, when "there went out a decree from Cæsar Augustus that all the empire should be enrolled" (Luke ii. 1). Then "God sent forth His Son, born of a woman, born under the law, that He might redeem them which were under the law, that we might receive the adoption of sons" (Gal. iv. 4, 5). The Emperor Augustus died nineteen years after this census, in which the name of the Son of God and the Saviour of men was enrolled among the eighty-five millions who formed the subjects of Rome. On the Emperor's death the vestal virgins produced his legacy to the Senate and to Tiberius, his successor, in the shape of a Breviarium or ledger of the empire. This census report briefly recorded not only the number of the citizens, subjects, and allies, but the resources and administrative details of the commonwealth, the provinces, and the dependencies. It closed with a solemn warning not to extend the frontiers beyond the lines of the Rhone and the Danube, the Euphrates and the Red Sea, the Atlas and the Ocean. The " Pax Romana " slowly taught the race the idea of its unity, and intensified the expectation of a longing for Him who had been described as the Desire, the Trust, the Consolation of all nations. From 170 millions, at the beginning of the nineteen Christian centuries, the race has grown to 1470 millions. Half of mankind, if not Christian, are ruled by professedly Christian powers. Great Britain alone rules one-fourth of the race, for whom the " Pax

Britannica" is doing exactly what God used the "Pax Romana" to do for the eighty-five millions around the Mediterranean Sea, where Jesus Christ began His brief three years' ministry.

In 1838 Mr. Gladstone thus described the fulness of the time, in his *State in its Relations with the Church* :—

"A brighter day, however, dawned, when the fulness of time had arrived and the whole world had been politically and socially re-cast, apparently in order to allow of a free, uninterrupted, and universal propagation of the liberated truth. God sent forth His Son, made of a woman ; and that which hitherto had but been chanted in the Temple, or echoed in the mountains of Judah ; that which had been enveloped in types and figures, symbolized in the visible institutes of sacrifice and purification ; that which had been known in the letter to a small and single people, and which in the spirit had been the precious food of a yet smaller and obscurer flock, was to be told upon the housetops, to be proclaimed, as with a trumpet, through all lands, beginning from Jerusalem, even unto the ends of the earth ; was to summon to its obedience every nation, every class, every character ; to purge, to chasten, to restore the whole of the fallen race of man.

"Such was the scheme of glory that appeared to be announced in the preaching of that gospel under which where sin had abounded, grace was much more to abound ; and where, by the disobedience of one, (the) many had been made sinners, so and much more by the obedience of One, were (the) many to be made righteous. The whole earth was to break out into songs of triumph and rejoicing, and was to be filled to overflowing with the universal knowledge of the Almighty in a more than golden age of light, and love, and joy,

"'Light intellectual, replete with love ;
Love of true happiness, replete with joy ;
Joy that transcends all sweetness of delight.'[1]

"The universality of this dispensation was its glory. Its message of mercy was to every child of Adam. Rob it of that characteristic, and you rob it of its crown, and St. Paul of his triumphant assertion. It becomes, with reference to the extent of its application, but as another form of Judaism. What matters it, in respect of universality, whether you take the whole of one nation, or an individual here and there from every nation ? There is a limit, a limit of principle, in either case alike, and upon such a supposition, one fixed by the will of the Author of the dispensation, not merely by the stubborn intractability of its recipients.

"But in the case of the Christian scheme, the limit is imposed, as Scripture informs us, only by the obstinate aversion of the human will from God, which induces it rather to choose misery and destruction, by blinding it in such manner that it is incapable of sober choice, and yet that it also remains persuaded of its power of sight. The difference, therefore, is this : now the mercies of the covenant are made ready for every one, are offered to and enjoined upon every one : ' Go ye into all the world, and preach the gospel to every creature.' Then the vast majority of mankind were left under the darkened natural law, and a covenanted salvation was not placed within their reach. Let us then keep steadily in view this universality or universal applicability of the Christian dispensation, as opposed to the limited applicability of the Jewish."

---

[1] Dante, *Paradiso*, c. xxx. v. 40. Conf. St. Augustine, *De Civ. Dei*, viii. 6.

The Jesus of History, the Son of God and the Son of Man, was a poor carpenter of Galilee, so little educated that His despisers asked how this man knew letters, never having learned. Yet He claimed, and He proved Himself, to be as universal as the humanity which He took upon Him; sinless by the confession of His enemies, and the friend of sinners, in whom He first created a conscience of sin, and then worked out a new creation of holiness like His own. He was a Teacher speaking as never man spake, with authority; and He closed His short career as the one Sacrifice of infinite value and universal applicability, having said of Himself, "The Son of Man must be lifted up, that whosoever believeth in Him should not perish, but have everlasting life; for God sent not His Son into the world to condemn the world, but that the world through Him might be saved." He came not personally to save individuals only, but to found a society coextensive with the race and with all time; to create a kingdom on earth, yet not of this world; to lay the foundations of the City of God visibly among men. To men He was and is God, with power to make them sons of God, by raising them to a brotherhood with Himself, in which they may at the same time recognise their equality with each other. This society, or kingdom, or Church is universal in its application and extent, as it is in its origin. It is marked off from all others, as Christ the equal of the Father is, by His alone claiming as Son of Man the power to forgive sins, not merely to teach that sin may be forgiven. The History of Missions is the history of Himself, as King of glory, sending forth His Spirit, working through the men whom He selected (Luke vi. 12), and trained to be witnesses, preachers, and organizers for Him among all nations; and of the men and women who ever since His ascension have shown faith and obedience enough to carry out His commission. He Himself was not a missionary, but the Incarnate God, who, historically, is Christianity itself. He gave to rebellious men the gifts of apostles, prophets, evangelists, and teachers when He ascended. But He left it to the Holy Spirit whom He promised, to apply those gifts. The History of Missions is thus a history of the dispensation of the Spirit.

The Relation of Christ to Jews and Gentiles in His brief ministry illustrates the universality of His nature, His claims, and His gospel, making Him very specially an example to the missionaries whom He sends. Jewish shepherds first received from angels the news of His birth in the great missionary song, and hastened with instant faith and eager obedience to adore Him. But the heathen world were represented at His cradle by its wisest sages, whom God Himself drew by the star in the East, identified by astronomers with one of the variable stars in connection with the conjunction of planets which marked that year. Thus to the chosen people and to all the race alike, to Jewish pride and Gentile culture, the angels and the star united to herald the greatest, the central event in the history of our earth: "Glory to God in the highest, and on earth peace, goodwill toward men," or, "On earth peace among men of goodwill," *i.e.* who are the objects of the goodwill of God. Again, He who, to try the faith of a heathen woman, said that He was sent only to the lost sheep of the house of Israel, declared that He had found the greatest faith in a Roman centurion. To certain Greeks who desired to see Him, there came a voice from heaven, and there was made the most gracious revelation of Himself yet vouchsafed: "Verily, verily, I say unto you, Except a grain of wheat fall into the earth and die, it abideth by itself alone, but if it die it beareth much fruit. . . . And I, if I be lifted up from the earth, will draw all men unto Myself." So to the outcast woman of Samaria He not only revealed the spiritual nature of His worship, which the Jews—even His own disciples—could not receive, but He used her report of Him to teach the apostles what harvest it was that He sent them to reap. As the crowds came from Samaria on the woman's report to see the wondrous prophet, He bade the Twelve lift up their eyes and behold "the harvest." But lest they should confound His teaching with the natural harvest, which was not due for four months, He pointed to the Samaritans flocking towards them, and said, "Say not ye, There are yet four months and then cometh the harvest? behold, I say unto you, Lift up your eyes and look on the fields, for they are white already unto harvest" (John iv. 35). It was a Samaritan who was the missionary in His parable. It was a Hellenist, Simon of African Cyrene, who, when our Lord was sinking beneath the weight of the cross, was pressed into the service of carrying it. It was a Roman governor who pronounced Him righteous, and would have set Him free but for the fury of the Jewish councillors and his own political fears; while to him Christ revealed the true nature of His kingdom. As Pontius Pilate was the civil, the centurion at the cross was the military representative of the Empire, and it was given to that Roman officer to declare, "Truly this man was the Son of God"

(Mark xv. 39), when all the disciples forsook Him and fled. It was the King, Christ Jesus, who from heaven called the persecuting Pharisee Saul, and made him the Apostle of the Gentiles, the first and greatest Christian missionary.

Christ's Missionary Methods may be studied in His selection of the Twelve, and their daily training by His side; in His instructions to the Seventy; in His preaching to the people who heard Him gladly,—to the poor; in His compassionate healing of the sick and feeding the hungry; in His answers to the cavillers of the bazaar, and the inquirers of the schools; and in His rebukes of the self-seeking, the self-righteous, the hypocrite, and the Sadducee. The Gospels thus form a code of the principles, as the book of the Acts of the Apostles is a manual of the history of the first purely Christian Missions. But all through the Gospels, above them and underlying them and between their lines, is the personality of Christ, Himself the subject as well as the teacher, the message as well as the trainer of the messengers, the model and the moulder in His own type of all whom He calls to witness, to preach, to live His life and death for sinners. Hence the History of Missions is the realization of Christ in time and in humanity. The career of every missionary, from Paul to Carey and Livingstone, from John to Duff and Wilson, is worthy of study in proportion as he lived the life of Christ, and loved sinful men as Christ loved the world. And thus the History of Missions is, in its widest sense, the history of civilisation as well as of redemption. All through the history we see the greatest, the most self-renouncing and successful, foreign missionaries reproducing Christ in their own life, their teaching, their converts. And we see missionary churches and societies ever turning to the Gospels, the Acts of the Apostles, and the Apostolic Letters, for their own guidance, and for charges to the men and women whom they send forth in Christ's name. When addressing the first two ministers of the Church of England sent to Ceylon as missionaries in 1814, Dr. Claudius Buchanan took as his model Christ's charge to the Seventy (Luke x.), and His parallel charge to the Twelve (Matt. x.). The missionary who has written most recently on vernacular preaching among the educated and the scoffing natives of India, exclaims of the preaching of the Holy Jesus,[1] "Oh what a perfect Missionary was He! What sermons of love did He preach! What inimitable answers

[1] *Church Missionary Intelligence*, p. 610, Oct. 1883.

did He ever give! Yet He allows us to follow in His steps; and never will you feel so much in His position as when you stand in an Eastern bazaar surrounded by a crowd of captious cavillers."

The Missionary Charge to, and Prayer for every Disciple, in which Christ gathered up His teaching, training, suffering, and glory, into one last commission, takes its place beside the memorial communion of His body and blood,—Baptism with the Lord's Supper. Both are the bonds of the new society, evidences of its Founder, rewards of His followers, gifts of His power, channels of His grace, proofs of His presence. In the very act of leaving the world He claims the right given Him by the Father from all eternity; He asserts the authority conferred on Him by the Father's oath, in language, if possible, more absolute and explicit than He had ever before used; He promises His own effectual presence with His obedient disciples all the days to the end of the world. Three of the Evangelists thus record the commandment which He gave "through the Holy Ghost:"—

MATTHEW.	MARK.	LUKE. Gospel,	Acts of the Apostles,
xxviii. 18-20.	xvi. 15.	xxiv. 46-49.	i. 8-10.
All authority hath been given to Me in heaven and on earth. Go ye therefore, and make disciples of all the nations, baptizing them into the name of the Father and of the Son and of the Holy Ghost: teaching them to observe all things whatsoever I commanded you: and lo, I am with you alway, even unto the end of the world.	*Go ye into all the world, and preach the gospel to the whole creation. He that believeth and is baptized shall be saved; but he that disbelieveth shall be condemned. And these signs shall follow them that believe: in My name shall they cast out devils; they shall speak with new tongues; they shall take up serpents, and if they drink any deadly thing, it shall in no wise hurt them; they shall lay hands on the sick, and they shall recover.*	*Thus it is written, that the Christ should suffer, and rise again from the dead the third day; and that repentance and remission of sins should be preached in His name unto all the nations, beginning from Jerusalem. Ye are witnesses of these things. And behold, I send forth the promise of My Father upon you.*	*Ye shall receive power, when the Holy Ghost is come upon you: and ye shall be My witnesses both in Jerusalem, and in all Judæa and Samaria, and unto the uttermost part of the earth.*

The Lord seems to have repeated three times in different words the great Charge to His Church—(1) to the affrighted eleven, as they sat at meat, recorded by Mark and Luke as above; (2) most fully, in the words with which Matthew breaks off his Gospel with sublime abruptness, to the eleven and the five hundred worshipping Him on the same Galilæan mountain, probably, where He had given the New Law; (3) to the eleven, "with the women and Mary the mother of Jesus, and with His brethren," on the Sabbath-day of the Ascension from the Bethany or eastern slope of the Mount of Olives, as detailed by Luke in his second treatise. The whole converse of the forty days after the Resurrection was of the things pertaining to the kingdom, and that converse is gathered up in the final commission from the Galilæan and Judæan mounts. The slope above Bethany, thus more hallowed by the presence of the Christ than any other, now looks down on the solitary hamlet built from the stones of the time of the risen Lazarus, whose name it bears (El-Azariyeh), nor has it been degraded by superstition like the other "holy places." From that spot as from the mount of the new law, there comes to each disciple the missionary charge in its *warrant*, "All power is given Me;" in its *marching order*, "Go ye, disciple and baptize all the nations;" in the *service* it claims, "Teaching them to observe all things whatsoever I commanded you;" and in its *promise*, "Lo, I am with you alway, even unto the end of the world." So (Eph. i.) the Father of glory "made Him to sit at His own right hand in the heavenly places, far above all rule and authority and power and dominion, and every name that is named."

The Risen Christ, the ascending King of the City of God, uses all power or authority, in heaven and on earth, to teach, to disciple, to evangelize the world, through eleven poor and puzzled fishermen, on whom He breathed the Holy Spirit, as the first gentle movement of the mighty rushing wind which was about to convert them and all true disciples into fishers of men. And, referring to these chosen eleven, He had said in His marvellous intercessory or missionary prayer before His crucifixion, "Neither for these only do I pray, but for them also that believe on Me through their word; that they may all be one, even as Thou, Father, art in Me, and I in Thee, that they also may be in Us; that the world may believe that Thou didst send Me. And the glory which Thou hast given Me, I have given unto them, that they may be one even as We are One" (John xvii. 20).

The Kingdom of Christ differs not only from all kingdoms of the world such as Satan offered in the temptation, and His own disciples expected up to the last hour He spent with them. It differs from all religious systems founded by men in this, that the founders claimed only a casual relationship to the doctrines they taught, while the person of Christ is an essential constituent of Christianity. Hence, as Dorner shows, "Christianity alone is the religion of redemption which is grounded in the person of Jesus, because of the unprecedented union of divine and human life in His personal nature, and in His action, a union certain to the believer." In the Scriptures which record the origin of Christianity, Christ is everywhere declared—declares Himself—to be the foundation-stone, the corner-stone of the kingdom of God. He is Life, and Light, and Power—the eternally ideal. He is Truth and Knowledge—the realization of the ideal in history (John xiv. 6). Hence He could say, what it is the function of every missionary to proclaim, "No man cometh unto the Father but by Me." While the other evangelists recorded the establishment of the kingdom of Christ among men, it was John's special duty, writing as the only survivor of those who had seen Christ in the flesh, to repeat that the ideal divine essence of the Truth was realized in historical facts: "The Word was made flesh and dwelt among us, full of grace and truth." "That which was from the beginning, that which we have heard, that which we have seen with our eyes, that which we beheld and our hands handled concerning the Word of Life, declare we unto you, that ye also may have fellowship with us." In Jesus Christ "heaven has stooped to earth, to the earthly present, in order to found the kingdom of heaven." Through Him "the union of the divine is transplanted into estranged humanity by the agency of the Holy Spirit, who actively proceeds from Him to the Church."

This kingdom, **John the Baptist**, closing the old covenant series of Messianic anticipations and its last martyr, heralded: "He must increase." Christ and His apostles preached it not as the Jews expected, but as the universal missionary covenant revealed it to Abraham. The kingdom began at the Nativity, and was described by Gabriel to Mary, the human mother of the King. Thou "shalt call His name Jesus. He shall be great, and shall be called the Son of the Most High; and the Lord God shall give unto Him the throne of His father David, and He shall reign over the house of Jacob for ever, and of His kingdom there shall be no end." The kingdom was entered upon at the ascension. It was first revealed to the new Christian world a few days after, at Pentecost, in the sound as of the rushing of a mighty wind and the tongues parting asunder like as of fire. It has been spread by the Spirit through the Church and every true disciple ever since. It will yet cover the whole earth and subdue every enemy of the King, who will then deliver up the mediatorial kingdom to God, even the Father (1 Cor. xv. 24–28). "But of the Son He saith, Thy throne, O God, is for ever and ever" (Heb. i. 8). Then shall the Redeemer's prayer to the Father be fulfilled: "Glorify Thou Me with Thine own self with the glory which I had with Thee before the world was." Such are the royal claims, such their historical realization, such the universal sovereignty of the King of the missionary host. "Whose I am and whom I serve" is the boast of every missionary disciple from Paul to the least in the kingdom of heaven.

The Parables of the Kingdom, in which our Lord teaches the theoretic or general truth concerning the divine kingdom, have been thus grouped and characterized.[1] The parable of the Sower shows the Word of the kingdom to be diversely received according to the moral condition of hearers. Those of the Tares and the Drag Net teach that there will be a mixture of good and evil in the kingdom till the end. In the Treasure and the Pearl we see the kingdom of God to be the *summum bonum*. The Mustard Seed and the Leaven assure us that the kingdom of God is destined to grow to greatness in numbers and influence. The Blade, the Ear, and the Full Corn, make the growth to be gradual and slow. The Selfish Neighbour and the Unjust Judge teach the certainty of an ultimate answer to persistent prayer for the coming of the kingdom. The parable of Extra Service suggests the exacting demands of the kingdom, and the temper needed to meet them (Luke xvii. 7–10). The three parables of the House, the Talents, and the Pounds relate to the problem of work and wages in the kingdom of God. The other two groups of parables, or those of Grace—such as the Lost Sheep, the Lost Coin, the Lost Son, and the Great Supper; and those of Judgment—such as the Barren Fig-Tree, the Wedding Feast, the Wedding Robe, and the Ten Virgins, were no less distinctive of Christ as the Missionary Teacher.

[1] Professor Bruce's *Parabolic Teaching of Christ*. 1882.

CHAPTER IV.

THE HOLY SPIRIT THE LEADER OF THE MISSIONARY HOST.

Christian Missions the Work of the Spirit—The First Christian Missionaries—Stephen, "the Crown"—Paul, the Apostle of the Nations—Christianity conquering the Cities—The Name Christian—Paul's Three Mission Tours from Antioch—John the Divine—The Missionary Apocalypse.

Christian Missions the Work of the Spirit.—Christ Himself ascribed His apparent failure to convert many of the Jews of Palestine, as Paul did at the close of the apostolic history among the Jews in Rome (Acts xxviii. 26), to the spiritual blindness of the covenant people predicted by Isaiah,—a blindness which nineteen centuries of Christian light seem only to have intensified. But, in harmony with the divine claims which He always made when on earth, He told the timorous, ignorant disciples of all ages that the conversion of the world to Himself was reserved for them. Marvellous are His words, "Verily, verily, I say unto you, He that believeth on me, the works that I do shall he do also, *and greater works than these shall he do*, because I go unto my Father" (John xiv. 12). The assurance would be incredible, followed as it soon was by His own breathing upon the eleven, and His declaration, "All authority hath been given to Me in heaven and earth; go ye therefore and make disciples," but for Pentecost a few days after. The last words of the eleven were stammering folly, after all that had happened, regarding the time of the restoration of the kingdom to Israel. Yet to such men, and to His disciples in all ages and of all races and degrees of culture, the ascending Christ, leaving few other followers, and to the world only the record of a malefactor's death, calmly promised the doing of "greater works" than His own, even the evangelization of all the earth. The incarnation, the public ministry, the death of the cross, the resurrection, the ascension, were all a preparation for the day of Pentecost. The Incarnate God whose veiled glory men beheld on earth for a time, gave place to a

Living Influence whom He had promised to send, and whom He did send to abide for ever. Is there any proof of the divinity of Christ, of the supernatural power and character of Christianity, greater than that? That is a proof which has continued growing in intensity and extent ever since the day of Pentecost startled the world, so that the History of Missions has a peculiar evidential value. If the Captain of salvation personally abstained from making many followers by putting forth a power which must have extinguished the first law of the Kingdom,—the individualism of the Church,—it was that He might do it through the impersonal life-giving influence of the Spirit and the co-operation of those whom the Spirit should graciously enable to do "greater works" than His. The miracle—and it is more—is perpetually repeated in the calling of every man and woman who is in any sense a missionary, and in the new birth of every soul. The King of the City of God is ever personally at the right hand of the Father: the Spirit whom He sends down is ever personally convincing the world of sin, of righteousness, and of judgment; is taking of the things of Christ and showing them to those who believe; is preparing the world for the missionary, and calling the missionary to go and help the world.

The First Christian Missionaries find their record in the book of the Acts of the Apostles, which has been described as the Fifth Gospel, or the Gospel of the Holy Spirit. From the foundation of the Christian Church on the day of Pentecost up to its establishment by the Emperor Constantine in 311 A.D., it may be said that every Christian was a missionary. Christ left "above five hundred brethren" (1 Cor. xv. 6), who were probably scattered in Galilee and elsewhere after the Passover and the forty days before the ascension. In Jerusalem there were "about a hundred and twenty" (Acts i. 15). There were devout Hellenist Jews, or Jews of the Dispersion, from the thirteen different countries mentioned in geographical order in Acts ii. 8–12, who witnessed and heard "the mighty works of God" on the day of Pentecost. Of these and of the residents of Jerusalem three thousand were baptized as the result of the **First Missionary Sermon**, which preached repentance, baptism, the remission of sins, and the gift of the Holy Spirit. That sermon was followed by the **First Christian Battle for Toleration** (Acts iv. 19), caused by the opposition of the Jewish priesthood and Sadducees to the success of the new gospel, for the number of the *men* who believed rose to five thousand, making a

Christian community in Jerusalem alone of fifteen thousand. The **Second Missionary Sermon**, which had for a text the first Christian miracle performed in "the name of Jesus Christ of Nazareth," further developed the gospel of the Messiah as offered to the Jews "first," to bless them in turning away every one of them from his iniquities, promising seasons of refreshing now and the times of restoration of all things (*apokatastasis*) when the Christ whom the heaven had received should come again. **Peter** was the preacher on both occasions, and John was his companion in working the miracle on the lame man, in entering the prison, and in boldly testifying before the rulers of the people and elders of Israel, who were compelled to set free these "unlearned and ignorant men" who were "filled with the Holy Ghost." The deliverance led to the **Church's First Missionary Hymn** (Acts iv. 24–31), based on Ps. ii., and a fresh outpouring of the Holy Spirit "when they had prayed," so that "the place was shaken wherein they were gathered together." Peter, thus early, began the work of building the City of God among the Jews, that, with the Jews, he might extend it among the heathen, beginning with Cornelius. But he never rose entirely above the level of the circumcision, of which he and **James** the Lord's brother, surnamed the Just, were the apostles. The one duty of bringing Jew and Heathen into the one fold thus became twofold, and another was wanted to do it,—a Jew yet not ignorant, so that he might present the gospel free from Judaistic forms, as universal good news; a Roman citizen and not unlearned, so that he might commend the gospel in all its fulness to the conscience of every man. Such was Paul, and his teacher in the school of Christ was Stephen.

Stephen, "the Crown."—The two elements in the growing Judæo-Christian Church were the Palestine or Hebrew, and the Hellenist or Greek Jews. From the latter, who complained that their widows were neglected in the administration of the common Church fund by the twelve Galilæan Apostles, seven deacons were chosen by the whole Church, and at their head were Stephen and Philip. Stephen (= "the Crown," known as the Archdeacon in the Eastern Church) was for this crisis, as the first martyr and as the teacher of Paul, greater than the apostles. He may have been a freedman of Rome, a goldsmith of the Empress Livia, converted to Christ on the day of Pentecost. Or he and Philip may have been of the number of the seventy missionaries sent forth by Christ, to precede Himself in every city and village. Hence the breadth of view, the charity, the Gentile leanings which he showed. Hence his remarkable familiarity with the very words of Christ. The inspired history almost lavishes on his character eulogies given to no other man, not even to Paul: he was full of the Holy Ghost and "wisdom," a word ascribed to him alone in the Acts; he was full of faith and the Holy Ghost; he was full of grace and power; he was of irresistible wisdom and spirit. All this appears in his missionary disputations (Acts vi. 10), in his development of the missionary meaning of Old Testament history, in his enthusiasm, in his vivid realization of unseen things, and in his martyrdom. He was the first Jew to understand and to apply Christ's words to the woman of Samaria on spiritual worship (Acts vii. 48), and Christ's rebuke of the "scribes, Pharisees, hypocrites." He saw and knew assuredly the coming glory as none had done since Abraham. His face kindled like an angel's when, charged with teaching the destruction of Jerusalem, he beheld the missionary future of the Church Universal. At the supreme moment, being full of the Holy Ghost, the first martyr "looked up stedfastly unto heaven, and saw the glory of God, and Jesus standing on the right hand of God." He died like his Master, praying for his murderers, as his martyred missionary successors have since done. Heber and Tennyson have both sung him, but Augustine's remark is more true to life than the poets':—"Si Stephanus non orasset, Ecclesia Paulum non haberet." The same Father suggests with reference to the observance of his martyrdom the day after Christmas day, that men would not have had the courage to die for God if God had not become man to die for them.

Paul, the Apostle of the Nations.—"The witnesses laid down their garments at the feet of a young man named Saul. And they stoned Stephen. . . . And Saul was consenting to his death." Every word of Stephen was burned into the heart of the young Pharisee, Gamaliel's student, who afterwards reproduced the more characteristic phraseology in his Epistles to the churches. The death which scattered the Christians of Jerusalem all over Syria, sowing the seed of the word, only intensified Saul's hate to "the way," to the Methodists of that time. But he had been separated, even from his mother's womb (Gal. i. 15), and called through the grace of God to preach among the Gentiles the Jesus whom he persecuted. The hour came, one midday in the year 34 of the Vulgar Era, when the voice which had called Abraham sounded to him from out of the light of heaven, above the brightness of the sun, "Arise, go." And then, as he afterwards told King Agrippa in open court, there was laid on him—on him first saying, "Lord, what wouldst Thou have me to do?"—a mission such as neither before nor since, in the splendour of its surrounding circumstances or in the amplitude of its terms, any human being has ever received—not Abraham or Isaiah, not David or Daniel, not Peter or John, not the whole Pentecostal band:—"To this end have I appeared unto thee, to appoint thee a minister and a witness both of the things wherein thou hast seen me, and of the things wherein I will appear unto thee; delivering thee from the people, and from the Gentiles, unto whom I send thee, to open their eyes, that they may turn from darkness to light, and from the power of Satan unto God, that they may receive remission of sins and an inheritance among them that are sanctified by faith in me." Read the life of Paul, to which the rest of the book of the Acts is devoted, and his writings, in the light of that charge, and behold the ideal missionary.

Christianity conquering the Cities.—Founded in Jerusalem, according to the Lord's command, the Church appeared to be only a sect of the Jews, until it assumed the catholic or universal form and the name of its Founder and Head at **Antioch,** then the Græco-Syriac capital of the East. Twenty miles from its port of Seleucia, in the corner between Syria and Asia Minor, where the Orontes, the greatest of the four rivers from Lebanon, passes between it and an offshoot of the Taurus range, rose this Greek city. Till supplanted by Constantinople, Antioch was without a rival, in the climate which attracted the wealthy of Rome, in the commerce which passed through it from east to west, in the wit which has been commemorated by the Emperor Julian as taking the form of a love of nicknames. If Peter was the first apostle to visit it, when he "passed through all quarters," as tradition tells, then he founded only a church of Jews. Even those missionaries whom the persecution that arose about Stephen sent to Antioch, as well as Cyprus and Phœnicia, preached to the Jews only at first, until some who had been broadened as "men of Cyprus and Cyrene" "spake unto the Greeks also," with such success that "a great number believed." In **Barnabas,** a wealthy gentleman of Cyprus who had thrown his all into the common treasury, the Church at Jerusalem had a missionary—soon to be made by the Holy Spirit an apostle—specially fitted to consolidate the work in a city with which he must have been familiar. Of his visit, also, it is recorded that "much people were added unto the Lord," so that he sought assistance from his friend Paul, then at the not very distant Tarsus, whom he probably had known, and whom, with the friendly grace which gave him the name of "a son of consolation," he had introduced to the naturally distrustful disciples in Jerusalem. "And it came to pass that even for a whole year they were gathered together with the church, and taught much people; and that the disciples were called (*Gr.* 'got the name of') Christians first in Antioch." Thus the first step of Christianity towards the world-wide power which it claimed and was soon to assert over the Roman Empire, was, having tarried for a time in Jerusalem, to appeal to the greatest heathen city of that neighbourhood, Antioch. So steadily did the gospel of the first ages work out from the cities, that the two names applied to non-Christians are villagers and dwellers in the open country, or *pagans* and *heathen*. The process is being repeated in North India before our eyes: Duff attacked Brahmanism from Calcutta, and Wilson, Parseeism and Mohammedanism from Bombay city.

The Name Christian thus first appears in history in the year A.D. 42 or 43, as a Latin word applied in scorn to the worshippers of Christ, and adopted by men whom Christ had taught to rejoice in reproach for His sake (Matt. v. 10–12). Hence Peter wrote (1 Pet. iv. 14–16), "If ye be reproached for the name of Christ, happy are ye. . . . If any man suffer as a Christian, let him not be ashamed, but let him glorify God on this behalf." Peter and John had left the court of the Sanhedrim "rejoicing that they were counted worthy to suffer shame for His name." The Church had now passed out of the narrow cradle of Jerusalem, and had measured strength with the Greek intellect and the Roman empire. Those who to themselves were "brethren," "saints," "believers," "disciples," "faithful," or "those of The Way," and to Jews were "the sect of the Nazarenes," required a historical and a catholic designation. That they got it from the Romans, the Latin form *Christiani* shows; that it was given in scorn was in keeping with the character of the wits of Antioch, and with the fact that believers never use it of themselves in the New Testament, save when Peter reasons from it as a term of reproach. Euodias, the first bishop of Antioch, is said by tradition to have adopted it; and Ignatius, his successor, not only frequently used it, but formed from it the derivative *Christianismos* = Christianity and Christendom. These two last words were long equivalent to each other in our own language. Chaucer writes, "Certes faith is the key of Cristendom;" and Froissart, that the creation of Urban VI. "was signifyed to all the churches of Christianitie." Roman governors and historians accepted the word as a respectful or at least neutral designation; thus King Agrippa: "With but little persuasion thou wouldest fain make me a Christian." Tacitus wrote in his *Annales:* "Nero falsely accused and punished most grievously certain people, hated for their wickedness, whom the common sort called Christians. The origin of that name was Christus, who, in Tiberius' reign, was put to death under Pontius Pilate." About the same time, the beginning of the second century, Pliny bore this reluctant testimony to Trajan as the outcome of his investigations among the Christians of his province: "This was the sum of their fault or error, that they were wont to meet together on a stated day before sunrise, and sing a hymn to Christ as God, and bind themselves by a sacramentum that they would not commit theft or robbery or adultery, that they would not break faith nor repudiate a trust." Glorious nickname, even in its other form of *Chrestiani*, from *Chrestos* = good, the word used by Peter also (1 Pet. ii. 3) of the Lord Himself, and translated "gracious." For is not that, in a sense, "the new name which the Lord shall name," when the Gentiles were to see the righteousness of Zion, as described by Isaiah (lxii. 2),—a name from "the Anointed," and exalting the Head of Jew and Gentile in the persons of "the members of His body," the partakers of "His life," the temples of His Spirit, those whom the Lamb is described in the new song (Rev. v. 10) as having purchased unto God with His blood of every tribe, and tongue, and people, and nation, and having made them unto God a kingdom and priests; and they reign upon the earth?

Paul's Three Missionary Tours from Antioch.—The first act of the Christians of Antioch was characteristic of the New Faith. Warned by the prophet Agabus of the approach of that famine which devastated Syria under Claudius Cæsar (A.D. 45), they sent relief, "every man according to his ability," to the elders in Judæa by the hands of Barnabas and Paul. These two returned to Antioch with John Mark, where they were formally set apart as apostolic missionaries to the heathen. As the presbytery of prophets and teachers "ministered to the Lord and fasted, the Holy Ghost said, Separate me Barnabas and Saul for the work whereunto I have called them. Then when they had fasted and prayed and laid their hands on them, they sent them away. So they, being sent forth by the Holy Ghost, went" (Acts xiii. 1–4). Thus the Church was moved by the Spirit to set apart, and the missionaries so set apart by the laying on of hands were sent forth by the Spirit, a gracious combination of the Divine and the human springing from the Risen Lord's Warrant, and effectual wherever followed all down the stream of mission history.

1. Paul's first tour was that of A.D. 45, in Asia Minor alone (Acts xiii., xiv.), during which he came into contact with heathenism in its lowest form, and the Jews again refused the gospel. Accompanied by Barnabas, and attended by John Mark, he left the new centre of Antioch for its port of Seleucia, where he took ship for the island of Cyprus, the native place of Barnabas. Landing at Salamis on the eastern end, they went right through the island for a hundred miles to Paphos, the western capital, where the Roman proconsul, Sergius Paulus, "believed, being astonished at the teaching of the Lord," where the Jew magician (Elymas = Ulema) Barjesus was struck blind for a season for opposing his conversion. Having sailed to the Pamphylian port of Perga, on the mainland, whence John Mark returned home, they advanced into the mountainous interior, encountering the unparalleled hardships described by Paul himself in 2 Cor. xi. 26. Rising through "the pass" where the two great roads meet, **Paul preached his First Sermon**, in Antioch of Pisidia, to the Jews, following the line laid down by Stephen. His theme, as it had been the Baptist's, and his Master's, and Peter's, was the glad tidings of forgiveness of sins—"through this Man is proclaimed unto you remission of sins." The common people heard him gladly, but the jealous rulers of the Jews thrust the gospel from them. "Lo," said Paul, quoting Isa. xlix. 6 regarding the Servant of the Lord, "we turn to the Gentiles; for so hath the Lord commanded us, I have set Thee for a light of the Gentiles, that Thou shouldest be for salvation unto the uttermost part of the earth." Thus Paul, recalling the trance in the Temple at Jerusalem (Acts xxii. 21), and the Divine words, "Depart, for I will send thee forth far hence unto the Gentiles," was shut up to his special mission to the non-Jewish world. Driven out, the two missionaries followed the high road to Iconium, where their success was such that they had again to flee to the rural town of Lystra; there the simple aborigines, like the hill tribes of India, at once welcomed and misunderstood their message. Returning and "making many

disciples" by Perga, they told the church at Antioch, and then at Jerusalem, "all things that had been done with them, and how that He had opened a door of faith unto the Gentiles." The **Council of Jerusalem,** consisting of "the apostles and the elders, with the whole church," and presided over by James, decreed that the Gentile Christians should not put on the yoke of the Mosaic ceremonial, while they should respect the ancestral prejudices of their Jewish brethren in matters of expediency. This first Presbyterian Council's decree ran thus: "It seemed good to the Holy Ghost and to us to lay upon you no greater burden than these necessary things; that ye abstain from things sacrificed to idols, and from blood, and from things strangled, and from fornication; from which if ye keep yourselves it shall be well with you." But it was long — long even after the fall of Jerusalem — till the Christian Church was freed from obsolete Mosaic prejudices. Even Peter, who had admitted Cornelius and had freely lived with the Antioch Christians, was ashamed to do so when messengers came from James, and was boldly withstood by Paul, the consistent champion of toleration and Christian liberty.

2. Paul's second tour (A.D. 51), with Silas and Timothy as his assistants (Acts xv. 36–xviii. 22), beginning again at the Syrian Antioch, was undertaken to confirm the Asian churches founded six years before, and to deliver to them the Council's decree. Passing through Syria and Cilicia, his native place, Paul again visited Lystra, where Timothy was given to him as the fruit of his first tour, and went through the region of Phrygia and Galatia, where he fell sick, the Celtic inhabitants receiving him "as an angel of God" (Gal. iv. 13). He would have gone farther northwest into Mysia and Bithynia, but "the Spirit of Jesus suffered them not." Divinely driven, they went down to the coast at Alexandria Troas, now to become memorable for a greater event in history than that sung by Homer. "A vision appeared to Paul in the night: there was a man of Macedonia standing, beseeching him and saying, Come over into Macedonia and help us." Southern **Greece, Europe, the whole Western World, cried for the Gospel** through the man of that vision, to the Jew of contemptible presence, who tossed restlessly on the Ægean shore, and rose "concluding that God had called us for to preach the gospel unto them." That day, when Paul and Luke sailed straight across to Samothrace, and landed at Neapolis, the port of Philippi, Christianity, leaving its Asiatic cradle, became evidently, historically, the one universal missionary, aggressive, transforming faith,

for the race, for world-empires and the barbaric hordes which were preparing to sweep them away, for nations yet unborn, for lands yet undiscovered, for seas and islands to be made by English-speaking peoples new centres of light, before which Rome and Greece, Antioch and Jerusalem, were soon to be only historic names. But at Philippi in the prison; at Thessalonica in an uproar, atoned for only by the nobleness of Berea; at Athens, where culture was crueller than the stones of Lystra; and at Corinth, where Gallio cared for none of these things,—such was the power of the devil, the world, and the flesh, Paul's reception augured as little of the assured success of a near future, as his Master's experience in Galilee and Judæa. Sailing from Cenchrea, the port of Corinth, he visited Ephesus, Cæsarea, and Jerusalem, and again remained some time in Antioch, his headquarters.

3. Paul's third tour (A.D. 54) from Antioch (Acts xviii. 23–xxi. 33) was devoted to Ephesus, after a loving run "through the region of Galatia and Phrygia, stablishing all the disciples." For three years at Ephesus he trained the eloquent Alexandrian **Apollos**, met Greek philosophy with the weapons of Christ, testified amid the idolatrous races of the Pan-Ionic festival of Diana, and was hurried away by his friends to begin his second European tour at Macedonia. After three months spent among the churches in Greece, he was forced by a Jewish plot to sail for Syria, but not before he had dared the perils of a secret visit to Philippi. As they coasted along Western Asia from Troas, amid the Cyclades to Tyre and Cæsarea, Paul received the elders of Ephesus at Miletus, where he spake an impassioned farewell to them and to all Asia, unmatched in literature, and a model for every missionary and preacher.

In A.D. 58, Paul was received at Jerusalem by a **General Assembly** of James and all the elders, to whom "he rehearsed one by one the things which God had wrought among the Gentiles by his ministry. And they, when they heard it, glorified God." Seized in the temple by a Jewish mob, he was rescued by the Roman soldiers, was sent to Cæsarea for trial, appealed to Cæsar, and, his judges declared, would have been set at liberty but for that appeal. His voyage from Cæsarea by Sidon, Cyprus, Myra, Cnidus, Crete, Malta, Syracuse, and Puteoli, in the Bay of Naples, and thence along the great Appian Way to Rome, was a fourth missionary tour. His first detention in Rome, A.D. 61, 62, as a state prisoner, when he preached to all, was succeeded by journeys eastward to Asia Minor, and probably westward to Spain, when he was a second time imprisoned in Rome, as a felon, during the persecution of the Antichrist, Nero. Then only Luke and Onesiphorus dared to visit him. His first examination resulted in deliverance. "The Lord stood by me, and strengthened me, that through me the message might be fully proclaimed, and that all the Gentiles might hear." Tradition tells that he was joined at this time, in the Mamertine prison, by Peter, whom he had not seen since he rebuked the apostle of the circumcision at Antioch (Gal. ii. 14). A few months after, in the year 67 (Eusebius), or 68 (Jerome), and when above the age of sixty years, "Paul the aged," as he called himself, writing to Philemon, realized the glowing anticipations which irradiate the close of his Second Epistle to Timothy with a divinely heroic lustre: "I have fought the good fight. The Lord will deliver me from every evil work, and will save me unto His heavenly kingdom : to whom be the glory for ever and ever. Amen. Grace be with you." On the Ostian road, at the Tre Fontane, Paul was beheaded. On the Janiculum hill, at the same time, after they had parted from each other, according to the story, Peter was crucified. The epistles of both, and especially of Paul, to the infant churches, form, with the book of the Acts, the Statute-Book and the Procedure Code of Missions.

John the Divine introduces the second missionary epoch of the Church, if we look upon the martyrdom of Paul and of Peter as the close of its first epoch. From Jerusalem and Rome, and even Antioch, the missionary centre becomes **Ephesus**, for John is there right on to the beginning of the second century. Thence (1) the churches of Asia—named as seven, the number of completeness—were extended, consolidated, edified, and made, in the modern sense, self-supporting and self-propagating. (2) The gospel was carried by the scholars of John and their assistants, like Pothinus, as far as Gaul, and probably to Britain, the missionary church of which always followed the Eastern or Greek rite. (3) John himself sent forth the fourth Gospel about A.D. 85 or 86, according to the statement of Irenæus, taught by Polycarp, the disciple of John, who was the martyr-bishop of Smyrna: "Afterwards John, the disciple of the Lord, who also leaned on His breast, he again put forth his Gospel while he abode in Ephesus in Asia." In a missionary sense the fourth Gospel is of peculiar value, for it records not so much the external events of our Lord's life, as His inner teachings on His person, and on His kingdom, its origin, growth, laws, and triumph, in opposition to the early heresies of Gnostic origin and the errors of heathen philosophy. The Greek Cerinthus in Ephesus had used Christianity, as the Jew Philo in Alexandria had used Judaism, to develope a human Gnosis (system of knowledge), which separated the Divine Christ from the human Jesus, and robbed Christianity of its whole meaning as the power of God and the wisdom of God for the salvation of all who believe. Against this **First Heresy** John is inspired to reveal Jesus Christ, whom he had known more intimately than any other human being, as the Son of God in whom the Divine and the human have their union and perfection, so as to form the only reconciliation of man to God. "These are written that ye may believe that Jesus is the Christ, the Son of God, and that believing ye might have life in His name." Hence John was called Theologos, the Divine, as giving the most distinctive account of Christ, which supplements the three earlier Gospels. Thus early (A.D. 85) in the history of the Church did the Spirit teach the lesson, that the nature and the claims of the Christ form the very essence of missionary teaching, without a jealous regard for which missions cease to be Christian. We shall see this necessity repeated in the Arian heresy and in the Reformation of the sixteenth century.

The Missionary Apocalypse.—John's special service to the missionary church consisted not only (1) in his preaching "the Word" as life, and so giving a full manhood to the early Christians and completion to the work of Jerusalem. It is seen (2) in his unveiling of the immediately partial and ultimately complete triumph of the Word as King of kings and Lord of lords; in his visions of the glorified Lamb of God calling the Gentiles to salvation, and of the saved multitude whom no man can number; in his confident and convincing announcement of the destiny of the Church in time and in eternity. It is not too much to say that without "the revelation of Jesus Christ which God gave him to show unto His servants," the missionary Church could not have borne the persecutions, nor have met successfully the heresies, of John's time, and of the many succeeding periods of trial and martyrdom, down to Eromanga. Criticism, from the Chiliastic hopes of the persecuted Christians before the establishment of the Church by Constantine, to the most recent and rich writings of Westcott and Godet on this subject, is divided on the two points of an earlier (A.D. 68-69) or a later date (A.D. 95-97) of the revelation, and of a Continuous, a Præterist, or a Futurist interpretation of its visions. We can only suggest here, as doing fullest justice to the inspired missionary character of the book, the superiority of the Præterist interpretation. That meets the immediate historical sense of a revelation of "things which must shortly come to pass," while it admits of the higher spiritual and continuous fulfilment which is being evolved in this modern missionary epoch.[1] It describes the spiritual principles and forces which will yet destroy all heathen and Mohammedan error, and will introduce the New Jerusalem, the City of God.

John, son of Zebedee and of Salome the sister of Mary, was the cousin-german of our Lord, the disciple whom Jesus loved, and, with his brother James and Simon Peter, son of Jonas, one of the inner group of three. Promised by our Lord a long life, which tradition developed into the legend of immortality, the man who was a son of Thunder in his youth, and the apostle of Love in his old age, certainly lived, according to Irenæus, for thirty years after the fall of Jerusalem had, as we believe, fulfilled the immediate predictions of the revelation, had swept away the old polity and temporary covenant of Judaism, and had introduced in its fulness the Christianity of the fourth Gospel. His charge of the Lord's mother, probably till death removed her before A.D. 51, may account for his absence from Jerusalem during the stormy times of Paul, Peter, and James, until the Council met, when he is mentioned (Gal. ii. 9) as one of the three "reputed to be pillars." Banished from Ephesus to Patmos during the reign of Nero, whose persecution of the Christians began in A.D. 64, he there received the revelation by an angel, and he wrote it between the death of Nero and the fall of Jerusalem (A.D. 70), in the reign of Galba or Vespasian. Standing on the rock of Patmos, and casting the eye of Divine vision from Jerusalem and Ephesus to Rome and the farther West, from dying Judaism to decaying paganism, what does he see? What, filled with the symbolism of Ezekiel and Zechariah, does he unveil in words which, while they rise above human historical conceptions, yet idealize and spiritualize these for all who are blessed to read and to hear the words of the prophecy?

A *prologue* (i.–iii.) pictures the persecutions, schisms, and backsliding of the Church and the suffering of the empire, and urges the churches to reform, to faithfulness. The angel-presbyters of the churches, as stars for the whole world, and candlesticks for their own missions, receive exhortations, censures, eulogies from Him who walketh among them, which should form the daily study of every missionary. *Part I.* (iv.–xi.), with its seven seals and seven

[1] See Dods' *Post-Exilian Prophets*, p. 31, in this Series.

trumpets, follows our Lord in describing the destruction of Jerusalem, "spiritually called Sodom and Egypt, where our Lord was crucified," which lasted three years and a half from the spring of A.D. 67 to August 70 (Rev. xi. 1–3). The woman's child is taken up to the throne of God, and she in her wanderings marks the dispersion of Israel ever since. Judaism is dead, is cast out. *Part II.* (xii.–xx.) shows us the birth of Christianity, the child of Judaism, caught up unto God and His throne from "the devil and Satan, the deceiver of the whole world," who with his angels "went away to make war with the rest of the woman's seed which keep the commandments of God and hold the testimony of Jesus." A series of terrible symbols denote the destruction of Babylon, Rome or heathenism, from Nero, the typical Antichrist, through all the wild bestial forms rising from the sea. Above all, John saw an "angel flying in mid heaven, having an eternal gospel to proclaim unto them that dwell on the earth, and unto every nation and tribe and tongue and people." Then heathenism, like Judaism, is destroyed, John hears the voice of the great multitude redeemed to God out of every nation and tribe and tongue, yea, he sees "the heaven opened, and behold, a white horse, and He that sat thereon called Faithful and True, . . . and his name is called The Word of God, . . . King of kings, and Lord of lords." Jerusalem and Rome, or Judaism and heathenism, have fallen; the deceiving devil is cast into the lake of fire and brimstone with the beast and the false prophet. The *Epilogue* (xxi.–xxii.) shows the universal triumph of Christianity as "a new heaven and a new earth;" the resurrection of the evangelized nations, and the judgment upon their enemies, typifying the final resurrection and judgment, and the everlasting glories of the holy city, the tabernacle of God with men, whose gates are never shut.

"The Lord, the God of the spirits of the prophets, sent His angel to show unto His servants the things which must shortly come to pass. And behold I come quickly. . . . I Jesus have sent mine angel to testify unto you these things for the churches. . . . And the Spirit and the Bride say, Come. And he that heareth, let him say, Come. And he that is athirst, let him come: he that will, let him take the water of life freely."

Fulfilled soon after in the destruction of Judaism by the fall of Jerusalem, and in the historical destruction of the heathenism of that day by the fall of the Roman Empire and the acts of Constantine, this revelation finds its fuller, its continuous and complete historical development in the History of Missions. Every period, from the weary empire of Nero to the longing but unconscious and dumb millions of modern days, echoes the refrain of the aged John, "Amen, come, Lord Jesus;" or mutely appeals to the Church in its too prolonged trance, "Come over and help us." The Triune God, in whose threefold name Christ commanded His disciples to baptize the nations, here repeats the threefold pledge of His willingness, and the Spirit assumes the Church and every true disciple as co-operating. Truly the present, the rapid conversion of the world depends now only on the faith of the Church, that is, on the faith and obedience of each of its members.

PART II.

LATIN PREPARATION, A.D. 70 TO 1784.

CHAPTER V.

THE ROMAN EMPIRE SUBDUED BY THE CITY OF GOD.

Christianity after the Fall of Jerusalem—Christianity and the Empire—The Ten Persecutions—The First Missionary Triumph—Pagan Idolatry utterly abolished—The Destruction of Paganism a Guarantee of Greater Triumphs—The Conversion of the Empire gradual—The Four Patriarchates of the East—Alexandria as a Missionary Centre—Pantænus and the Catechumens' School—Constantine—Constantine's Christian Legislation—The Council of Nicæa—Theodosius and the Code.

Christianity after the Fall of Jerusalem.—Spiritually Judaism perished, the Judaic covenant had fulfilled its temporary purpose and ceased, when the veil of the temple was rent in twain during the Jews' crucifixion of their Messiah, the Saviour of the world. Historically Judaism was swept from the face of the covenant land when, in spite of Titus, a Roman soldier fired the inner doors of the Holy of holies, and the Temple itself was burned to the ground. As a national cult or faith the practice of Judaism had been sanctioned by Roman law and usage, precisely as the British Government of India tolerates all the religious customs of its peoples which are not inconsistent with the very basis of morality. But this same law placed Christianity beyond all toleration, because it was believed to be a dissent from Judaism which it was neither politically nor morally desirable to encourage or even protect. From the time when all classes of the Jews had united to crucify Jesus Christ, and the zealots had stoned Stephen, the first Christian martyr, the Jews had been the most bitter enemies of the Christians who charged them with having crucified the Lord of glory, though "in ignorance." In the banishment of the Jews from Rome under Claudius, the Christians had shared the common fate. The fall of Jerusalem changed all that. Individual Jews and Jewish communities might be, for a time, not less bitter in their denunciations, and Roman emperors and governors not less severe in their persecution of the Christians. But Christianity at least came gradually to be understood to be a faith which was not disloyal to the empire, and a cult which was not only not immoral, but was marked by an ethical perfection and spiritual self-devotion so exalted and courageous, as to be a silent reproach to paganism. The first act of the Imperial Government after the final conquest of Judæa, begun by Pompeius 134 years before, was to recognise the universal expectation of a Deliverer, by prosecuting all who claimed to be descendants of David. The result opened their eyes to the fact that the Christians had no objection—nay, were required by their faith—to call Cæsar master. Gradually there stole over the whole empire the conviction of the truth which Christ had told Pilate, that the kingdom sought by the Christians was not of this world, but was therefore all the more subtle and powerful and dangerous. Hence the panic-stricken character of the persecutions which followed, the emperor and his subordinates, priests and mob, striking wildly at a force which they could not grasp, and, when they yielded to it, yielding as Constantine did to visions and signs created by the imagination and the conscience.

Christianity and the Empire were born at the same time, and the Christians were the most loyal subjects of a power which persecuted them by irregular outbursts of cruelty, only winning for them the martyr's crown. Not till Trajan was Christianity prohibited by law, and the law was not universally or stringently enforced. But as a persecuted faith, Christianity was pure and bright and missionary in the noblest sense of Christ Himself. Even before Paul lived in Rome and near the Prætorium, he had sent greetings to more than twenty persons there, slaves and freedmen of the emperor in the Palatine, which was far from the Prætorium. From the earliest days the emperor's palace was one of the chief seats of the growing Christian Church in Rome. Soon the faith won over the very highest classes, men and women. In the year 58, **Pomponia Græcina**, the wife of the consul Plautius, conqueror of the Britanni, was a Christian. A coin recently discovered gives historical ground to that interesting mission book, *The Acts of Paul and Thecla*, written in the second half of the second century, in which Tryphæna, the queen of Polemon in

Asia Minor, showed kindness to the martyr Thecla, a disciple of Paul. Tryphæna was related to the Emperor Claudius. In 96, Domitian put his cousin-german T. Flavius Clemens, a consul, to death for his leaning to Judaistic doctrines and atheism. His wife was Domitilla, who was banished for Christianity, as John was, and was the mother of two princes whom Domitian had once shown as heirs-apparent to the throne. Inscriptions lately discovered in the great catacomb of Domitilla leave it without doubt that, between fifty and sixty years after Christianity had reached Rome, a daughter of the emperor embraced the faith; and thirty years after the fearful persecutions under Nero, the presumptive heirs to the throne were brought up in a Christian house! But these were exceptional cases till the time of Septimius, when the Church became a political and religious factor in the empire.

The **Ten Persecutions** by which paganism thus sought to destroy the power which ignorance feared, have been stated by historians according to the vision of the Revelation (xvii. 12–14), "The ten horns which thou sawest are ten kings, . . . these shall make war with the Lamb." The persecutions are generally given thus, but a fuller and more distinct classification might be made:—

A.D.	EMPERORS.	A.D.	EMPERORS.
64	Nero.	235	Maximinus.
95	Domitian.	249	Decius.
107	Trajan.	257	Valerian.
163	Aurelius Antoninus.	274	Aurelian.
201	Severus.	303	Diocletian.

More hostile to the progress of Christianity than even the worst of these bloody outbursts, were the occasional attempts of all that was best in paganism at a revival, especially in the age of the Antonines. The philosophers and philosophic emperors thought that what they could not extirpate they might overcome by imitation. But paganism, its priesthood and philosophy, its ritual and ethics, was already corrupting. Disappointed of its Deliverer, whom it thought it had found in the cradle of Bethlehem and the cross of Calvary, and might see returning from the conquest of Syria, the world became ever more weary, till after Diocletian it ceased to strike, and at last learned to adore. What the troubled conscience and longing heart of the empire found not in the destruction of Jerusalem, it discovered and acknowledged in the fall of its own mighty capital. It was when, in 410, Alaric sacked Rome that Augustine wrote his *City of God*. Then Christianity openly triumphed over paganism, as it had not done in 325 in the Council of Nicæa, nor in 390, when Theodosius legally suppressed the heathen worship.

The First Missionary Triumph — Pagan Idolatry utterly abolished.—In less than four hundred years after the Incarnation, the religion taught by the carpenter of Nazareth to eleven fishermen of Galilee, and by the Spirit of Jesus after His ascension to His disciples, everywhere, by peaceful persuasion only, swept away the last and greatest of the four world-empires and world-idolatries. The claim to universal sway based on universal authority, the command to preach the gospel to every creature accompanied by the certainty of the Spirit's perpetual presence, had been vindicated with a completeness which, up to this century, forms the most remarkable fact in history, sacred and secular. This fact of "the early, wide, and, within certain limits, absolutely irresistible diffusion" of Christianity, has been used by apologists, from Augustine to the present day, as the first argument for its truth; and to explain it away by secondary causes, Gibbon vainly applied his unmatched historical powers. We find the latest apologist thus writing of it:—

"The classic paganism, Greek and Roman, the Syrian, the Egyptian, and North African, the Druidic, and ultimately the Teutonic, have all fallen to rise no more; and at this moment there is not on the face of the earth a single worshipper of 'the great goddess Diana' or 'the image that fell down from Jupiter,' of Baal or Dagon, of Isis or Serapis, of Thor or Wodin. They are preserved in imperishable literature, and in equally imperishable art. Homer and the great tragedians have enshrined them; Virgil and Ovid; even Milton in his *Paradise Lost* and *Christmas Hymn*, to say nothing of that wonderful Book, which, in revealing their abominations, will be found to have carried farthest and widest their memory. But not a single shrine remains to them in the proper sense of the word, not even where the Apollo or Venus, the Minerva or Hercules, enchains universal admiration. They are abolished as idols, while immortalized as relics; and not even the exquisite beauty lavished upon them can hide the moral deformity to which they owe their downfall. It is long centuries since one single soul regarded them with anything of the feeling with which the African trembles before the rudest fetish, or the Hindu before the most unsightly of his divinities. Another conquest so complete and absolute does not mark the history of the world. All ranks and classes passed through the revolution. The husbandman had to give up his offerings to Liber and Ceres, the sailor his votive tablets to Neptune, the soldier his chaplets dedicated to Mars. The youth had to forget his place in the procession, the virgin her part in the dance or secular games. The senator had to forego his libation on entering the senate; the general his search after the omens before battle; the very emperor, the honour of his own coins and titles of divinity. What but an immense and boundless power could have wrought this change, and wrought it not by constraint but willingly, through the force of persuasion? It cannot be denied that some of the later conflicts with paganism were unfair, and that Christianity denied to idolatry the civil justice which it had so nobly and passionately claimed for itself by act and suffering. But in the decisive stages of the contest nothing prevailed, or could have prevailed, but moral influence; and the preacher, the apologist, the martyr, secured a pure and bloodless victory.

"'The difficulty of this gigantic task has been underrated by Gibbon, with his characteristic skill in finding some shadow of foundation for his assertions, and then exaggerating them beyond reason. The shadow of truth is the weariness of unsatisfied longing which idolatry had diffused. But this did not lead men to quit it, even nominally, any more than the weariness of men in the service of sin begets a universal repentance. The force of habit—even the returning fear of superstition—to say nothing of the dread of state convulsion and the bias of manifold selfish interest, upheld the great fabric long against all assaults; and even philosophy did its best, by surrendering so much of paganism, and trying to improve the rest, to avert the impending destruction. Idolatry died so hard that we find the Emperor Julian, in the fourth century, still needing to be refuted by the very arguments, at the hands of Cyril of Alexandra, that had done service in the days of Clement and Origen; nor could Augustine, in the full blaze of Christian triumph, overlook the prejudice which traced the capture of Rome by the Goths to the anger of its neglected deities. But though Christianity had to complete its work slowly, it did it, and did it alone; and thus there was ended a revolution greater than if the idolatries of India, China, and Japan—such as we know them in our days—were one and all to fall; for these are not the leading nations of the world, nor will their thought affect all time; whereas paganism then died in the very centre of the world's life and greatness, and the thought from the midst of which, as by a mighty hand, it was torn out, has lived on to affect all literature, and even the Christianity that overmastered it, to the end of the world. It is true that the victory of Christianity was not perfect, and that paganism shrunk back into a subtler and more spiritual form, waiting its opportunity again to rush forth amidst congenial darkness, and in the very name of Christ to enslave mankind. But the deliverance, though not final, was yet unspeakably great and blessed; and the unreason, the blight, the continued burden and shadow with which polytheism in its gross and open prevalence afflicts the nations, for ever passed away."[1]

The Destruction of Paganism a Guarantee of Greater Triumphs.—The extirpation of Greek and Roman paganism has more than an apologetic or evidential value of the first order. It is a spiritual and historical pledge to the Church ever since, that the Spirit will enable it to do "greater works than these." The Second Missionary Triumph followed close on the first, in the eleven centuries from the fall of imperial Rome to the blow struck

---

[1] Principal Cairns, D.D., on *The Success of Christianity and Modern Explanations of it.* 1883.

by the Reformation at papal Rome, or the conversion of Europe. We are now approaching the close of the first century of the Third Missionary Epoch, which is universal or extensive in a sense unknown to its two predecessors. What Greece did in the first, and Rome in the second, England or English-speaking people are now called to do on a far wider scale, co-extensive with the whole race. Christianity took four centuries to subdue the empire to Christ; it took eleven more to bring Europe under His sway. Eighteen hundred years have been required in the providence of Him with whom a thousand years are as one day, to begin, even, the universal missionary era.

The Conversion of the Empire was gradual.—All the statements and allusions in the contemporary Christian and non-Christian writers, as explained by the first modern critics Gibbon and Bishop Lightfoot, "bear witness, with one exception, rather to the wide diffusion than to the overflowing numbers of the Christians." Dr. Lightfoot takes the middle of the third century, when the gospel had been preached for nearly two centuries and a quarter, amid all the discouragements of a worldly opposition, but with all the zeal of a new-born enthusiasm. **Origen**, who wrote his treatise against Celsus about A.D. 246, describes the Christians then as "very few indeed" in comparison with all the subjects of the Roman empire. **Gregory Thaumaturgus**, his pupil in Neo-Cæsarea, chief town of Pontus, found only seventeen Christians there in A.D. 240, and left only seventeen heathen in 265. From a letter of Cornelius, Bishop of Rome at the same period, we gather that there were 50,000 Roman Christians only, or one-twentieth of the whole population of a million, an estimate confirmed from the sepulchral monuments. So much for the two great centres of Asia Minor and Rome. Turning to Gaul, and excluding the Greek and Asiatic settlers who had suffered in the martyrdoms at Vienne and Lyons two generations before, Dr. Lightfoot is of opinion that Native Gaul was not more Christian than Native India was ten years ago. Certainly the spread of Christianity was very rapid between the persecutions of Decius and Diocletian in the latter half of the third century. After Diocletian it went on with accelerating force; but Chrysostom states the Christian population of Antioch, about A.D. 400, as a bare majority. The united conclusion of Gibbon and Dr. Lightfoot is that in the middle of the third century the Christians were one-twentieth of the subjects of the empire, and one hundred and fiftieth of the whole human race. That is, after the period of two centuries since the man of Macedonia stood before Paul at Troas, during which Christianity was propagated under the most favourable circumstances, one human being in one hundred and fifty was Christian. Now the proportion, at least one in five, is fast becoming one in four.

The Four Patriarchates of the East, Jerusalem, Antioch, Alexandria, and Constantinople, were successively, with Rome, the great missionary centres of the empire. Of **Jerusalem** we have already seen that James the Just (*Sadeek*), the Lord's brother, was the moderator or bishop of the Church of the circumcision. He perished as a martyr in A.D. 62. His brother **Symeon**, chosen by the Church as his successor, after a service of more than forty years, was denounced to Hadrian as the representative of the royal line of David. At the great age of a hundred and twenty years, he testified to the Divine claims of the Son of David, and was crucified. His successors of the circumcision ceased when Hadrian built Ælia Capitolina on the site of Jerusalem, and excluded every Jew from the settlement. A Gentile Church arose under one Marcus; but **Justin Martyr**, a Samaritan proselyte of the second century, bewailed the desolation of the Church which Mohammedanism swept away. **Antioch** became the patriarchate of all the East till eclipsed by Constantinople. Its second bishop, **Ignatius**, alike as a writer of Epistles and a martyr under Trajan (107), was a successor worthy of Paul. **Theophilus**, who was fourth in succession from him, was a stout defender of the purity of the faith against the growing heretics of the time. Antioch promised at one time to be a light to the whole of Asia. It sent off a Catholicos into the far East. The city where the disciples were first called Christians, despatched missionaries to Cape Comorin and farthest China. From the Nestorian as well as orthodox churches of Antioch, missionaries went into "the territories of the Lama, into the strongholds of Buddhism, into the foul abominations of Shamanism," and promised to conquer Eastern and Central Asia for Christ, till overwhelmed by Saracen and Tartar. Antioch, once the city of half a million, that vied with Rome itself, now a squalid village with not a vestige of its ancient glory, still sends bishops to India and China, still watches over the descendants of the churches which it founded in the fervour of its first love. Through Antioch and Alexandria, the great Alexander's Hellenic conquests were made subject to Christ for a time.

Alexandria, as a Missionary Centre, however, distanced Antioch. The Roman conquest of Egypt (B.C. 32) prepared North and East Africa, and South-Western Asia, which had been under the rule of the Ptolemies since B.C. 304, through Alexandria, just as Antioch, the capital of the Seleucid successors of Alexander, prepared the rest of Asia. As the meeting-place of Greek philosophy, Jewish thought, Roman provincial polity, and Oriental commerce, Alexandria became the intellectual centre of the world, just as Christianity became a missionary faith. The first Ptolemy had formed a royal school of learning in the two departments of the Museum or University in his own palace, and the library with its 700,000 rolls and volumes which had overflowed into the Serapeum or temple of Serapis. These two cornerstones of Greek and Roman paganism were so won to Christ, that before the successive waves of Vandals and Saracens obliterated the Church, North Africa was the most advanced portion of Christendom. In their own quarter of the city, the Jewish scholars, under royal patronage, had produced the Greek version of the Old Testament known as the **Septuagint,** which has been justly called by a recent popular writer "the first apostle of the Gentiles." Just before **John Mark** preached Christ in the halls of Alexandria, following the Jews of the Dispersion who had been converted at Pentecost and had returned to Cyrene with the good news of God, **Philo** the Jew, a contemporary of Jesus Christ, had formulated a theosophy from the later theology of the Rabbis and the teaching of Plato, which for many became a stepping-stone through the Gospel of John to the unclouded revelation of God in Christ, just as happened this century in the case of Neander. The Emperor Hadrian, in A.D. 134, in a flippant letter to his brother-in-law preserved by Vopiscus, writes of the Christians in Alexandria in terms which lead us to the conclusion that, a hundred years after the death of Christ, they were nearly as numerous as the heathen. "The city is rich and populous, no one lives there in idleness. They have one God; Him the Christians, Him the Jews, Him all the Gentile people worship; and I would that this city were of purer morality, since it merits by its magnitude the supremacy of Egypt." Charles Kingsley's *Hypatia* is a vivid picture of the fermentation of belief, thought, and life in ancient Alexandria, which marks Calcutta, Bombay, and Madras under parallel conditions at the present day. Like these too, after Claudius, in the second half of the first century, from the discovery of the monsoons of the Indian Ocean and the decadence of the Parthian empire, Alexandria absorbed all the trade of the East.

Pantænus and the Catechumens' School.—From the self-sufficiency of the Stoics, Pantænus was won to sin-revealing, sinner-saving Christianity about A.D. 180. He probably established, he certainly adorned as its president, the great missionary college which destroyed the heathen Serapeum in time, known as the Didaskaleion Catechumenorum. That was at once the defence of the orthodox faith against the Gnostic heretics Basilides, Valentinian, and the Ophites, and the institute from which missionaries and Christian teachers went forth to all lands from North-Western and Eastern Africa to Arabia, India, and Ceylon. This first Missionary Institute gradually developed from a school in which inquirers and neophytes were taught the simplest elements of the doctrine of Christ, to a college of divinity and evangelistic method, in which advanced Christians were trained to meet the systems of pagan philosophy, and heathen thinkers were invited to attend. Doubtless **Clement's** *Pædagogue* and his *Exhortation to the Heathen* were originally delivered by him as lectures in this college. Its nearest modern analogue is found in the institutions or colleges, first established by the Scottish Free Church Missions, and notably by Duff and Wilson, in the great cities of India. Pantænus may be pronounced the first historical missionary to India, in response to messengers who came praying him that teachers of Christ might be sent to their country. Whether by "India" was meant the Hindoo Peninsula, or Ethiopia, or Arabia Felix, or only the Upper Nile country, is not certain. We know from Eusebius that the Thebaid, the first home of monasteries, contained so many Christians soon after, that they witnessed "a splendid martyrdom under the sword of Severus." Jerome states that Pantænus found on his arrival, "that the Apostle **Bartholomew** had already preached the coming of Jesus Christ according to the Gospel of St. Matthew, which he brought back to Alexandria written in Hebrew." The traditions regarding the preaching of the Apostle Thomas in India, and his martyrdom a little south of the present city of Madras, have doubtless only this basis of truth, that the descendants of Christian converts by his preaching in Syria settled in South India. **Clement the Alexandrian** and **Origen** succeeded Pantænus, and carried Christian scholarship, strict textual study of the Holy Scriptures, and missions, to a height which culminated in Augustine, the greatest of the Latin

Fathers. Origen's **Hexapla**, or six-version edition of the Hebrew Scriptures, was the greatest work of the kind until Erasmus gave the Church the Greek text of the New Testament twelve centuries afterwards.

Cosmas, the merchant-missionary, may be taken as a representative of the large class of Christian traders who, like the mercantile marine of England now, carried Christian influences with them from the head of the Red Sea to the Malay Archipelago. After travelling over the greater part of the world as then known, he retired to a monastery, and in A.D. 535 issued his *Topographia Christiana*. The book, intended to prove that our world is a solid plane, has its interest concentrated in the writer's own travels and descriptions of Christian settlements. He did not visit China, then reached by Nestorian missionaries overland; but he writes of it as the country of silk, lying to the left as you enter the Indian Sea, on the very borders of the habitable world, and yet within reach of Western merchants. He gives no Christians to China, though we know that both Jews and Christians were there. Everywhere he found the Christian Churches to be of Persian, Antiochian, or Nestorian origin. In Ceylon, on the Malabar coast, at Kalyan, now a Free Church mission station near Bombay, and on the semi-barbarous island of Sokotra, he found Christian communities, churches, and bishops. "In Bactria, too, and among the Huns and other Indians, and indeed throughout the known world, were numberless churches, bishops, and multitudes of Christians, with many martyrs, monks, and hermits." Such is Mr. Priaulx's summary of the information of Cosmas Indicopleustes. Alas! Islam was soon to sweep away all these churches except those protected by Hindoo and non-Christian rulers in South India. And Indian Buddhism, which ought to have attracted the study and the missionary efforts of the Christian Church, had spread its baleful pantheism over all Eastern and Central Asia, from Ceylon and Burma to Peking and Lhasa, which it still grips with an ever-weakening hold.

In the nine hundred years from Alexander's conquest of India to the close of Justinian's reign, the Eastern world was prepared for and received Christ. In the next nine hundred, to A.D. 1498, when India was re-discovered by Europe, the Eastern world fell away from Christ because the Church had failed to be a missionary, an aggressive power.

Constantine placed Christianity on the throne of the empire, to the damage of the Church. The emperor, who under paganism had been worshipped as a god, and whose picture the Christian martyrs had refused to adore, now adopted Christianity as a substitute. Thus from the pagan side at first, and following the imperial law and custom, Church—the Christian Church—and State were united. The emperor, says Harnack, was now obliged to give way as deity, but "the God-favoured imperial Lord" only shone with the greater glory. If not born in York, yet proclaimed emperor there, and the man who built London wall, Constantine has been claimed as an Englishman. His conversion —if that word may be applied to an event which certainly turned his face from paganism and set it firmly towards Christ—is the greatest event since the death of the Apostle John, and is the first of a series of royal accessions to the Church like those of Clovis the Frank, Vladimir of Russia, and many Keltic and Saxon princes. The cross—with its legend "In this conquer"—which, when praying, he saw in the heavens as he approached Rome for the decisive conflict of the Milvian Bridge (312), may have been nothing more than such an appearance as that of the aurora borealis in 1848, which France regarded as forming the letters L N of the president's name. Constantine himself may have been as inferior to Marcus Aurelius as Mr. John Stuart Mill laments that he was. But that vision, followed by the Council of Nicæa (325), the foundation of "the City," as Constantinople was called (330), and by the growth of the papal power in Rome, which he abandoned to it, did more to affect the Church for good and evil than any event from the dispersion on the martyrdom of Stephen to the Reformation. From a purely missionary point of view, it began the system of compromise with error,—of nationalism instead of individualism in conversion,—which in the East made the Church an easy prey to Mohammedanism, and in the West produced Jesuit missions.

Constantine's Christian Legislation began, the year after his conversion, with an edict of toleration, although he was often afterwards intolerant. In 321 he forbade all secular labour and civil action on Sunday, except the emancipation of a slave, and he encouraged the army to attend on that day the public prayers which contained one germ of the *Te Deum*. He abolished crucifixion, infanticide, private divination, gladiatorial games, and licentious and cruel rites; but he still remained chief pontiff of

Jupiter, "best and greatest," while he allowed prayers to be addressed to the genius of the emperor.

The Council of Nicæa.—As consecrated chief of the Roman people and of the Roman religion, Constantine summoned "the great and holy synod," the first of the Seven General Councils, to meet at the Bithynian city of Nicæa,—the Council whose Creed has ever since been held by universal Christendom. All its members were bishops, unlike the first Council in the Acts of the Apostles. Of the 318 members who signed its decrees, eight only were from the West. Among these were John the Persian, Metropolitan of India, and Theophilus the Goth, the predecessor of Ulfila, from the far North. They sat around a copy of the Holy Gospels, and at their head sat Constantine. They settled three controversies— the Arian, regarding the nature of Christ; the Paschal, as to the time of keeping Easter; and the Melitian, an obscure dispute which affected the Church of Egypt only. The Creed and Twenty Canons were written in a volume. **The Nicene Creed**, pronounced by Stanley "simple, moderate, and comprehensive," went forth to every missionary Church, establishing in the word **Homoousion** the truth of the Incarnation, the essential divinity of Christ, which from Athanasius to Luther was pronounced the *propugnaculum fidei*, the outpost of the faith.

Theodosius consolidated and completed the transition work of Constantine, in the Council of Constantinople (381), which established the Nicene faith, in the abolition of paganism by the Senate, and in the special commission which shut the temples, destroyed the idol vessels, abolished the priesthood and confiscated the property. The Serapeum of Alexandria was levelled with the ground. In 390 the last edict ran thus: "It is our will and pleasure that none of our subjects, whether magistrates or private citizens, however exalted or however humble may be their rank and condition, shall presume, in any city or in any place, to worship an inanimate idol by the sacrifice of a guiltless victim." The publication of the Theodosian Code by his grandson, in 438, may be taken as the close of paganism. The Church started on its missionary career from this point, established, corrupt, secular, destroying the freedom and the purity of apostolic communities like those which had already Christianized most of Western Europe, yet with a true faith which saved the northern barbarians from the fanatical heathenism of the Arian heresy.

CHAPTER VI.

THE CONVERSION OF THE SCOTS AND ENGLISH.

Britain from the first a Missionary Land—The Romano-British Church—Gildas and his History—Albanus and the Proto-British Martyrs—The Scots of Ireland — The Scoto-Irish Church — Sukkat or Patricius—Columba—The Culdees—The Man Columba—Lindisfarne—The Columban Church — The Papal or Romano-English Church — Gregory the Great—St. Augustine—Absorption of the British by the Papal Church—Paulinus—Fursæus—Aidan—Colman—Hild and Cædmon—Cuthbert—Archbishop Theodore, the Greek Monk.

Britain from the first a Missionary Land.—The same insular position and commercial facilities which have made Great Britain the abode of constitutional freedom and the head of the most powerful civilising empire the world has yet seen, early caused it to receive and to propagate the gospel of Jesus Christ. What, physically, Palestine was before the days of the apostles, as the cradle of Christianity, that the two little British Isles have been ever since as its nursery. Each, Palestine and Scoto-Ireland, has been in succession the holy land of missionary preparation and propagation—Palestine, from Abraham to Christ; Britain, from the Celtic Patrick and Columba and the Saxon Boniface and Wiclif, to the English Carey and the Celtic Duff. Paul declared his design to visit Spain, and from a passage in an Epistle of Clemens Romanus, the chief missionary apostle has been set down as the Apostle of Britain. Clement represents Paul as "coming to the extremest limit of the West." In the five or six years between his first imprisonment at Rome and his martyrdom, there was time for the apostle to visit not only Spain but Britain, which had close commercial relations with that peninsula.

The Romano-British Church.—The Roman dominion in Britain lasted for five hundred years, from the first landing of Julius Cæsar in B.C. 55 to about A.D. 446. But the actual conquest did not begin for a hundred years after Cæsar's landing, and with that conquest the progress of Christianity was co-extensive for four centuries before the flood of Saxon heathenism checked and for a time almost extinguished the light of the gospel in England south of the Humber. We may say that our Celtic precedessors or forefathers were converted to Christ—(1) by Roman soldiers and officials; (2) by captives from among ourselves, who learned the truth at Rome and returned; (3) by visits from traders from Spain and missionaries from Gaul, into which last Pothinus had introduced Christianity from Ephesus, and where his successor Irenæus died in 202. The apostolic origin of the Church, whether from Ephesus or Rome, or both,—whether from St. John's immediate disciples, or from Paul himself, or both,—is seen in its purer doctrine and freedom and in the time of its celebration of Easter, when it came into conflict with the papal Church in the seventh century.

Gildas the Wise, a Welsh monk (A.D. 520), is the only British authority, in his *History* and *Epistle*, on the subject of the introduction of Christianity into the island of Great Britain. His language deserves study, when he writes of the conquest of the south in the days of the Emperor Claudius, and of the slaughter when Boadicea revolted: "In the meantime, Christ, the true Sun, afforded His rays, *i.e.* His precepts, to this island benumbed with icy coldness and lying far distant from the visible Sun: I do not mean from the sun of the temporal firmament, but from the Sun of the highest arch of Heaven, existing before all time, which manifested its brightness to the whole world during the latter part of the reign of Tiberius Cæsar." The period of the military occupation of Britain was a time when every Christian was a missionary. For thirty-three years, from A.D. 43, when Aulus Plautius brought over four legions, the country was garrisoned by 48,000 Roman soldiers, or as many as held all British India just before the Mutiny of 1857. The conquest of Anglesey in 59 by Suetonius Paulinus, which destroyed Druidism in its stronghold, was followed not only by the slaughter of Boadicea's hosts, but by the sending of many captives to Rome. The Welsh Triads tell how **Cunobelinus**, the father of Caratâcos, was kept seven years as a hostage at Rome, where he learned Christ, and whence he returned a missionary to his countrymen. This is tradition; but the highest authority on the subject (Rev. F. Thackeray) observes of the family and other captives who accompanied Caratâcos himself, that Paul during his first imprisonment may have become acquainted with some of these, "and that through their representations he might have been induced, when liberated from his confinement, to undertake a voyage to Britain." Tertullian (208) boasts, without challenge, that even those parts of the British Isles which the Romans had not reached, were yet subject to Christ. Two centuries later, Chrysostom writes of continued missionary extension: "Although thou didst go unto the ocean and the British Isles, . . . thou shouldest hear all men everywhere discoursing matter out of the Scripture." Referring to this time, Gildas thus describes the constitution of the Church: "The Church is spread over the nation, organized, endowed, having sacred edifices and altars, the three orders of the ministry, monastic institutions embracing the people of all ranks and classes. It had spread, moreover, into Ireland and Scotland. It was also a learned Church; it had its own version of the Bible and its own ritual." And it had its martyrs, in the persecution of Diocletian, the two first being **Albanus** at Verulamium, now St. Albans, and Amphilalus; and Julius and Aaron at Caerleon-on-Usk. Probably at the great Council of Nicæa (325) and that of Sardica (347), certainly at those of Arles (314) and Ariminum (359), British bishops were present. And, once fairly constituted, this early British Church was, in the modern sense, a missionary Church. In 401, **Ninian** (St. Ringan), Bishop of Withern in Galloway, then the frontier Roman province in Britain, converted many of the South Picts between the Firth and the Grampians. At this time there were twenty-eight cities, of which two were "municipia" (York and St. Albans) and nine were colonies, under the Roman rule; and the Church must have been strong when, after three successive centuries of Saxon devastation, England was still thought able to support twenty-six missionary bishops. **London**, destroyed in the Boadicean revolt, became a city in the time of Antoninus Pius, and soon the site of a monastery. But centuries were to pass before London could grow to be the centre of the missionary world. Iona and Lindisfarne, Canterbury and York, even little Kettering, were to lead the way. **Kentigern** or Mungo ("darling") continued, from Glasgow to St. Asaph's and North Wales, the work begun by Ninian, and to both was soon added Columba from Ireland. In the famous meeting of these two aged missionaries, we see the virtual unity of the Scotic and Pictish Churches.

The Scots of Ireland.—As the most remote and insular of all the Celtic lands, and therefore most secure against the war and piracy which ravaged Europe, and even England, from time to time, Ireland became for the next eight Christian centuries the missionary school of Christendom, in a higher sense than degenerating Constantinople or secularizing Rome. The **Scoto-Irish Church** shone with a brighter because purer gospel light, and spread that light more extensively over what has ever since been the Christendom of Europe, than these centres of the Greek and Latin Churches. This purely British Church, which sprang from Ireland, maintained its independence till 1172; then, compelled by Pope Adrian IV., an Englishman, and Henry II., the Synod of Cashel bound it to the Romanized Church in England. Had the Scoto-Irish Church not been subjugated by papal Rome, we might have seen another case like that of the Waldensian Church. No Reformation might have been necessary, and Ireland and Scotland combined might have continued all through the Middle Ages their pure missionary influence. Throughout that time the monasteries of Ireland are described by Neander as schools where religion and science were fostered in close connection with one another; from which, at the same time, Christianity and the seeds of scientific culture were transported to other countries. In the later time of Charlemagne, Alcuin required of the Irish monks that thenceforth it should be their endeavour "that through them and from them the light of truth might shine to many parts of the world," reminding them that, in ancient times, the most learned teachers came from Ireland to Britain, France, and Italy. Hence Ireland was everywhere known as "Insula Sanctorum," the Isle of Saints, the "University of the West."

Sukkat or Patricius.—First and greatest of these teachers was the missionary best known as St. Patrick (395–493). To the Christians already there from an earlier period, described as "Scoti in Christum credentes," Pope Celestine had sent Palladius, who, after landing at Wicklow for a short time, died at Fordun in Kincardineshire on his way back to Rome. Son of a deacon, and grandson of a priest, Patrick was born at "Bannavem Taberniæ," a place which some believe to have been Boulogne, but which the best Keltic and German authorities identify as Bonaven or Kilpatrick, near Alclwyd or Dumbarton. We know more, and more accurately, of the man who became the apostle of Ireland, than of almost any missionary before William Carey, for we have still his autobiography in his *Confession to the Irish People*, and in the famous hymn, known as his "Breastplate," which he composed at Tara, on the eve of that interview with the heathen king which ended in the conversion of Ireland. The Scottish lad, when sixteen, was carried off to Ireland by pirates of the same Scots race whose fathers had settled the west and central portion of what came to be known thenceforth as Scotland. During six years of hardship, as herd-boy in the service of a heathen chief, he tells the people: "I was re-formed by the Lord, and He hath fitted me for being at this day what was once far enough from me, that I should concern myself or take trouble for the salvation of others, when I used not to think even of my own." The record of his missionary call is tinged by that of Paul, whose transcendent words, "the Spirit itself maketh intercession for us," and whose experience of the man of Macedonia, sank into the young man's heart. After a second but short captivity and a second escape to his father's house, he saw in a vision of the night a man who carried many letters, and one for him which was headed, "Words of the Irish People." As the awestruck youth read, he seemed to hear the sound of many voices from the Irish coast, "We beseech thee, child of God, come and again walk among us." His parents and friends resisted his desire to obey the heavenly vision, but again, after the fashion of Him who had said to Paul, "I am Jesus whom thou persecutest," it thus came, "He who gave His life for thee, He speaks in thee." With joy he returned to the people from whom he had made his escape, in 431, the year after the papal Palladius had given up his happily brief and fruitless mission. But he first sought systematic instruction and received ordination in the Gallic monasteries of the stern Martin of Tours and Germanus of Auxerre, whose work in Europe it was reserved for him and his successors to carry on.

For the third of a century Patrick spent himself in evangelizing Ireland, and establishing the schools whence missionaries were sent forth for four centuries after his death. From Saul, in county Down, where the ruins of Sabball Padruic, the "barn of Patrick," may still be seen, to Tara, the capital of King Leogaire and the centre of Druidism, the missionary, and his first son in the faith and successor, whom he named Benignus, preached the gospel. Like Elijah in his conflict with Ahab, Jezebel, and the priests of Baal, Patrick so witnessed for Christ one Easter morn before the worshippers of fire who would have put him to death, that a fire was kindled which will yet do for Ireland itself what it was thus appointed to do for all Europe. Thus it was that Patrick mused and prayed when the Druids were about to bring him before the king. The verses, literally translated from the closing passage of his hymn, show what was the faith by which he lived, and which he spread among our fathers.

> "May CHRIST, I pray,
> Protect me to-day
> Against poison and fire,
> Against drowning and wounding;
> That so, in His grace abounding,
> I may earn the preacher's hire!

> "CHRIST, as a light,
> Illumine and guide me!
> CHRIST, as a shield, o'ershadow and cover me!
> CHRIST be under me! CHRIST be over me!
> CHRIST be beside me
> On left hand and right!
> CHRIST be before me, behind me, about me!
> CHRIST this day be within and without me!

> "CHRIST, the lowly and meek,
> CHRIST, the All-Powerful, be
> In the heart of each to whom I speak,
> In the mouth of each who speaks to me!
> In all who draw near me,
> Or see me or hear me!

> "At Tarah to-day, in this awful hour,
> I call on the Holy Trinity!
> Glory to Him who reigneth in power,
> The God of the elements—Father, and Son,
> And Paraclete Spirit—which Three are the ONE,
> The ever-existing Divinity.

> "SALVATION DWELLS WITH THE LORD,
> WITH CHRIST THE OMNIPOTENT WORD,
> FROM GENERATION TO GENERATION—
> GRANT US, O LORD, THY GRACE AND SALVATION."

His methods and results resembled those of modern Protestantism rather than those of the sacramentarian missionaries of Romanism, from Boniface to Xavier. Preaching from the Scriptures the Christ of salvation, with a persuasive power peculiarly his own, he won over individual hearts, of noble and peasant, and thus gradually moved whole tribes of Kelts, whom he then instructed and built up in the faith, training the best of them as missionaries in their turn. His tongue was the vernacular Irish; he gave woman her proper place in the work of proselytism and in the family life; he opened schools everywhere, and had boys and girls taught the alphabet which he had invented for them. He completed his evangelization of Ireland, a country not larger than the jurisdiction of many missionaries in India now, but destitute of all means of civilisation till he introduced them, by the conversion of Ulster and the adoption of Druim-sailech, the "hill of the willows," as his northern centre. Around the church which he then built, and the house in which he died, there grew up the city of **Armagh**, to become the seat of a primacy which would have had a far brighter history had its archbishops been allowed to remain faithful to the teaching of Patrick.

Patrick's, or the old British, Church was tribal and monastic rather than parochial in its organization, but it was not Episcopal in the sacerdotal and sacramentarian sense. Amid the savagery of the times, married missionaries gathered together in brotherhoods, and unmarried women and widows in sisterhoods. The former were under a moderator or abbot, who might be a bishop, but frequently himself trained and sent forth bishops or superintendents of native churches. The women's societies, of which that of Brigid at Kildare, the "cell of the oak," became the most famous, consisted of women who were under a vow of celibacy while in the sisterhood, and who with prayer and meditation gave their lives to home mission work, such as the relief of the poor and care of the sick.

Colum or Columba.—Crimthan ("wolf") or Columcille ("dove of the churches") was one of the many youths of noble birth whom Patrick, Benignus, and their successors at Armagh, attracted to the missionary's as the greatest of all careers. He was born in 521 at Garitan in the Donegal hills, and was educated in Finnian's schools at Moville and Clonard. When he had been ordained to the ministry, he cut down the oaks on the shore of Loch Foyle, and there built the monastery which grew into the city of Londonderry. That done, he founded other schools of the prophets mentioned by Bæda. He might thus have continued to make foreign missionaries rather than himself to become one, when the same Providence who had sent a Scottish youth to Ireland to herald the great light, sent back from Ireland a missionary to Scotland. A man of great force of character and burning zeal, he is said to have become involved in a battle which led the Synod to decree that he should gain from heathenism to Christ as many souls as had perished in the contest. His old teacher Finnian and another protested, but we can believe that a sentence of exile for such a purpose was not distasteful to Colum. From his own Lough Foyle he had often seen Kintyre and the isles of the Southern Hebrides, where sixty years before, Eric, chief of the Uist Scots, had founded a kingdom of Dalriadic Scotia on the fringe of the Caledonian wood. There, besides boars and wolves, the heathen Picts under Brude of Craig Phadrick, near Inverness, must have made life bitter for the colonists. To his countrymen lapsing into heathenism, and to the savage Picts, Columba came, as oft since missionaries have gone for service to both. To this one man the world owes it that not only the name Scot, but the whole character and results which that name has since implied, was given to the peoples of North Britain, to whom the Saxon element was soon to be added.

Columba was forty-two years old when, in 563, he and his twelve associates stepped out of their *curach*, coracle or hide-bound wicker-work boat, on the strand of the islet called I, Ia, or Hii, or by its adjective from Ioua, which a misprint of his biographer Adamnan's writing has for ever consecrated into the word **Iona**. Guided by Dr. Skene's *Celtic Scotland—Church and Culture*, the visitor can, at the present day, trace the outlines of the position of the Columba family, seen amid the partially restored ruins of the Benedictine buildings of the thirteenth century, which stand on the sites of the first Scottish missionary's wooden abbey or wattle and daub cell. The key to the whole position is the mill stream immediately to the north of the present "cathedral" boundary.

As you coast along in the boat towards the landing-place, you can just descry the thin line of green grass through which the water trickles down to the ocean. Pass on, however, and land at Columba's own harbour, the creek now called Port Na Muintir, or the harbour of the community. Opposite you, across the sound, is the *portus insulæ* on the coast of Mull, whence a road led across that island, eastward to the branch settlement in the island of Hiuba, under Ernan, Columba's uncle. Here it was that the dying Ernan landed when he had desired to be taken back to Columba, who, having set out from his cell to meet the aged saint, saw him fall to the ground and expire not far from the shore. Adamnan's description of that touching incident, and the fragment of a poem attributed to Columba, enable us to trace the road from the Port Na Muintir to the cell. Pass up the old causeway, leaving the Romish nunnery chapel to our left, and we are at the Benedictine abbey, or so-called Romish cathedral.

which stands on the site of Columba's abbey. Cross the mill stream almost at the old kiln where the oats for the brotherhood were dried. Leave to the left the swamp which they embanked into the Lochon Mor to feed the stream and the mill, and climb the vallum surrounding on two sides the elevated site on which Columba built his wooden cell, overlooking the abbey and all this side of the island, and sheltered by the Dunii Hill from the Atlantic. Here realize the first missionary to savage Picts and Dalriadic Scots, as he sat and wrote and read, while an attendant, and occasionally one or two of the brethren, stood at the door awaiting his orders; as he slept on the bare ground with a stone for his pillow; as he prostrated himself in prayer for the land and the people of whom are we, with our divided and warring kirks; and as he looked across the Sound of Iona and across the hills of Mull, to that more beautiful Sound, where, in after days, from Lismore, Romish bishops undid his work.

The Culdees.—The Columban Church of Iona was as much a mission from the Irish Church as Dr. Duff's in Calcutta was from the later Church of Scotland. It was "essentially a monastic Church: we find in it neither a territorial Episcopacy nor anything like Presbyterian parity, but the same anomalous position of the Episcopal order." We may continue the parallel with the Free Church India mission, by saying that the Scottish and foreign missionaries are practically bishops, while the native converts ordained to preach or teach, correspond to the presbyters of the Irish and Iona Churches. Columba and the Culdees taught the comparatively pure doctrine, on essentials as distinguished from Church organization, of the Second General Council held in 381, as against the growing errors of the Bishop of Rome. Columbanus tells us that the Columban Church "received nought but the doctrine of the Evangelists and Apostles." The ninth successor of Columba at Iona, his biographer Adamnan, declares the foundation of Columba's preaching and his great instrument in the conversion of the heathen, to have been the word of God. Similarly the Culdees, up to their obliteration or absorption by the Romish Episcopate of Scotland, were *Keledei, Ceile De, Cœlicolœ*, or Colidei, who first appear as "Culdees" in the eighth century, three hundred years after Columba. They were the *socii, mariti*, or *servi* of God, which is the meaning of "Ceile." The so-called "Culdees" of popular belief—a word utterly unknown to Adamnan, Eddi, and even Bæda—are one of the numerous fictions of Hector Boece. Dr. Skene proves that they "originally sprang from that ascetic order who adopted a solitary service of God in an isolated cell as the highest form of religious life, and who were termed *Deicolæ;* that they then became associated in communities of anchorites, or hermits; that they were clerics, and might be called monks, but only in the sense in which anchorites were monks; that they made their appearance in the eastern districts of Scotland at the same time as the secular clergy were introduced, and succeeded the Columban monks who had been driven across the great mountain range of Drumalban, the western frontier of the Pictish kingdom; and that they were finally brought under the canonical rule along with the secular clergy, retaining, however, to some extent the nomenclature of the monastery, until at length the name of Keledeus, or Culdee, became almost synonymous with that of secular canon."

The **Man Columba** is not quite so clear to us as Patrick has made himself by his autobiography, but we have this nature psalm from his pen:—

"Delightful would it be to me to be in *Uchd Ailiun*
   On the pinnacle of a rock,
That I might often see
   The face of the ocean;
That I might see its heaving waves
   Over the wide ocean,
When they chant music to their Father
   Upon the world's course;
That I might see its level sparkling strand,
   It would be no cause of sorrow;
That I might hear the song of the wonderful birds,
   Source of happiness;
That I might hear the thunder of the crowding waves
   Upon the rocks;
That I might hear the roar by the side of the church
   Of the surrounding sea;
That I might see its noble flocks
   Over the watery ocean;
That I might see the sea monsters,
   The greatest of all wonders;
That I might see its ebb and flood
   In their career;
That my mystical name might be, I say,
   Cul ri Erin (Back turned to Ireland);
That contrition might come upon my heart
   Upon looking at her;

> That I might bewail my evils all,
>   Though it were difficult to compute them;
> That I might bless the Lord
>   Who conserves all,
> Heaven with its countless bright orders,
>   Land, strand, and flood;
> That I might search the books all,
>   That would be good for any soul;
> At times kneeling to beloved heaven;
>   At times at psalm-singing;
> At times contemplating the King of Heaven,
>   Holy the chief;
> At times at work without compulsion;
>   This would be delightful
> At times plucking duilisc from the rocks;
>   At times at fishing;
> At times giving food to the poor;
>   At times in a *carcair* (solitary cell).
> The best advice in the presence of God
>   To me has been vouchsafed,
> The King, whose servant I am, will not let
>   Anything deceive me."

Adamnan's biography gives us the gentler features of the character of the exiled missionary, who to the power of all master minds and leaders of men, that of swaying others to his will, joined a tenderness which drew forth passionate devotion: "From his boyhood he had been brought up in Christian training, in the study of wisdom, and by the grace of God had so preserved the integrity of his body and the purity of his soul, that though dwelling on earth, he appeared to live like the saints in heaven. For he was angelic in appearance, graceful in speech, holy in work, with talents of the highest order and consummate prudence; he lived during thirty-four years an island soldier. He never could spend the space even of one hour without study, or prayer, or writing, or some other holy occupation. So incessantly was he engaged night and day in the unwearied exercise of fasting and watching, that the burden of each of these austerities would seem beyond the power of all human endurance. And still, in all these, he was beloved by all; for a holy joy ever beaming on his face, revealed the joy and gladness with which the Holy Spirit filled his inmost soul." Columba is credited with not a few of the Latin and Gaelic hymns which have survived the ravages of war and intolerance and time in the *Leabhar imuin* (book of hymns) now in Trinity College Library, Dublin, and in the *Bangor Antiphonary* in the Ambrosian Library, Milan. The hymns were called Loricæ or breastplates to protect the singers against evil on a journey, during a storm, and amid similar dangers. This is a specimen[1] of the *Altus* of Columba:—

> "The judgments of Heaven shall be scattered abroad
> On all who deny that our Saviour is God;
> But we shall be raised up with Jesus on high,
> To where the new mansions all glorious lie."

After a busy and hardy missionary life of thirty-four years in Scotland, during which he and his associates founded churches and schools from the farthest Orkneys and Hebrides, south to the Humber, so that **Lindisfarne** became in modern England the daughter of Iona, through his pupil Aidan, "the apostle of Northumbria," Columba entered into rest on Sabbath morning the 9th June 597. His last work was to transcribe the thirty-fourth Psalm, stopping with the eleventh verse: "They who seek the Lord shall want no good thing," and saying, "The next words, 'Come ye children, hearken unto me,' belong to my successor rather than to me." His children became known as the Schotten or Scotsmen of the next four centuries all over Europe, as representing at once pure gospel teaching and discipline, sound learning and Christ-like zeal. In time the true apostolic succession was seen when, from the least famous of those Schotten klöster, that of Erfurth, there came Martin Luther. Of this school were **Columbanus**, who preached from Burgundy to Lombardy and the Roman Apennines, and **St. Gall**, whom we shall meet with again in Switzerland; **Kilian** of Franconia, whose martyr dust lies in the Wartzburg Cathedral; **Virgilius**, who brought Carinthia to Christ from Salzburg as a centre; **Fridolin** "the traveller," who lies in Sekingen Abbey, after preaching the cross in many lands and Christianizing the Alemanni; and **Willibrord**, who carried the truth he had learned in Ireland to Friesland, Westphalia, and Batavia. The visitor to Milan may still see in its libraries copies of the Bible marked with the commentaries in Irish of these Scots missionaries, to the Teutonic, Scandinavian, and even Italian peoples of the dark ages.

The **Columban Church** was established in Northumbria by King Oswald in 635, and became the means of the permanent conversion of the Angles there. Bæda writes thus in his history: "Churches were built in several places; the people joyfully flocked

---

[1] Rev. N. MacNeill in the *Catholic Presbyterian* for December 1883.

together to hear the word; possessions and lands were given of the king's bounty to build monasteries; the younger Angles were by their Scottish masters instructed." When Aidan was first made Bishop of Lindisfarne, "he received twelve boys of the Anglic nation to be instructed in Christ." Mailros, or Old Melrose, not far from the present abbey, had as its abbot one of these boys. The king's half sister Æbba founded Coldingham, just south of Saint Abb's Head, which has ever since borne the name of the saintly woman missionary. For seven hundred years this free church lasted, as in Ireland also, from Ninian to King David, the "sore saint," who in 1124 completed its absorption by Rome.

The Papal or Romano-English Church was introduced into England by St. Augustin, prior of St. Andrew's Monastery on the Cælian Hill of Rome, and first Archbishop of Canterbury (596–607). He, his fellows and successors, were missionaries to the Saxons of Kent and the south-east, whom the pure gospel, as held by the remnants of the Romano-British Church in Wales and Cornwall, had not touched, and whom the zealous and cultured preachers of the Scoto-Irish Church had not reached. But the mission of the papal St. Augustin was also directed against these purer churches, and it succeeded in gradually destroying them in all save a few obscure parts, especially of Scotland, where the Culdees and Wiclif's Lollards afterwards kept bright the torch of gospel truth till it merged in the widespread light of the Reformation of John Knox. For the first time we now meet with the Romanist missions of compromise between Christianity and heathenism, which culminated in the order and the policy of the Jesuits, and have given to India and other countries thousands of caste Christians but little removed in belief and life from the idolators around them. But at so early a period as the sixth century, St. Augustin's mission, and that of Boniface to Germany, which sprang from it, was as far superior to that of Xavier as his was to that of his successors in Southern India and China, although its discipline and teaching contained the seeds of a crop of errors, most of which Wiclif and Luther burned up.

Gregory the Great, Benedictine monk, when passing from his monastery of St. Andrews through the Forum of Rome one day, beheld three Yorkshire boys exposed for sale. Attracted by their flaxen hair and fair complexion, he asked the Jew dealer whence they came. Learning that they were Angles, he exclaimed, as if by a sudden inspiration of more than human pity and scholarly wit, "Non Angli, sed Angeli forent si essent Christiani," and went straight to the bishop-pope for permission to devote his life to England as its missionary. He set out secretly with companions, and was already three days' journey on the way when he was recalled. The times were very evil in Rome, in Italy, and in Constantinople, and he alone could set them right. The missionary was forced by the people of Rome into the papal chair, and five years afterwards he sought for another to do the work in England which he had coveted for himself. It was well that he found a far weaker man in the prior of his old convent. Had the great Gregory established the Roman hierarchy in England and Germany, had he become the apostle of the Teutonic peoples, the brighter light of the British Church must have been sooner quenched and the Christianity of Europe have become more speedily unlike that of Christ.

St. Augustin seems to have been a missionary of the Jewish stamp of Jonah. Pope Gregory, hearing that the Saxons of Kent had applied to the neighbouring Frankish bishops for missionaries, had instructed them to buy English slaves of from seventeen to twenty years of age, and train them to be preachers to their countrymen. The year after this order, in 596, he sent forth Augustin with forty associates to convert England. It was summer, and the party had reached the south of France on their way, when they heard such tales of the savagery of the Saxons that Augustin went back to Rome to ask that they might be recalled. In his reply to "the timid servants of the Lord," as in his censure of the rich bishop who would not help the poor, and of the lazy bishop who said he had no leisure to read the Scriptures, Gregory was at his best. Back went Augustin, like another Jonah; but so slowly did the Benedictine brotherhood proceed, that more than a year had passed before they landed on what was then the Isle of Thanet, on the spot first touched by the Saxon Hengest in 449. Æthelbert, king of Kent, was in his wooden capital of Canterbury. His wife Bereta (Bertha) had given herself to Christ when yet a girl in her Frankish home, and she worshipped in a little Roman-British church outside the city. Predisposed by his believing wife, the king of all the Saxons south of the Humber granted toleration to the magnificent Augustin, who marched before him as he sat under an oak. On the Whitsunday, 2nd June 597, which recalled the Pentecostal effusion, the king was himself baptized;

and on the subsequent Christmas day, after the Witena or parliament of the people had adopted the faith, upwards of ten thousand were immersed in the Swale, two and two performing the baptism on each other at the command of Augustin, while, according to the legend, the crowd were miraculously delivered from drowning. A contrast this to the slower but equally widespread and more scriptural work of individual conversion granted to the prayers and the labours first of the early Christian missionaries of the Roman army, and chiefly of Patrick, Colum, and their followers! Four years thereafter, Gregory sent other missionaries, such as Melitus, Justus, and Paulinus, to help in the advancing work, and these took with them not only gifts of the Bible, complete and in portions, and other books, but relics, vestments, and vessels. Augustin was created Metropolitan or Archbishop of **Canterbury**. Rochester and London were made bishops' sees. He was empowered to place a metropolitan at **York** so soon as the Romanist form of Christianity had extended into regions evangelized by Aidan and the followers of Columba. He was instructed to use the idol temples as churches after purifying them with holy water, and not to abolish but to convert into Christian saints' days and festivals the times of heathen observance and sacrifice.

Absorption of the British by the Papal Church.—The prelatic arrogance of Augustin defeated the first formal attempt at union between the two Churches. In a letter, which Neander justly characterizes as a most precious admonition for every one in any age who is tempted to glorify himself on account of what God has effected by his instrumentality, Gregory warned Augustin against the want of humility which had exalted the once recreant missionary into a proud priest:

"Glory be to God in the highest, peace on earth, and good-will amongst men, that the grain of corn has fallen in the earth and died (John xii. 24), in order that *He* should not reign *alone* in heaven by whose death we live, by whose weakness we are made strong, by whose sufferings we are redeemed from suffering, out of love to whom we seek our brethren in Britain whom we knew not, by whose grace we have found those whom we sought without their knowing it. Is it not the work of Him who said, 'My Father worketh hitherto, and I work;' and who, in order to show that He will convert the world, not by human wisdom but by His own power, chose unlearned men for His apostles; the same thing which He does now, since He has condescended to effect mighty things among the English people by weak instruments? But, my beloved brother, there is something in this heavenly gift which, along with your great joy, gives reason for much fear. You must rejoice that the souls of Englishmen have been led by outward miracles to inward grace, but you ought to fear lest the miraculous works which have been performed should puff up your own weak soul; for we must remind one another that when the disciples returned with joy from their mission, and said to their heavenly Master, 'Lord, even the very devils are subject unto us through Thy name,' they were at once told, 'In this rejoice not that the spirits are subject unto you, but rather rejoice because your names are written in heaven.'"

In 603, under the tree which in Bæda's time and afterwards was famous as "Augustin's Oak," Romanist and British clergy met in conference. The threefold ultimatum was proposed to the British from far Flintshire and farther Northumbria,—Keep Easter according to the Roman, and not the earlier Greek time; baptize as the Romans do, that is, with the rite of confirmation, or with the trine immersion; help Augustin to evangelize the Saxons on these methods. The demands were made as a right due to the Bishop of Rome. It amounted to a claim practically to stop all missionary effort which did not proceed on sacerdotal and sacramentary lines sanctioned by what every successive century made more and more a mythical apostolic succession, contrary alike to the teaching of Scripture, the facts of history, and the liberty that is in Christ Jesus. The same claim has been made—and repelled—ever since, not only by the papal Church, which shows some logical consistency therein, but by Anglican bishops of the Reformed Church in India, in Africa, and in Madagascar. The Romanist fiction of the grace of orders has been a pernicious obstruction in the way of Christian unity, purity, and success.

The British missionaries, like all their evangelical successors ever since, refused to submit their spiritual independence and divine views of truth to the yoke, and Augustin followed them with priestly threats. His successor Lawrence, a year after, so embittered the controversy by his attempts, that one Irish bishop refused even to eat with the men who would have unchurched him. The Romish Church so declined, on the death of King Æthelbert, that Lawrence contemplated a retreat to France. But the marriage of his Christian daughter to Edwin, king of Northumbria, and the zeal of Paulinus, who accompanied the princess to her heathen home, resulted in the adoption of the faith by the Witena. It was on this occasion (627) that one of his heathen nobles, feeling after God, thus addressed King Edwin :—

"The present life of man, O king, may be likened to what often happens when thou art sitting at supper with thy thanes and nobles in winter time: a fire blazes on the hearth, and warms the chamber; outside rages a storm of wind and snow; a sparrow flies in at one door of thy hall, and quickly passes out at the other. For a moment, while it is within, it is unharmed by the wintry blast, but this brief period of happiness over, to the wintry blast whence it came it returns, and vanishes from thy sight. Such is the brief life of man; we know not what went before it, and we are utterly ignorant as to what shall follow it. If, therefore, this new doctrine contain anything more certain, it justly deserves to be followed."

The high priest of Odin himself was the first to pull down the chief temple, and soon the gospel spread. For a time the chants of Gregory were heard everywhere as Paulinus and his fellows preached and baptized. Missionaries came even from Ireland, like **Fursæus** the Scot, who in his cell at Burgh Castle, as Sir Francis Palgrave writes, kindled the spark which, transmitted to the unharmonious Dante of a barbarous age, occasioned the first of the metrical compositions from whose combination the *Divina Commedia* arose. Oswald "the Fair," or "Free of Hand," one of Edwin's successors, sent to Iona instead of to Canterbury for preachers; and in 635 the monk-bishop Aidan, second only to Columba himself, was despatched, as we have seen, to become the founder of Lindisfarne, the second Iona. He so spread the British Church in Wessex and Essex, that again a conflict with the Romish priests became inevitable. To the dispute about the time of keeping Easter was now added that concerning the form of the clerical tonsure. Patrick and Columba had followed the usage of their predecessors in shaving the fore-part of the head from ear to ear, like a crescent. Designing to represent the crown of thorns, the Romans shaved the crown so as to surround it with a circle of hair. To this had Gregory's well-meant aggression come. In 664, Oswiu king of Wessex presided over the Synod of Whitby, and by a jest regarding Peter as the door-keeper of heaven, decided in favour of the Roman customs represented by Wilfrid of York, after **Colman** of Lindisfarne had declared for those of the earlier and purer Church. Colman retired to Scotland, but his colleagues and successors yielded. The Church in England, and ultimately in Scotland and in Ireland (1172), thus became Romanized with woeful results, which in Ireland we are still reaping.

Hild or Hilda (614-680), of the royal house of Edwin,—whose frontier was our modern Edinburgh,—may be taken as the worthy representative of the many noble and educated women who at this period gave themselves to a missionary life. When Edwin, her grand-uncle, was baptized in 627, she received baptism as a girl of thirteen. Under Aidan's teaching she organized the monastery of Whitby, which, like the Irish house of St. Brigid at Kildare, became the great missionary school of its day, for both men and women. "The Mother," as she was called, was under God the means of sending forth from her simple and primitive school, conducted like that of Iona, the principal clergy and bishops of what afterwards formed the province of York. She adhered to the Scottish rite, and condemned the appeal of Wilfrid to the Bishop of Rome. She was further honoured to be the instructress of **Cædmon**, the peasant tenant of the monastery, who may be called the first English poet and paraphraser of Scripture, the Saxon Milton.

Cuthbert (630–687) was the Scottish shepherd who became the apostle of the people of Northumbria, as his predecessors had converted their chiefs. When tending his sheep near Lauder,—which long after sent forth John Wilson to Western India from a similar home,—he was called by an angelic voice, he ran to Old Melrose, and, hearing of Aidan's death, he went south to Ripon, and then to Lindisfarne, where he submitted to the Roman rite. Bæda became his biographer, in one of the best mediæval lives which have come down to us. The work of Christianizing England was completed by Wilfrid in Sussex.

Theodore, sprung from Paul's city of Tarsus, as Archbishop of Canterbury consolidated the Roman hierarchy through the Synod of Hertford (689), while he established schools of learning. What Augustin weakly began in 596, Theodore vigorously completed, on both the literary and ecclesiastical sides, in 689. Thus "the Church of England owes its organization to a Greek monk." In less than a century Saxon England was at once Christianized and Romanized, the former chiefly by Scottish missionaries, the latter by Benedictine monks. England also was now made ready to become a missionary land to Germany and the Northern nations, as Ireland and Scotland had long been not only to Europe, but to England itself.

CHAPTER VII.

THE CONVERSION OF THE GOTHS AND THE FRANKS.

The Gothic Nation — Arianism a Compromise with Heathenism — Ulfila, the Apostle of the Goths—Chrysostom—Valentinus and Severinus, Jerome—The Franks—Martin of Tours—The Anti-Arian Baptism of Clovis—Honoratus—Germanus and Lupus—Eligius of Noyon—Columbanus—Gallus, Kilian, and Tradpert.

The Gothic Nation, extending across middle Europe from the Black Sea to the Baltic, pressed south upon the Danubian frontier of the Roman empire, and west upon the Franks and Germans, all through the third of the Christian centuries, at the close of which Diocletian reconstituted the imperial administration on an Oriental basis. In the fourth century, from Constantine to Theodosius, the emperors had gradually allowed them to settle on the south side of the Danube, using them as a buffer against their then northern brethren as we use Afghanistan, and employing them also as mercenaries in distant provinces like our Sepoys. The Ostrogoths roaming over the steppes of Scythia and Sarmatia, and the Western or Visigoths more settled on the Danube and the Alpine slopes, were forced to cease their intestine struggles by the pressure from the north-east of another and Mongolian horde, the modern Huns. These succeeding Kelt, Teuton and Slav, formed (374) the fourth prehistoric wave of migration from Asia into Europe. But a Christian missionary had been at work among the Goths so as to give a new aspect to the whole history of East and Central Europe. The half-Christianized Goths turned to Rome, which had done so much for many of their brethren, as the Government of British India now is the protection and asylum of fugitives from the despotism of Central Asia. Headed by the Christian chief Fridigern, a body of 200,000 men, women, and children, standing on the north bank of the Danube, clamoured for lands in the fertile plains of Mœsia.

Arianism, a Compromise with Heathenism.—The Emperor

Valens, busy with theological controversy in distant Antioch, and watching the Persians on the Euphrates, temporized and deceived the starving multitude in a way which their race afterwards avenged. But, for the time, there was only one man, like Schwartz in Haidar Ali's time, who could meet the difficulty, and he a missionary. Ulfila assured the emperor that all were in the way of becoming Christians. The emperor demanded that they should adopt his own **Arian Confession,** as opposed to the Nicene Creed, and to this Ulfila, loving Christ much but knowing theology little, consented. It was an unhappy concession, for Arianism was in the early missionary Church what Romanism especially in its Jesuit form was and is in the later,—a compromise with heathenism. Athanasius had done well to hold against the world the hypostatic union, the identity in substance of the Son and the Father, else would Arius have only anticipated at an earlier date the Mohammedanism of the Saracens and the Turks, which sprang out of, and is still kept in existence by, a corrupt Christianity. Such is the vital necessity of declaring to the heathen the whole counsel of God, of meeting the sin and the idolatry of mankind with the twin truths of the old missionary covenant, that Christ is God, and that the Spirit of God applies the salvation secured by the incarnate Christ. Arianism became the creed of the half-instructed materializing heathen nations, both Goths and Franks, and centuries of un-Christian war were necessary before the heresy was rooted out by the Scots and English missionaries. If Ulfila was guilty, in simple-minded ignorance, of the weakness which led to this, he nobly atoned for it by being the first to give the non-Christian races the Bible in their own vernacular, and that vernacular the future mother-tongue of the English-speaking and English-reading peoples, who were to evangelize regions which the Romans never knew.

Ulfila, the Apostle of the Goths (318–388).—Among the Goths of Eastern and Central, as among the Kelts of Western Europe, Christianity was first taught by devout Roman soldiers and by captives. Of the latter was the boy Ulfila, a Teutonic word meaning "the little wolf," who, like Patrick near Dumbarton, had been carried off during a Gothic raid into Cappadocia. He was seven years old when the Council of Nicæa met, and so far had Christianity spread among the Goths at that time, that they sent out a bishop, Theophilus, whose name appears at the foot of its decrees. As Ulfila, who became his successor, grew up, he was frequently employed by the Goths in political missions to the Roman authorities. While still short of those fifty years which prudence has fixed as desirable for the office of a bishop, he was selected by the Emperor Constantine himself, and consecrated by the imperial chaplain, Eusebius of Nicomedia. Settling south of the Danube, as we have seen, he was hailed by his Gothic converts as a second Moses, who had led them into a fat and peaceful land. Sent forth from Constantinople, he had come "from the metropolitan temple of the Holy Wisdom of God, bearing the written tidings of salvation to his admiring and expecting countrymen." It was the conviction of the Barbarians, says Ozanam, "que le fils de la louve ne pouvait faire mal." They had lost the art of writing during their migrations and wars, if they ever possessed it, and Ulfila designed for them an alphabet, that he might give them the word of God in their own tongue. That was the most fertile idea in the centuries of Christian missions from Jerome's Vulgate till the Reformation. The Greek Church which sent him forth, the Latin Church which, following the British Church, sought to reconvert the northern nations from Arian error, despised all tongues but two as barbarous and unfit to express the mysteries of the faith. Ulfila took from the Greek and Roman alphabets such letters as were suitable, and to these he added others expressing sounds unknown to the fastidious refinement of the two classical languages, making, however, only twenty-four in all. The historian of the science of language may well exclaim: "It required a prophetic sight and a faith in the destinies of those half-savage tribes, and a conviction also of the effeteness of the Roman and Byzantine empires, before a bishop could have brought himself to translate the Bible into the vulgar dialect of his barbarous countrymen." Thus was the whole Bible preserved, as it were, during the convulsions of Europe till the art of printing, save, it is said, the four books of Kings, which might have stimulated the martial ferocity of the people. We still possess, as a venerable relic, the greater part of the Gospels and other fragments of this translation, as it is in the Codex Argenteus, which, after a strange history, was carried off by Gustavus Adolphus to Upsala. To study the beautiful silvered letters of the parchment there, scholars make pilgrimage to what we may call the northern shrine of Ulfila. We have other examples of missionaries of the Greek Church thus translating the Scriptures. A century after, Miesrob, royal secretary, did the same for the Armenian Church, which has survived all the attempts of Zoroastrians and

Mohammedans to destroy it, and still prepares the noblest of the Oriental Churches for the Reformed teaching of the American Presbyterian missionaries. If the Goths spread Arianism, they carried with them the Bible of Ulfila all over Italy and Spain.

Chrysostom (404), most eloquent if not greatest of the Fathers, takes an honourable place in the History of Missions. When in the fulness of his power, he was the first to found a missionary college, in Constantinople, to continue and extend the work of Ulfila, by training Goths and other converts to preach to their countrymen. He spent the three years of his exile amid the hardships of Mount Taurus, in appealing to his friends for money, which they gave him liberally, and in stimulating missionary work not only among the northern races, but in Phœnicia and Persia. He redeemed captives and made missionaries of them. He encouraged all the churches by epistles full of fire, in which he points now to the example of Paul, now to the glory yet to be revealed. So humanizing did the missionary work of Ulfila, Chrysostom, and their successors prove to be, even where it did not effect individual conversion, that Augustine almost forgives the Visigoths and Vandals their Arian heresy, for the charity and clemency which marked conquerors like Alaric in the first sack of Rome (410), an event which pagans and Christians alike regarded as "the turning-point in the providential government of God."

Valentinus (440) around the modern Passau, and **Severinus** (454–482) in Bavaria and Austria, were early missionaries who sought to win the Arians as well as the heathen to Christ. From his retreat in an Eastern desert, whither he had fled in his youth after encountering a great danger, Severinus declared that Divine voices had summoned him to prove his love to Christ by evangelizing the tribes of the Upper Danube. His love to Arian and orthodox, to barbarian and Roman, to bond and free, made him the friend of all. He saved Vienna, almost like the later Sobieski; he induced the king of the Alemanni to spare Passau and restore all captives. Odoacer sought him as a friend. This joyous man of God, for thirty years an angel among the most savage races, sang as he lay a-dying the psalm which his brethren could not chant for sorrow: "Let everything that hath breath praise the Lord."

Jerome looked out from his cell at Bethlehem on such outpouring of the Spirit on all flesh, while he translated the Greek Testament into the Latin Vulgate, wrote to two Gothic correspondents who had consulted him as to the different versions of the Psalms in circulation: "Who would believe it that the barbarous Gothic tongue should seek the truth of the Hebrew; that while the Greek is slumbering or wrangling, the German should explore the sayings of the Holy Spirit? Of a truth I know that God is no respecter of persons; but that in every nation he that feareth God and worketh righteousness is accepted of Him So the hands once hardened by the sword-hilt, fingers once fitted to the bowstring, have turned to the stylus and the pen; the fierce heart of the warrior is softened to Christian mildness. Now we see fulfilled the prophecy of Isaiah, 'They shall beat their swords into ploughshares.'" To another correspondent he thus completes the contemporary picture: "Lo the Armenian lays down his quiver; the Huns are learning the Psalter; the frosts of Scythia glow with the warmth of faith; the ruddy armies of the Goths bear about with them the tabernacles of the Church; and therefore, perhaps, do they fight with equal fortune against us, because they trust in the religion of Christ equally with us."

The Franks of Ancient Gaul received the gospel through the Roman Provincia almost as soon as Rome itself, and held it with such tenacity and purity for a time, that the martyrs of Lyons and Vienne, in the reign of Marcus Aurelius, have made noble confessions. **Pothinus**, the first missionary bishop, so early as the middle of the second century, was succeeded by the famous **Irenæus**, the pupil of the Apostle John's disciple, Polycarp. But the faith did not spread beyond single churches in the midst of the mass of heathenism of which Julius Cæsar gives us glimpses, till towards the end of the fourth century. And even then the Frankish Church continued so lifeless that it was deaf to the appeals of the Saxons of England for missionaries, and to its duty to Germany, and had itself to receive new life from the Scots.

Martin of Tours (374–397) was literally a soldier rather than a missionary of the Cross, violent against the Arians who persecuted him much, the author of ascetic monasticism in France, and a priest of exceeding pride for those early days. Born in Pannonia and educated at Pavia, he withstood his parents, who would have kept him from Christ, led a military life which coloured all his career, studied under Hilary of Poictiers, and finally devoted himself to the service of God as a missionary-monk. He was the Iconoclast of his day. From Tours as a centre he led an army of military monks like himself over the land, so that the fear of the Christians' God fell upon the Franks, who saw their idol temples and groves swept away, while the missionary's voice proclaimed the one God, living and true, and salvation through Christ alone. The times made such evangelizing methods seem less evil than they really were, and the positive truth preached was blessed to many. But from Martin, its ecclesiastical founder, to the present day, the Gallic Church has preferred such methods, with results which the best of its sons bewail, as we ourselves do in Ireland.

The Anti-Arian Baptism of Clovis, which took place a century after Martin's death (496), introduced a new era in Frankish history. Chlodwig or Clovis (Louis) had, at fifteen, become chief of the Salian Franks, settled along the eastern land of the Rhine, from its junction with the Maine to its mouth. In a few years after he attained manhood he extinguished the Roman power, and conquered a territory corresponding to modern France, which marched with that of the Visigoths at the Loire. His wife was Clotilda, the daughter of the King of Burgundy, and she was an orthodox Christian, though brought up amid Arian influences. When, at Tolbiac, the Alemanni contended with him for the supremacy of Gaul, and he had implored the aid of his own gods in vain, he bethought him of Clotilda's teaching, and vowed to be baptized if he were victorious. With three thousand of his soldiers, on Christmas day, he knelt before the font at Rheims, while Remigius, the bishop, said: "Sicambrian, with meekness bow thy head; burn that thou didst adore; adore that which thou didst burn." Clovis arose the one ruler in the West who accepted the Nicene Creed, and he lost no time in following in the footsteps of St. Martin of Tours, who was by this time accredited with miracle-working. He carried fire and slaughter into Burgundy, he added Arian provinces to his kingdom, and he returned red with Arian blood to the shrine of St. Martin, where Anastasius, the Greek emperor, caused him to be invested not only with the old Roman office of consul, but with the new title, of unhappy augury for France, "Eldest son of the Church."

Honoratus.—Off the Mediterranean coast of France are the Lerins group of islands, one of which was long famous as the prison of the man with the iron mask. From 410 to 429, the young noble of Belgic Gaul, Honoratus, converted the desolation of the island which now bears his name into a garden and nursery of missionaries. Hilary of Arles, his successor, was his most famous disciple. From this Iona of the Gallican Church there went forth many who, during the next century, spread the gospel to Nice and Metz, Troyes and Lyons.

Germanus of Auxerre (418–448) and **Lupus of Troyes**, his contemporary, redeem the early history of the Gallic Church, by their missionary visits to Britain chiefly to oppose the spread of the Pelagian heresy, and by their influence over Attila and his Huns. **Cæsarius of Arles** (born 470), trained in the famous monastery of Lerins in Provence, did much to arrest the threatened relapse of the people into barbarism, by incessant gospel preaching and the education of Christian teachers for regular services in village churches; his sermons and appeals may be read with profit at the present day, and they possess a historical significance. After forty years' toil as a missionary bishop, during which he suffered much from the Visigoths, and his holy life and words compelled the admiration of Theodoric, the Arian king of the Ostrogoths, before whom he was summoned at Ravenna, Cæsarius died the day before that kept in memory of the great Augustine's death, 27th August 542. "Ye know," he said, "how I have loved him as a teacher of the truth, and how great the distance is between him and me in point of worthiness." **Eligius of Noyon** (588–658) is another light of the Frankish Church. Sprung of an old Christian family, he became goldsmith to King Clotaire II., and won in his daily life such reputation for self-sacrifice, that he was elected bishop in 641. He who had spent his all on the poor and in ransoming hundreds of the slaves of Roman, Gallic, Moorish, and British descent, but especially Saxons who were sent to Clotaire's court for sale, when bishop of a large German-speaking diocese, won by his Christlike life the Pagans to his Master, and built them up in the faith by sermons, of which fragments of powerful simplicity and persuasiveness have come down to us. Such were the true founders of the Gallican liberties of the fair Church of France, the true ancestors of the Huguenots, the true predecessors of the Protestant missionaries who are opening up Basuto and Zambesi land to the gospel to-day.

Columbanus (559–615) was the most remarkable of the Irish missionaries who evangelized both the Franks and the Germans. Born in Leinster, and trained at the famous Ulster monastery of Banchor, he was thirty years of age when, with the usual brotherhood of twelve companions, he landed in Gaul. Gontran, grandson of Clovis, would have kept him in Burgundy, but he would not rest until he had passed over the Vosges to the fierce Suevi. Amid their gloomy defiles and dense forests he planted the settlements of Anegray and Luxeuil and Fontaines, on the stern rule of self-denial for Christ even to death. The simpler and purer customs and beliefs of the missionary abbot of Luxeuil, brought from Ireland, excited the hostility of the Frankish bishops, while his evangelizing methods were too stern to win the Suevi. Settling on the lake of Constance, he established a new centre of light at Bregenz, which had lapsed from the faith under the incursions of the Alemanni. Thence he passed into Lombardy, where he founded the monastery of **Bobbio** as a third Iona or Lindisfarne, and there he died at seventy-two. His monastery continued down to 1803, and became farther famous for its library, in which Cicero's *De Republica* and Irish MSS. had been preserved. His name is still perpetuated in St. Columbano, near Lodi.

Gallus (died 627), the best known of the companions and disciples of Columbanus, remained at Bregenz, from which he restored the churches in all the region from the Black Forest and around Constance, and became the apostle of Switzerland, where his name survives in that of the Canton of St. Gall. **Kilian**, of the Iona order, in Thuringia and **Tradpert**, in the Black Forest, fell martyrs to their zeal and consistent purity of life and doctrine.

CHAPTER VIII.

THE CONVERSION OF THE TEUTONS AND THE NORTHMEN.

The Scots and Anglo-Romish Missionaries contrasted—Winfrith or Bonifacius—Walpurga, Leoba, and Thekla—Bæda—Alcuin—King Ælfred—The Northmen or Normans—Anskar—Norway—Hakon, Olaf Tryggvason, and Olaf the Saint—The Conversion of Western Europe completed.

The Scots and Anglo-Romish Missionaries contrasted.—The German theologian and historian who, on his own conversion from Judaism, through Platonism, to evangelical Christianity, took the name of Neander, "a new man," bursts forth into an exclamation of grateful joy, as in 1846 he contemplates the successive steps by which the Scots and English missionaries brought the Teutons of Germany to Christ: "What would have become of our fatherland if God had not, by His Spirit, awakened that missionary zeal? . . . As we now with joy look back with gratitude on the labours of those heroes of the faith, to whom we owe the blessings of Christianity and of all mental culture, so hereafter, the churches gathered from among the heathen in South India, Asia, and Africa, when they have received, through Christianity, the abundance of all earthly and heavenly good, will look back with gratitude on the commencing missionary zeal of the present day." But, hearty Lutheran though he was, Neander carefully discriminates between the merits of the earlier and purer British preachers, representing a free Church and a full gospel, and those of the English bishops and priests who spread the hierarchical organization and ritualistic observances of the papal Church over Europe; especially from the close of the seventh century. The mission of Augustin and his immediate successors in the sees of Canterbury and York had so limited the field of the Scoto-Irish missionaries at home, that they swarmed like bees—to use the expression of contemporary annalists—into the dark places of heathen Europe. Left alone, the churches and communities which they formed might have developed into free national churches, of the Culdee or Waldensian type. But, in Europe as in England, the Romish missionaries built on their foundation, overlapped their mission fields, consolidated and organized the free nascent Christendom of Northern Europe into a powerful ecclesiastical system, with Rome as its basis, and the new Roman Empire of Karl the Great and his successors as at first its protector and then its *protégé*. "The missionary," writes Neander, "requires especially the spirit of Christian freedom that he may not obstruct the work of God in the soul by human alloy, or prevent Christ, whose organ alone he ought to be, from obtaining in every nation that peculiar form which is exactly suitable to each one." The first apostle of the Germans acted on lines so contrary to this, that a second apostle became necessary to Germany and Christendom, even Luther. But, looking at the seventh and eighth Christian centuries, it must be admitted that, if the British and Irish missionaries were superior in freedom of spirit and purity of Christian knowledge, Rome was better able to consolidate the outward framework of the infant Church against the assaults of Paganism and of Arianism, a subtle compromise with it.

John Richard Green, the latest and ablest historian of *The Making of England*, writes of the Scoto-Irish Christianity, that "when it burst on Western Christendom it brought with it an enthusiasm, an energy, a learning greater than any it found there. For while in Italy, or Gaul, or Spain, Christianity had spent its vigour in a struggle for self-preservation against the heathen invaders, in winning them to its creed, in taming them by its discipline, in bringing to bear on them the civilisation which it had alone preserved through the storm of conquest, Ireland, unscourged by assailants, drew from its conversion a life and movement such as it has never known since. The science and biblical knowledge which fled from the Continent, took refuge in famous schools which made Durrow and Armagh universities of the West. The new Christian life soon beat too strongly to brook confinement within the bounds of Ireland itself. . . . For a time it seemed as if the course of the world's history was to be changed, as if the older Celtic race that Roman and German had driven before them had turned to the moral conquest of their conquerors, as if Celtic and not Latin Christianity was to mould the destinies of the churches of the West."

Winfrith or Bonifacius, born at Kirton, in Devonshire, in 680, spent the forty years of his missionary life from 715 to 755. Born of Christian parents, who planned for their son a secular life, Winfrith early received the missionary's call, which none can mistake or resist to whom it comes. He became a monk at Nuteschelle, in Hampshire. He frankly confesses, in one of his letters, that to the fear of Christ there was added a passion for foreign travel, just as Cook's voyages in later days fired William Carey and many of the earlier modern missionaries. He had the English impulse for the sea, for colonizing, for raising savage races to the platform of Christian civilisation. This craving, guided by the word of God, the Spirit sanctified. Under the influence of Egbert, an English priest who had vowed to take the gospel to the German tribes, but had been prevented, Willibrord of Northumbria, but educated in Ireland, had begun the Friesland mission. The tales of his sufferings at the hand of the heathen prince Radbod, were told in every English monastery. They roused Winifrith, now known as the monk Bonifacius; he set out with three associates, only to find that Friesland was at war with Charles Martel, and, for the time, shut to the gospel. But he did not forget his first field. Setting out the second time to preach to his kinsmen after the flesh, after refusing to fill the place of abbot, he obtained a commission from Pope Gregory II. to preach in Germany, and, adding to this "an ample supply of relics," he made Thuringia his first centre. Refusing to succeed Willibrord in the see of Utrecht, he evangelized Hessia and Saxony, also with such success that the Pope made him regionary or general bishop in 723. By his oath of obedience over the grave of Peter, he bound the German Empire to the Pope with bonds which are still fast over half its extent, in spite of the Reformation: "I vow to thee, the first of the apostles, to thy vicar, Pope Gregory, and his successors, that, with God's help, I will continue in the unity of the Catholic faith, . . . in close adherence to the usages of thy Church," etc. His many letters and his life thenceforth prove that while he was a sincere and loving missionary of the word of God, he was above all things a Romish missionary. Writing to his friend the Abbess Bugga in England, he said: "Since I am the last and most unworthy of all the messengers which the Romish Church has sent out for the publication of the gospel, may I not die without having brought forth fruit."

The victories of Charles Martel co-operated with the zeal of Boniface. Finding on his second return from Rome that many of his converts had returned to their Thor-worship, he determined himself to strike a blow that would shatter all belief in the thunder-god. In presence of the enraged heathen and trembling half-Christians, he cut down the sacred oak of Giesmar in Hesse. As the mighty tree crashed to the ground, the people shouted, "The Lord He is God," and on the spot a Christian church was built of the timber. The mission spread, so that he addressed a circular letter to the clergy in England for help: "Have pity on the Pagan Saxons, for they themselves were used to say, 'We are of the same flesh and bone.'" Many missionaries, men and women, left the now pleasant retreats of English monasteries for the German forests, where not only converts arose to train native missionaries, but industrial and agricultural schools, like those which are converting the great Kafir tribes of Africa into peaceful and prosperous subjects. Those who remained behind he implores, "Support us by your prayers,—us who labour and scatter the seed of the gospel among the rude and ignorant tribes of Germany." Not again would he run the risk of a relapse into heathenism, such as had marred his own earlier efforts, and had wasted the Frankish Church. Copying the Scots, and true to the spirit which has ever identified the Benedictines with useful and godly learning, he set up the school for the young beside the church, and made the Scriptures the substance of the teaching. His letters to Cuthbert and others in England are full of requests for MSS. of the Epistles of St. Peter in gilded letters, that he might have the words of his predecessor ever before him, for copies of the Scriptures in a good clear hand, suitable for his weak eyes, and for expository commentaries, especially those of Bæda. Having founded many bishoprics in Germany, he obtained in Rome the higher powers of legate, he reorganized the Bavarian Church, and in 743 he called the first synodal council held for eighty years. Amid many desirable regulations for the good of the churches, both German and Frank, this synod extended the papal power over national churches, and further crushed, in the spirit of a bitter intolerance, the Scots missionaries. Men like **Clement the Scot**, propagating a purer gospel than Boniface, much as he excelled his successors in devotion to the word of God, were condemned for holding the faith in the purity of apostolic times, as to the freedom of the Church, the sole authority of Scripture, and the right to marry, along with Origen's views about Hades. When, from the metropolitan see of Mainz, Boniface exercised his jurisdiction also over Worms, Spires, Tongres, Cologne, Utrecht, and the four heathen peoples beyond, and was now seventy years of age, he retired to **Fulda**, the great missionary monastery in Buchwald, which, under his own eye, his son in the faith, the Bavarian **Sturm**, had caused to arise as a second Nuteschelle. But there came back on him the desire of his youth, to finish the work of Willibrord in East Friesland. The old saint of seventy-five, taking with him the treatise of Ambrose on *The Advantage of Death*, and sundry relics in his shroud, met with the missionary martyr's death from the heathen ancestors of the Dutch, as he lay, with a volume of the Gospels for a pillow, on the shore of the Zuyder Zee. Thus lived and died the Englishman whom all Teutonic Europe has justly commemorated since that 5th of June 755 as the father of its civilisation. **Gregory of Utrecht**, his disciple, founded at that city the great missionary college of the time,—the best memorial of Boniface.

Walpurga, who at the special request of Boniface had accompanied her brother Winibald and kinsman Willibald from Dorsetshire to help the much-toiling missionary in Thuringia, represents a band of devoted women who founded sisterhoods in many parts of Germany, and tamed the people by their Christ-like tenderness and self-sacrifice. Of the thirty companions the best known are **Lioba** and **Thekla**. Lioba became the friend of Charlemagne's queen, whom she drew to Christ.

Bæda (673–735), Alcuin, and King Ælfred represent the literary side of the English missionary movement. After Gildas, Bæda's *Ecclesiastical History of the English People* is our second great authority for its facts, as *The English Chronicle*, first compiled at Ælfred's court, is the third. Only two centuries separate Bæda from the landing of the first English colonists in Thanet. At Jarrow or Wearmouth he carried on his studies amid what Dr. Stubbs calls all the existing sources of learning in the West,—the Irish, the Roman, the Gallican, and the Canterbury learning. He had the then rare knowledge of Greek and Hebrew, and seems to have read all the literature preserved up to that time. This enabled him to help in the foundation of the great missionary school at York, from which the light of the West was rekindled over England and Europe. His missionary work lay not so much in his *Historia Ecclesiastica* and other works, as in his translation and commentaries on Scripture. He died when translating the 9th verse of the 6th chapter of John's Gospel, and repeating the Gloria Patri. His disciple Egbert, Archbishop of York, handed on the torch of Divine learning to a descendant of the same noble house as that from which Willibrord, apostle of the Frisians, had sprung.

Alcuin (735–800) added to his studies at York the breadth of view and knowledge of men which travel gives, and which enabled him to educate Europe. From the school at York he was called by Karl the Great to complete that strong ruler's third of a century's struggle with Saxon barbarism, which had carried the light to the Elbe and the North Sea, but had again imperilled the Church by seeking an outward and a rigid conformity without knowledge and without faith. "Carry on the publication of the Divine Word according to the example of the apostles," he said to the Emperor. "Of what use is baptism without faith?" he asked of the Bishop of Salzburg. "And faith is a matter of free will, not of compulsion, as the holy Augustine says. Man must be instructed and taught by repeated preaching, and especially we must implore for him the grace of God." The letters, and poems, and theological works of Alcuin mark him out as the teacher and missionary civiliser of the eighth and ninth centuries, from the great Karl himself and the princes of the Palatine school. Justice has not yet been done to his life and influence.

King Ælfred (849–901).—Northumbria, first Christianized by Scots, and raised to supremacy under Ethelfrith, Edwin, and Oswiu, yielded to Mercia, or central England, during the eighth century under Offa (758–796), who held London. That in turn paled before the West Saxon power during the Danish or Scandinavian invasions of the ninth century under Egbert, "first king of all England," as he virtually was. Then Ælfred, his grandson, came to the front. A hard fighter, he had learned from his mother, and when he visited Rome in his youth, how rude his people were. He first formed a regular army and built good ships. He translated Bæda, Orosius, Boethius, and Gregory into English; above all, he began the *English Chronicle* in the vernacular for the people. The Bible, he urged, even at that early time had hold on the nations through versions in their own tongues. Englishmen might know it, as they might know the other great books of the world, in their own English. He made English, according to the late Mr. Green, the earliest prose literature of the modern world, little thinking that he was preparing the weapon wherewith the English were to attack the idolatry of India and the barbarism of the dark races in these later days. He feared God and loved man. His missionary zeal extended far beyond his own people and the Danes, for he sent gifts to Rome, Jerusalem, and to the distant shrine of Thomas in India. He was a keen geographer for those days, and a lover of strangers. The Danes had shaken the Christianity of Mid-Britain as previously the Saxons had done, and it is the glory of Ælfred to re-create what he had seen as a child, "how the churches stood filled with treasures and books, and there was also a great multitude of God's servants," as he tells us in the preface to his translation of Gregory's *Pastoral*. It was to Wales that he sent for Bishop **Asser** to help him, but for a national literature he did most himself.

The Northmen or Normans.—The age of the great Karl and our own Ælfred was succeeded by the last wave from the North. During the ninth century the Scandinavian Northmen swept over the civilisation which missionary Christianity had united with Roman polity to create. But here, as in every great world-movement since Abraham, it was the Divine or Christian element alone which at once made the civilisation permanent, and in time absorbed, with its spiritual transforming influences, the new invaders. In 826 the news of the German-Frank Emperor's death affected Europe as that of Alaric the Goth's first capture of Rome had done. Had the world, the new Christian world, come to an end when the conqueror of Saxon and Frank descended into the tomb he had dug for himself at Aachen, weeping for the woes that the pirates of the North were to bring on his empire? For already, from the icebound lakes and stormy fiords of Scandinavia, the Wikings or "creekmen" were threatening, with their long ships, every river and harbour, every valley and shore of Germany, France, and Britain, with the nascent commerce, the growing wealth, the learned monasteries, the village churches which centuries of missionary toil had created. **Liudger**, friend of Willibrord, and grandson of one of the Tuscan chiefs whom he had converted, after studying at Utrecht and under Alcuin at York, had, at the close of the eighth century, proposed to the emperor to begin a mission to the Northmen. **Willehad**, from Northumbria, began in 779 the completion of Willibrord's work, and, becoming the first Bishop of Eastern Frisia and Saxony, at Bremen, evangelized the fringe of the Danish territory on the north bank of the Elbe. But it was reserved for a missionary of another and higher type to become the apostle of the North,—for Anskar, who was the John, as Boniface was the Peter, of these messengers of Christ.

Anskar of Corbie, a French convent near Amiens, was a boy of thirteen when it was told throughout the empire that the great Karl was gone, leaving nought but a corpse sitting in silk and pearls, "his closed eyelids covered, his face swathed in the dead-clothes, girt with his baldric, the ivory horn slung in his scarf, his good sword Joyeuse by his side, the gospel book open on his lap, musk and amber and sweet spices poured around." When only five years old, the boy had learned what death was by the loss of his mother, and had then received his first call to be Christ's. But that the great emperor should die, after crimes as well as services to the Church like those of Clovis and Constantine, seemed too terrible. Anew was the youthful ascetic summoned to the life hid with Christ in God. Vision succeeded vision before the fasting meditative monk. Once he dreamed that he was taken to the assembly of the blest by two guides, Peter and John, and there placed before the boundless light, out of which the Divine Majesty spake with him in tones inexpressibly sweet: "Go hence and return to Me with the martyr's crown." The un-modern idea of martyrdom apart, it was precisely such a dream that the young Alexander Duff had, and repeated as his missionary call when he lay dying. Once again Christ appeared to Anskar, and, after his confession of sin, fully commissioned him, as Isaiah was sent, with the words: "Fear not, I am He that blotteth out thy transgressions." The missionary call and the missionary training were complete, even as Saul became Paul. The work was ready.

Harold Klak, King of Denmark, and his queen, when on a visit to the Emperor Louis the Pious, had been baptized in the cathedral of Mainz in the year 826. The event had a special significance. Nine centuries afterwards, it was Friedrich IV., a king of the same country, who was the first to send forth Protestant missionaries to India and to Greenland. With the Lord a thousand years are as one day. The good emperor sought for a missionary daring enough to go back with the royal convert and face the fierce sea-kings of Jutland and Sweden. Anskar was chosen, was ready, when only one of his brethren could be found to volunteer to accompany him, and even he timidly asked Anskar whether he really persisted in so dangerous an enterprize, receiving the answer: "When I was asked whether I would go for God's name among the heathen to publish the gospel, I could not decline such a call. Yes, with all my power I wish to go hence, and no man can make me waver in this resolution." Like the Scottish missionaries long after in India, Anskar opened at Hadeby, in Schleswig, a school in which to train native boys for the ministry. The teaching of Christians carried captive by the

Northmen of Sweden, had prepared that country for the gospel, and thither Anskar went in 831. From the old capital of Sigtuna on the Mälar Lake, he so spread the true light, that Hamburg was created an archbishop's see for the northern missions, and **Gauzbert**, his nephew, became first bishop in Sweden. The Pagan Normans were roused, they sacked Hamburg, ravaged the diocese, and expelled the Christians from Sweden. But the faith of Anskar never wavered; for he lived by prayer. Both Christians and heathen ascribed to him the power of working miracles, because, with the skill of a medical missionary and the tenderness of a woman,—he opened an hospital at Bremen,—he healed the sick. But he disclaimed any such power, in language which is a pregnant commentary on all legendary miracles: "If I were thought worthy before my God of that, I would beseech Him to grant me this miracle, that by His grace He would make of me a holy man." Prayer and pains prevailed, as John Eliot long after taught. King Horik of Denmark and King Olaf of Sweden ceased their intolerance so far as to recognise the Christians' God, and to allow the building of churches where the people could be persuaded. As Anskar was the first medical missionary, so he distinguished himself above all friends of the slaves, white and black, till the nineteenth century, led to this by a vision of Christ Himself, as he asserted. For thirty-four years he was a martyr for Christ in the sense of his prototype John. After labours and sufferings more abundant than those of any of his successors, he died in 865 with the last words of Stephen on his lips. The harvest which he sowed was first reaped nearly two centuries afterwards, when, in 1030, **Knut** (Canute), having married an English wife, and become King of England, forbade the rites of heathenism, and sent forth missionaries to the North to complete the conversion of Scandinavia, from Greenland (the first time under Eric the Red) and even North America and Iceland, to **Norway** and the Western **Lapland**, which was the last part of Europe to become Christian.

Norway, the extreme nursery of the Northmen, received Christianity from England (957–963) during the brief reign of **Hakon**, who had been educated at the court of our King Athelstan. The Wiking **Olaf Tryggvasson**, who had been confirmed as a Christian by Alphegé, Bishop of Winchester, and was elected King of Norway in 994, has been called the Northern Mahomet, because of his violent measures for the extermination of Odin-worship.

These led to his death in battle in the year 1000, when, rather than yield to the heathen Danes and Swedes, he leaped into the sea, and became the hero of many a Saga. Another of the same name, **Olaf the Saint**, in 1015 brought Norway, Denmark, and Sweden under one rule, destroyed the great image of Thor, as Mahmoud of Ghazni did that of Krishna at Somnath about the same time, and fell in battle in 1030, becoming ever since the patron saint of Norway. Thus Odinism gradually disappeared; but the first to attack it were the Scots missionaries known as "Papar," who had crept northward in their curachs to the Hebrides, to the Orcades, to the Faroes, to Iceland, where, on the re-discovery and colonization by the Norwegians in 874, traces of them were found. It was from Iceland that Greenland was first Christianized; it had seventeen bishops in succession up to 1408, after which the "black death" decimated the settlers, and the Eskimos exterminated the rest. Tradition tells of a Scots missionary, who from Greenland found his way to North America, and there died a martyr for the faith.

Meanwhile the earlier Scandinavian pirates, who had been settled for a century along the Seine, under the Christianity which was imposed on them as a condition of settlement, became strong and wise for the last conquest of England, although in France they had exchanged their free institutions for feudalism.

The Conversion of Western Europe may be said to have been nominally or historically completed when, in 1066, the Normans, Christianized, became conquerors, under William, of the Saxon and ultimately the Celtic peoples, who had been the chief instruments in God's hands of turning the Northern nations from nature-worship and hero-worship, animal sacrifices and human sacrifices, and dumb idols like the colossal Irmin-Saule and Thor, to the living God. First the Scoto-Celt transformed the Saxons so that they should not give England back again to a demon-driven barbarism. Then Christian Celt and Saxon became the missionaries to Frank and Goth, Hun and Scandinavian, who, as one historian writes, were tracked in their native deserts by "a missionary Christianity, —Christianity in her simplest and most persuasive guise, as the faith of the earnest, the loving, the self-devoted: before, they found Christianity in the empire,—Christianity refined and complex, imperious and pompous, Christianity enthroned by the side of kings, and sometimes paramount over them." Had the Gothic races not been thus taught to kneel in humble adoration, and turn in loving imitation, not to the Christ of the Arians,—as at first,—but to the only wise God our Saviour, before they conquered the empire, they might have swept away with it the Christianity which they had had neither time nor training to gaze at and adopt. As it was, the empire which consolidated the Church soon made it so corrupt and intolerant of all freedom, like that of the British missionaries, that a reformation became necessary, if the people of Christ were to recover for themselves spiritual and civil liberty, and to give both to the down-trodden nations. Western Europe was saved by the Christianization of the Northern nations from the fate which was fast overtaking Eastern and Southern Europe, where the Saracens and then the Turks swept away Church and State, creed and polity together, even in the lands where Christ had taught and suffered, where His followers were first called by His name, and His apostles found centres whence to evangelize Africa, India, and Spain.

CHAPTER IX.

MISSIONS TO SLAVS, MOHAMMEDANS, AND JEWS.

The Slavs—Cyrillus and Methodius—Adalbert of Prussia—Nilus—Otto of Bamberg—Vladimir of Russia's Baptism—The Saracens and the Crusaders—Francis of Assisi—Marco Polo and Franciscan Missions to Cathay—Raimundus Lullius, the First Missionary to the Mohammedans—Monte Corvino—Intolerant Missions.

The Slavs formed the last wave from Asia westward. Patient shepherds and husbandmen settling along the lower Danube, they soon became so oppressed by the German and the Turkish races as to have given their name to the most permanent and hopeless form of bondage. Driven north, they took possession of the plains and lakes of Modern Russia, and did not stop till they held the southern shore of the Baltic, which the Hohenzollerns have since made the head of a third empire. To-day they form a threefold difficulty, centring in the Eastern Question,—to complex Austria, which seeks to dominate them in their earliest European seats along the Danube; to Germany, which has never lost its old race hostility to them, and claims the Lithuanian portion of the Baltic shores, which they still hold; and to Russia, the German governing class of which uses them to recover Constantinople from their Turkish foes, but is being absorbed by them into an empire, which would be more dangerous to its neighbours if it enjoyed even the beginnings of free institutions. What we may now call the Austrian and Russian Slavs became Christian during the barren tenth and eleventh centuries. But it was the imperial Greek Church in its decay which Christianized them. The Prussian Slavs were won to Christ by German missionaries, and became absorbed, spiritually as well as geographically, in the great Lutheran movement.

Cyrillus and Methodius.—The first of the Slavonic peoples to adopt Christianity were the Bulgarians, who, after long oppression under the Turks, are destined to play a part in the future of the

Eastern churches and states. The Prince **Bogoris**, influenced by his sister, who had learned Christ when a captive in Constantinople, was baptized (861) by Photius the patriarch, and received a Greek archbishop, who spread the faith among the Servians to the Adriatic and in Greece and the Crimea. Those in Moravia, stretching from the Danube across the Carpathian Mountains to Southern Poland, had been compelled by the great Karl to profess Christianity and accept a regionary bishop under the metropolitan see of Passau. But, desiring preachers in their own vernacular, they wrote this appeal to the Greek Emperor Michael: "Send us teachers who may explain to us the Scriptures and their meaning." The request is prophetic of that brotherhood which long after inherited the name Moravian, and carried it to the confines of the heathen world. The emperor sent to them two brothers from Thessalonica, scholars described as familiar with the Slavonic language and clever philosophers, Methodius and Constantinus or Cyrillus. They proved to be missionaries specially qualified for the work to be done, to which, like all their wise successors in India, especially in modern times, they adapted their methods. As, long before, Ulfila had done for the Goths, they reduced the language to writing, using an alphabet of forty Greek, Hebrew, and Armenian letters. The Gospels, the Acts of the Apostles, and the Psalter were soon translated, and in four years the word of the Lord grew mightily and prevailed as of old. The Romish missionaries of Germany by this time had as little tolerance for the Scripture-reading of the Greek as for the freedom of the British churches. Methodius was summoned to Rome, where, by producing so sensational a relic as the alleged body of St. Clement of Rome, and satisfying Pope Adrian as to his creed, he was created metropolitan of Moravia and Pannonia. Neither then nor under the Pope's successor did he surrender the root principle of missions, that every people shall read the Bible and worship God in their mother tongue. He conceded, however, the use of a mass service in Greek or Latin. His version of the Scriptures kept Divine truth alive in this portion of the Greek Church for ten centuries, until the old Slavonic became a dead language and modern Russian took its place.

Adalbert of Prussia.—Soon after the death of Methodius, about 885, Moravia became part of the kingdom of **Bohemia**, which Methodius had nominally Christianized in continuation of the Scoto-German influences from Regensburg or Ratisbon. Then the infant Church passed through persecutions not unlike those of

Madagascar in modern times, till the proselytizing emperor Otho I. interfered, and a bishopric was established at Prag. There Adalbert was born, and in 982 became Romish bishop. What with Pagan customs and Slavonic liberty, which had not yet changed these, Adalbert thrice left Prag, seeking counsel, as so many of the godly of the tenth century did, of the Greek monk **Nilus**, who, in an age when faith and morals seemed dead, and hypocrisy ruled the Church, was in his Italian cell something like an incarnate conscience to Christendom,—its great home missionary. Nilus made Adalbert a missionary. After influencing Stephanus, who became the first King of **Hungary**, and established Christianity there, the ardent bishop raised the standard of the Cross at Dantzig, then the border between Poland and Prussia. That he might give himself irrevocably to the work, he sent off his ship with its crew, keeping only two associates. Repulsed again and again, and beaten nearly to death, they went from place to place about the mouth of the Pregel river, now singing the gospel, now declaring to the infuriated savages, in winning tones, the gospel message, "For your salvation I am come, that, forsaking your deaf and dumb deities, you may acknowledge your Creator, beside whom there is no god; that, believing in His name, you may receive eternal life, and be made partakers of an imperishable existence of heavenly joy." Transfixed with a lance by a priest, the martyr missionary died in 997, praying to the Lord for his own salvation and that of his murderers. The prayer was answered, after a terrible fashion, by a crusade against Slavonic heathenism far more sanguinary than those against the Saracen and the Turk. Or shall we not rather believe that it was first fully answered when German Prussia, from Berlin and Halle, began to atone for the butcheries of the Order of Teutonic Knights by sending its sons to the Hindoo and the Kafir?

Otto of Bamberg, a noble of Swabia and a bishop, a century after Adalbert (1124–1139), followed him through **Poland**, which was gradually Christianized from Moravia and Romanized, into Pomerania, of which Stettin was the capital, and the island of Rügen the heathen centre. Where a Spanish priest, Bishop Bernard, had failed, Otto succeeded, but as the splendid representative of the King of Poland at the head of a band of envoys and soldiers. At Pyritz seven thousand accepted baptism. Stettin itself had been prepared for the faith by the return of a captive lady, who had learned Christ in her exile, and whose sons were the first converts. As the Slavs saw their idols and temples falling before the axes of the missionaries, they helped in the work of destruction, declaring, like the people of Polynesia centuries after, "What power can these gods possess who cannot even defend themselves?" To Rome he sent the triple-headed idol Triglav, as in later days the mission-houses of London contain grim memorials of old superstitions presented by the devotees who have abandoned them for Christ. Rügen was the last to fall. There, in Arcone, its capital, the most terrible of the gods of the Slavs of the Baltic had for centuries reared its head. Within a temple of carved wood, hung with tapestry and adorned with paintings, stood the sanctuary of Sviantovit, surrounded by the four-faced god of the seasons and the seven-faced god of war, as described by the contemporary Danish historian Saxo Grammaticus. The monster Sviantovit rose to an awful height, its four heads resting on two bodies; the right hand holding a horn annually filled with mead, the left bent like a bow; a flowing robe half revealed, half concealed the demon; beside it were the gigantic bridle, sword, and silver scabbard, used when the god led the people to victory on a white horse. A sacred regiment of three hundred cavalry guarded the fane and levied the taxes which enriched its priests. Even yet the scene of that old Oriental devil-worship amid the storms of the Baltic is so awful, that Duff declared he had never seen any spot in modern heathendom like it. Otto more than once braved these storms and the heathen defenders of the shores of the Baltic, but it fell to a successor thirty years after (1168), and the dread idol was committed as fuel to the flames. Otto spent his closing years in building up the churches and redeeming the slaves whom pirate chiefs by sea and Jewish dealers by land still sold in the semi-barbarous courts of Europe.

Vladimir of Russia's Baptism.—The eastern Slavs were turned in a body to Christianity, after the fashion of the Franks and Clovis, by the baptism of Vladimir. The Norman or Varangian Runic had laid the foundation of the Russian Empire in 862. A century after, Olga, a princess of his house, when on a visit to Constantinople, was baptized. After personally studying the representations of Mohammedans, Jews, and missionaries of the Latin and Greek Churches, her grandson Vladimir sent envoys to other lands to report to him on the different religions. Constantinople and Justinian's Church of St. Sophia captivated the reporters, who confirmed the teaching of Olga. Such is the story of the Russian chronicler. Married to Anne, sister of the Emperor Basil, Vladimir and his twelve sons were baptized at Kieff in 988, the idol Peroun was sunk in the Dnieper, and the whole population immersed themselves in its waters, while Greek priests read the baptismal service from the banks. The books of Methodius and Cyrillus were read in their own tongue. Thus arose, in full stature, the most Erastian of Christian churches, and therefore intolerant to missionary efforts not conducted by its own hitherto half-educated and hereditary priests throughout what has become a vast semi-Asiatic empire. To this day Russia has shown a spirit of hostility to the Jews. We shall see how its Government drove out both Scottish and Moravian missionaries. With one missionary movement only has the Greek Church of Russia been always honourably if not energetically identified, from the days of Ulfila and Methodius,—the circulation of the word of God. Its relation to Mohammedanism has been political rather than spiritual. The Greek Church, which is identified with the autocratic and anti-popular government of the Czar, still awaits a Reformation. Such a revival, to be probably not unaccompanied by political revolutions, should make the Church of Chrysostom the most powerful missionary agency to Eastern Europe, and all Northern and Central Asia.

The Saracens and the Crusades.—At the opening of the thirteenth century, Europe was nominally Christian,—was, indeed, the only part of the whole world which could be called Christendom. For, parallel with the success of the Scots and Saxon missionaries in the West, Islam had been annexing the lands first evangelized by the gospel. The kaliph successors of Mohammed and their hosts of Saracens had spread like locusts from Arabia north and west and east. At the very time when the Scottish Aidan was founding an English Iona on Lindisfarne, the Saracens took the holy city Jerusalem (637), and overran Syria and Egypt. When the Saxon Winfrith or Boniface was preparing himself for the evangelization of Germany, the most bitter enemies of the Cross of Christ were obliterating all vestiges of the great churches of North Africa, which had given us Augustine. They had occupied nearly all Spain, a land identified with his own missionary policy by the Apostle Paul himself. They penetrated to Tours, the centre of the Frankish Church, before they received the first serious check (737) from Charles Martel; two years afterwards they threatened Rome itself. The letters of Boniface send to his correspondents in England echoes, even at that early time, of wars and persecutions, which issued in the six **Crusades**, from 1096 to 1248.

"God wills it" was the enthusiastic cry with which the chivalry of Europe, rich and poor, sought, not the conversion of the Muslim, but to recover from Antichrist the holy places of the Lord's birth and crucifixion and death, to which the legends of superstition and the fury of the sects had given a fictitious importance. The days of the apostles and the apostolic missionaries, who had subdued the cultured East, the apparently impregnable Empire, and the savage North, by weapons which were not carnal, to a kingdom which is not of this world, were forgotten. The seeds which the first Christian emperor had sown, had in Asia grown to be Islam, in Europe to be the Church and the polity of the Holy Roman Empire. The solitary contribution which the crusades made to the missionary efficiency of the Church of Christ, as some recompense for the evils which they did in at once perpetuating Islam, falsifying His kingdom, and introducing the leprosy of the East into Europe, was this,—they gave dumb, ignorant Christendom a knowledge of foreign lands and faiths, which grew into the discoveries of the fifteenth century, and are not without fruit in the true missionary crusade of the nineteenth century. But even amid the animalism and the din of the thirteenth and fourteenth centuries, there were a few choice souls whom the Spirit of God enlightened to wield those spiritual weapons which are mighty to the pulling down of strongholds.

Francis of Assisi, near Naples (1182–1226), son of a rich merchant, lover of pleasure, and imprisoned in his youth for a brawl, was suddenly arrested by the Spirit of God. Hearing the voice amid the loneliness of the Umbrian Hills, "My temple is falling into ruins, restore it," he took poverty as his bride. He founded the Order of Seraphic Brethren, Minorites or Greyfriars, who from their number and care for the poor have been called the democracy of Christianity. He lived a life worthy of the eulogy of his biographer, the great Dante, who describes him as a splendour of cherubic light. His special merit is that, during his life at least, he changed an army of monks into missionaries, sending them all over the West, from Morocco to find martyrdom, to Oxford to become professors. For himself he reserved the evangelization of the Saracen hosts, then (1219) besieged in Damietta by a mass of crusading Franks. Although there was a price on every Christian's head, the missionary, in his mendicant's grey robe and cord of self-denial, chaunting the 23rd Psalm, crossed over to the infidels, and was hurried into the Sultan's presence, to whom he declared, "I am sent not of man, but of God, to show thee the way of salvation." His courage, which to the Oriental seemed the inspiration of madness, was his safeguard: he was dismissed with honour, and he lived to induce the Sultan Meledeen to treat the Christian captives kindly, and to give the Franciscans the guardianship of the sepulchre of Christ. His method was magnificent, but it was not missionary in Christ's sense. Still, with Dante and Bossuet, we must admire the devotion of the man who, in the thirteenth century, left all to follow Christ, to tend the leper, and challenge the Moslem.

Marco Polo and Franciscan Missions to Cathay.—In the year 1260, Kublai Khan, grandson of Chinghiz Khan, was ruling from Peking over the mightiest empire the world had seen, over Cathay, which included all Asia except its southern peninsulas. It seemed to depend on an accident whether the prevailing religion there would be Christianity, Mohammedanism, or Buddhism. The Khans were "deists," indifferent to, but, for political reasons, curious about all religions. Kublai and the subordinate Khans of Persia and Western Asia were anxious to unite with the Christian powers of Europe against the Mussulmans, and the Popes and the Kings of France and Spain were nothing loath. Franciscans were used as the envoys, nominally as missionaries of the Cross, really as diplomatists. **William de Rubruquis** was sent by Louis IX. of France in 1256 to the Great Khan. Before this, when the father and uncle of **Marco Polo** first visited his court, Kublai sent them back as his own envoys to the Pope with a remarkable letter. He begged for a hundred Christians, "intelligent men acquainted with the sacraments, able clearly to prove by force of argument to idolators and other kinds of folk that the law of Christ was best, and that all other religions were false and naught: if they would prove this, he and all under him would become Christians and the Church's liegemen." The only result of this was that, in 1271, two Dominican preaching friars were sent with the two Polos and young Marco, but they fled back from Layas, the old port of Cilician Armenia. Latin Christendom, in its apathy and ignorance, threw away the opportunity of doing, through Kublai Khan, for Asia what the gospel had done through Constantine and Clovis.

Raimundus Lullius has a position of his own in the golden book of missionary biography. He was the first missionary to the

Mohammedans, in the modern sense, and as yet, we must confess, he is the greatest. His call was more remarkable than that of Loyola or Xavier. He was a philosopher, yet a fanatic in the highest sense; a scholar, yet a martyr; and all these that, by persuasion alone, "by love, by prayer, by proclaiming the word of truth rather than by force of arms," he might bring the Saracens within that kingdom which is love and peace and joy in the Holy Ghost. Crusade had succeeded crusade, leaving the Saracen stronger, calling out in the Turk a more terrible foe, before whom Constantinople itself was to fall and distant Vienna to tremble, and plunging Europe and the Church in deeper corruption. Raimund Lull was raised up as if to prove, in one startling case to which the eyes of all Christendom were turned for many a day, what the crusades might have become, and might have done for the world, had they fought for the Cross with the weapons of Him whose last words from it were forgiveness and peace.

The First Missionary to the Mohammedans was a young noble, born in 1236 in Palma, capital of the kingdom of Majorca, who rose to be seneschal in the court. As his father had served with the King of Arragon in the wars against the Saracens, Raimund Lull was familiar from his youth with the story of the crusades. To the Church of the Peninsula had been committed the special duty of evangelizing the Mohammedans and the Jews, and the many new lands soon to be discovered by its fleets. Raimund, all unconscious, as Paul had been, that he was to lead the way,—in which, alas! he had no followers,—spent the first thirty years of his life in sensuality and poetic trifling. As to the self-righteous Pharisee when on the path of persecution, so to the libertine when in the act of writing a sensual song, Christ appeared, but as the crucified One. That sad form of Love incarnate never left his imagination: he was drawn from sin, from the world, from himself, to the missionary career. It was Love that forgave him, purified him, sanctified his intellect, and cast him a whole burnt-offering on the altar of martyrdom. We have the whole story from his own pen in that work *On Divine Contemplation*, which may be put side by side with the *Confessions* of Augustine and Patrick, and the *Grace Abounding* of Bunyan. When the evil past would recur, and old habits would trouble him, he learned from a preacher how Francis had renounced the world for Christ. Thus was his covenanting with God: "To Thee, O Lord God, I offer myself, my wife, my children, and all that I possess. May it please Thee, who didst so humble Thyself to the death of the cross, to condescend to accept all that I give and offer to Thee, that I, my wife, and my children may be Thy lowly servants." Selling all that he had, and providing for his family only, he left his home, as he thought, for ever. His work was threefold, and in each part of it original. He devised a philosophical or educational system for persuading non-Christians of the absolute truth of Christianity; he established missionary colleges for training men in Arabic and other languages; he himself went and preached in Mohammedan lands, till he was the first to die for Africa.

1. The *Ars major sive generalis* of Lull was in intention what theologians call apologetic: he sought to prove the agreement between the truth of revealed religion and that which is founded in the nature of the human mind. He had induced the great Thomas Aquinas to attempt the same task in his work, in four volumes, *On the Catholic Faith, or Summary against the Gentiles.* The same problem has occupied the best minds in all generations since, though in very different ways, according as the enemy to be grappled with is deism or agnosticism or atheism. Not only do Islam and Brahmanism and Buddhism still demand similar efforts, but our own day, since Butler, abounds in treatises to meet the difficulties of those who are falling away from Christianity itself, or to win for Christianity the discoveries of new, if partial truths, by science and philosophy. The Lullian art was very famous in its day.

2. But the philosophic missionary could do nothing without the language, and so "he bought a Saracen," and from him learned Arabic for nine years. Then he became filled with the idea of missionary colleges. Reflecting that many forsook the world that they might be partakers of glory in another, he thus bursts forth: "I find scarcely any one who, out of love to Thee, O Lord, is ready to suffer martyrdom, as Thou hast suffered for us. It appears to me agreeable to reason, if an ordinance to that effect could be obtained, that the monks should learn various languages, that they might be able to go out and surrender their lives in love to Thee. . . . O Lord of glory, if that blessed day should ever be in which I might see Thy holy monks so influenced by zeal to glorify Thee, as to go into foreign lands in order to testify of Thy holy ministry, of Thy blessed incarnation, and of Thy bitter sufferings, that would be a glorious day, a day in which that glow of devotion would return with which the holy apostles met death for their Lord Jesus Christ!" The writer who prayed further that "monks of holy

lives and great wisdom should *form institutions in order to learn various languages, and to be able to preach to unbelievers,*" approached very near to the great modern conception and agency of societies and churches organized for foreign missions. One step farther, but some slight response from his church or his age, and Raimund Lull would have anticipated William Carey by exactly seven centuries. Failing in such a response, he succeeded in inducing James, King of Majorca, to found a convent for the instruction of at least thirteen Franciscan missionaries in Arabic. He visited Rome twice, to ask for a decree that a missionary institute of this kind should be attached to every convent, so as at once to give a practical direction to the monastic life of both sexes, and to convert the world. In 1311 he induced the Council of Vienne—place of missionary memory—to pass a decree that professorships of Oriental languages be established in the Universities of Paris, Oxford, and Salamanca. This Spaniard would have made England missionary once more. Now he expounded his *Ars* in the University of Paris, now in his native Palma, till the schools of Europe rang with praise of what they would see to be only a philosophical method, and would take no account of as a missionary key to the hearts and understandings of Mohammedan and heathen. He wrote another treatise *On the Discovery of Truth*, but that age would not see that the truth which fired his soul, and which the Spirit breathed on the pentecostal Church, was Christ crucified. Whatever we may think of the scholastic method to which that time was in bondage, can any praise be too high for the man who, after his first missionary visit to Tunis, and while waiting at Rome in the vain hope of influencing two successive Popes to adopt his mission, could thus anticipate the most fervent Protestant utterances as to the unity of truth and the triumph of Christ as the Truth by love alone?

"We have composed this treatise in order that believing and devout Christians might consider, that while the doctrines of no other religious sect can be proved to be true by its adherents, and none of the truths of Christianity are really vulnerable on the grounds of reason, the Christian faith can not only be defended against all its enemies, but can also be demonstrated. And hence, animated by the glowing zeal of faith, may they consider (since nothing can withstand the truth, which is mightier than all) how they may be able by the force of argument, through the help and power of God, to lead unbelievers into the way of truth, so that the blessed name of the Lord Jesus, which is still unknown in most parts of the world, and among most nations, may be manifested, and obtain universal adoration. This way of converting unbelievers is easier than all others. For it must appear hard to unbelievers to forsake their own faith for a foreign one; but who is there that will **not** feel himself compelled to surrender falsehood for truth, the self-contradictory for the necessary? . . . Of all methods of converting unbelievers, and reconquering the Holy Land, this is the easiest and speediest, which is most congenial to love, and is so much mightier than all other kinds and methods, in the proportion that spiritual weapons are more effective than carnal ones. This treatise was finished at Rome in the year 1296, on the holy evening before the feast of John the Baptist, the forerunner of our Lord Jesus Christ. May he pray our Lord, that as he himself was the herald of light, and pointed with his finger to Him who is the true Light, and as in his time the dispensation of grace began, it may please the Lord Jesus to spread a new light over the world, that unbelievers may walk in the brightness of this light, and be converted to join with us in meeting Him, the Lord Jesus Christ; to whom be praise and glory for ever!"

3. In despair of influencing others, this worthy prototype of David Livingstone—whom Humboldt in his *Cosmos* describes as at once a philosophical systematizer and an analytic chemist, a skilful mariner and a successful propagator of Christianity—landed in Africa in 1292, at the great Mohammedan city of Tunis. He had made the attempt to sail from Genoa some time before, but on the first occasion his courage failed him; and on the second, when he had constrained his friends to carry him on board, with his loved books, fever compelled his return. No such enterprise had ever been attempted in the history of the Church. This was no careless Crusader, cheered by martial glory or worldly pleasure. His was not even such a task as that which had called forth all the courage of the men who first won over Goth and Frank, Saxon and Slav. Raimund Lull, refused aid and sympathy by Europe, was going forth alone to preach Christ to a people with whom apostasy is death, who had made Christendom feel their prowess for centuries, who had steadily advanced and rarely retreated, who up to this hour have yielded the fewest converts to the gospel, and have attracted the fewest missionaries to attempt their evangelization, even in British India where toleration is assured. In the light of all subsequent missions to the Mohammedans, Raimund Lull's first hesitation at Genoa is a small thing, and it was soon purged away by the martyr's crown. He had hardly placed his foot on the deck of the ship in which he finally left Italy, when the fever of soul and body left him, and from that hour he never faltered. "Would I go back? Oh no," wrote Henry Martyn in later days, as he saw the Cornwall coast for the last time, and the misery of a hopeless human love was added to the weight which his faith had to bear. Full of his scholastic *Ars*, and burning with love to Christ, Raimund's first act was to invite the Maulvies or Mohammedan doctors of Tunis to a con-

ference, just as Ziegenbalg did afterwards with the Brahmans of South India, and John Wilson with the Pandits and Dastoors of Bombay. The Trinity as ascribing to the Godhead the divinest perfection and completeness of attributes, and Christ the Son of God with power dying for man,—such was the burden of his message. The teachers of the Koran, who had crowded to the conference with the hope of an easy victory, feared the effect of the Christian's zeal and eloquence. One only was found to commend the devotion of the missionary, whose life was spared. But he was cast into prison till he should be deported. After lying in wait for three months seeking opportunities to preach to the mass of the people, he reluctantly returned. Naples and Rome would give him no help, so he gave himself up for a time to evangelizing the Jews as well as the Mohammedans of his own native island Majorca. Thence he carried his Divine message to Cyprus, with its varied population, not only of Mohammedans, but of Nestorians and Jacobites, who were even then becoming the chief obstacle to the conversion of the Muslim. Nay, still farther, like the American missionaries who have given themselves to this special field, he went east to Armenia. As Livingstone did with success long after, he appealed to France and Italy for a Universities' Mission to Africa. It was vain. In spite of the threat that he should be stoned to death if he showed himself again in North Africa, he went there in 1307, as the Gordons gave themselves to the martyrs' death in Eromanga after Williams. At Bugia he proclaimed Christ in the market-place, denouncing Mohammed as a false prophet; the Maulvies rescued him from the mob, and during his imprisonment for six months plied him with all the sensual temptations of Islam to deny Christ. The old saint's answer, as he lay silenced in his dungeon, was to write a defence of Christianity, which the local sultan answered by again deporting him. Those Saracens, with whom learning had found an asylum when it fled from Europe, had respect for the fanatic and the philosopher. On his way back his ship was wrecked near Pisa, and several were drowned, but Raimund Lull escaped, though without his "books and parchments." With new experience, but the same fruitlessness, he appealed to the Church to preach Christ to the Mohammedans. "The Saracens write books for the destruction of Christianity; I have myself seen such when I was in prison. . . . For one Saracen who becomes a Christian, ten Christians and more become Mohammedans. It becomes those in power to consider what the end will be of such a state of things.

God will not be mocked." His latest proposal was a union of the many religious orders of knighthood for a new, a spiritual crusade.

To this day do all need the alternate warnings and appeals of this the greatest missionary orator of history:—"O Thou True Light of all lights, as Thy grace, through the true faith, has enriched Christians before unbelievers, so they are bound to demonstrate the true faith to unbelievers. . . . The holy Church, which consists of the souls of just catholic men, would be far more beautiful, if there were men acquainted with different languages who would go through the earth, that unrighteous and unbelieving men might hear the praises of Thy glorious Trinity and of Thy blessed humanity and of Thy painful passion." Let this be recorded, that there were found at Genoa pious noblemen and ladies who subscribed 30,000 guilders. In England there is a trace of Raimund Lull in the legend which represents him as having, at St. Catherine's Hospital, written a work on alchemy. When he was seventy-eight years of age, in 1314, about the time Scots and English were busy on the field of Bannockburn, this Paul-like missionary crossed the Mediterranean again to Bugia, where he had left a small band of converts. To these for a year he ministered in such quiet seclusion as Judson was constrained to observe in his early days in Burma. But the old burden lay upon him, weightier than that of bard or poet, "Woe's me if I preach not the gospel!" He called on the people to renounce Mohammed, and he was stoned to death, say some, or so nearly to death, say others, that he died at the age of seventy-nine, in the vessel in which some friendly merchants were taking him back to his native land. This end fitted well such a life. His name appears in no mere calendar of saints, in no historic roll: Raimund Lull was known to the thirteenth and fourteenth centuries rather as an ingenious schoolman, and to modern times as an independent inventor of the mariner's compass. But no Church, Papal or Reformed, has produced a missionary so original in plan, so ardent and persevering in execution, so varied in gifts, so inspired by the love of Christ, as the saint of seventy-nine whom Mohammedans stoned to death on the 30th June 1315. In an age of violence and faithlessness he was the apostle of heavenly love. Let this motto from his own great book be adopted by all his true successors: "He who loves not lives not; he who lives by the Life cannot die."

Monte Corvino (1305) deserves mention, as a Franciscan missionary who, in Tauris or Tabreez, India and Peking, preached so as to call forth the opposition of the Nestorians. He translated the New Testament and Psalter into Tartar, purchased a hundred and fifty boys, whom he trained in Latin, Greek, and psalmody, to be choristers and priests, won the regard of the Emperor of China, and baptized six thousand Chinese in two churches built beside the walls of the palace. He was made Archbishop of Cambalu or Peking, and was joined by seven other Franciscans.

Intolerant Missions.—So far before his time was Raimund Lull, that the Inquisition, which the Council of Toulouse had created in 1229 to punish a namesake of his, and extirpate the Albigenses, was in 1478 introduced into Spain to deal with Mohammedans and Jews, and all Christians whom Rome pronounced "heretics." In the little state of Asturias, Christianity so recovered its ground by means of the same physical force which Mohammed had preached, that by 1502 the Moors were expelled from Spain. The Jews, who had formed a highly-organized guild of foreigners in every country, and had carried out in a materialistic sense the prophecy of Isaiah, "Ye shall eat the riches of the Gentiles," had two years' respite, during which the priests plied them with Cardinal Mendoza's Catechism. So the evangelical preacher and pope-maker, Bernard of Clairvaux had, in the twelfth century, when heralding the Second Crusade, urged the soldiers of the Cross not to slaughter the people "who were scattered among all nations as living memorials of Christ's passion," while our own charitable Anselm of Canterbury had written a *Dialogue between a Jew and a Christian on the Christian Faith*. But in 1481 Seville was the scene of the burning of 291 Jews. In the next twenty years, the infamous Inquisitor-General Torquemada burned 10,220 persons, chiefly Jews, condemned in absence; he burned in effigy 6860, and compelled 97,321 to conform. A century of this work did not suffice, nor could the Jews purchase toleration by the tempting offer of thirty thousand ducats to coerce the Mohammedans. In 1492 the decree went forth which drove from the Peninsula the ablest of its population into other lands, and gave to England not a few of its greatest families, as well as the Disraelis. The Jew, like the Mohammedan,—twofold offspring of Abraham after the flesh,—is still the opprobrium of missions.

CHAPTER X.

THE REFORMATION ONLY INDIRECTLY MISSIONARY.

The Reformation a Home Mission to Christendom — The Discovery of America and the Opening up of India—John Wiclif—Martin Luther—Melanchthon—Erasmus—The Missionary Treatise of Erasmus—Coligny and Calvin—Gustavus Vasa of Sweden—Oxenstierna.

The Reformation, from Wiclif and Huss to Luther and Knox, **was a Home Mission to Christendom,** that the Church might be purified and again enlightened to preach the true gospel which Christ had given as a message to all nations. Directly, the Reformation of Luther became a foreign mission only by stirring up the Latin Church to conquests in the New World as a compensation for what it had lost in the Old. For three centuries before Luther it had been doing nothing; twenty years after, in 1541, it sent forth Xavier to India. But as a Protestant Foreign Mission the Reformation had only indirect or long-delayed results, and for two reasons. The spiritual conflict against so tremendous a power as papal Rome required and received the aid of—(1) Political and civil authority, through which it worked out personal liberty in Europe, but sacrificed or obliterated the duty of every individual Christian to propagate the gospel; (2) Reason or intellect as a basis of private judgment and necessary for the study of the Bible and elaboration of Divine truth, but this became exaggerated into the intellectual orthodoxy of the seventeenth and the repellent rationalism of the eighteenth century.

Historically, the Reformation was the beginning of that series of revolutions which, from the refusal of reform at the Diet of Worms to the independence of the United States of America and the destruction of the monarchy in France in 1793, when William Carey landed in Bengal, introduced Modern Missions. "Now," wrote Erasmus, the year before the Diet of Worms, when Luther issued his treatise *Against the Bull of Antichrist*, "I see no end of it but the turning upside down of the whole world." So had the book of the Acts of the Apostles described missionaries (xvii. 6). All the evangelical Reformers showed a remarkable ignorance of the doctrine of the Kingdom. They had the prejudices of the age against the outside world, just as the apostles had for a time; and, unlike the apostles, they never had these prejudices removed. Great mission fields lay round about them, especially in North Africa and Western Asia, which had been for the first five Christian centuries nurseries of the faith, and had become the strongholds of Islam. Large communities of Jews were scattered among them, and the case of Nicolas de Lyra, a learned convert, showed that the evangelization of these was a task not without hope, and certainly devolving upon them. The Reformers' doctrine of the Kingdom was narrowed and obscured by their eschatology, their teaching as to the end of the world and the judgment. Just as they confined the use of Christ's charge to an attack upon Rome, so they anticipated the end of the world as the near result of their preaching the pure gospel within the Church. The nations or Gentiles were not the heathen of their own day, but the Christians as opposed to the Jews. The apostles had at first made the same mistake, believing the fall of Jerusalem to be the proximate end of the world. The fathers, John Chrysostom and Jerome, Ambrose and Augustine, had been similarly led by the political convulsions of their day, to find in the sack of Rome and the devastation of Christian lands by the Vandals the predicted end. At the very time that, as we saw, the eloquent Patriarch of Constantinople was most zealously promoting the conversion of the Arian Goths and heathen barbarians, he considered himself to be hastening the consummation, for which he fixed the definite date of 400 years after Christ. Ambrose saw the Gog and Magog of Ezekiel and the Apocalypse in the Goths of his own day. All through the twelve centuries down to John Knox, the most spiritual and the most orthodox theologians and ecclesiastical leaders used the pregnant saying of our Lord in an anti-missionary sense: "This gospel of the kingdom shall be preached for a witness to all nations, and then shall the end come" (Matt. xxiv. 14).

The Discovery of America and the Opening up of India (1492–1508) formed an almost ironical commentary on such views. Truly God's ways are not as man's ways, nor His thoughts as the thoughts of even the best and wisest of His servants. Each of these two, America and India (including Africa), meant to the world and to the kingdom of Christ, empires wider than Rome at its greatest, spheres of missionary effort and triumphs compared with which the conversion of the northern nations was in itself a little thing; churches and Christian nations of the future worthy of the inspired language of prophet, of psalmist, of apocalyptic seer, yea, of Christ Himself when He said, "All power is given unto Me in heaven and earth. . . . Go ye therefore. . . . Lo I am with you all the days, even unto the end of the world." Luther was ten years old when Columbus returned with his story of San Salvador and the New World, but the age was not ripe, in any respect, as it became when William Carey was fired by the South Sea voyages of Captain Cook. The Reformers of the sixteenth century, in Germany and Switzerland, France and Sweden, Scotland and England, lived right through the greatest age of discovery the world has ever yet seen, but in vain so far as foreign missions are concerned. *That* was not their work. Not only were they theologically and ecclesiastically unprepared for it, but they were cut off from immediate contact with the new lands and heathen peoples. Spain and Portugal were first in the race of discovery, and their dead Church carried a gospel of compromise or extirpation to races who have died out before it. Germany, which led the Reformation, has not a colony to this day, or has only just acknowledged a small strip of the south-west coast of Africa. The Danes were the first Protestants to do their duty to the heathen, with German assistance, but on a small scale. The Dutch came out of their own national baptism so earthy, that when they supplanted the Portuguese in the East, they failed as missionaries by adopting the same method of compromise from its secular side. It has taken six centuries, from Wiclif to Duff, to train the British churches, for the second time, to become the missionaries of Christ and Christian civilisation to the nations. The nineteenth century has become the missionary century, and English-speaking men and women of Great Britain and America, aided by their German cousins in lands under British influence, are its missionaries.

John Wiclif (1320–1384) has a distinctly missionary interest not merely as the Morning Star of the Reformation. By his Yorkshire descent we might consider him the representative, as he was the successor, of the Scots missionaries sent by Columba into Northumbria, which they evangelized from Aidan's school of Lindisfarne. But historically he taught a purer gospel than even Luther long after him, especially against the subtler forms of the heresy of transubstantiation; his teaching made him the spiritual father of **Huss and Jerome of Prag** (1415), and so of the missionary church of the modern Moravians. His methods created "poor priests" and Lollards, who not only prepared England for the full noon of the Reformation, but have formed ensamples to modern missionaries. Finally, he first gave us the English Bible, which, more than its Hebrew and Greek originals, has become the model and even the basis of translations into all the vernaculars of nineteenth century heathendom. That which cost forty pounds sterling for one copy in 1414, when the decree of a persecuting Church and court went forth that all who read the Scriptures in the mother tongue should "forfeit land, cattle, life, and goods from their heirs for ever," has been carried by Wiclif's descendants over the world in three hundred vernaculars, in each of which it may be bought for a shilling. Truly the sound has gone out into all the world, but so far are we from the end of it that even the nineteenth century missions are but the day of small things.

Martin Luther (1483–1555), miner's son and Augustinian monk in a Scot-founded monastery at Erfurt, drew the Reformation from the pure and only fountain of truth in the word of God, finding there the mercy of God in Christ alone. A few years after, another monk, of knightly birth, Ignatius Loyola, struggled as Luther had done, in the monastery of Montserrat, and he sought peace in the adoration of the sacramental Body of Christ and of Mary the Dispenser of Mercy. The difference has marked ever since, as by a wide gulf, the doctrine, the methods, the results of missions as conducted by the Reformed and the Romanist Churches. Luther struck away the lordship over the Church of Pope and Emperor, restoring the freedom of every believer and the purity of the message to every sinner,—God just and yet the justifier of him who believeth in Jesus. Loyola became the slave of the new Romanism which the Council of Trent formulated, and the Society of Jesus above all its orders proclaimed to the heathen. We can forgive Luther for the failure—which Dr. Warneck, the first authority on Lutheran missions, most fully confesses—to think of the duty of the Church to any non-Christian peoples, except the Turks, for whom, indeed, he called believers to pray, but whom more frequently his rude vigour and the intolerance of the time led him to curse. When, occasionally, the spirit of the Renaissance burst through the great Reformer in spite of himself, he would break forth with such remarks as these, recorded in that remarkable book his *Table Talk*, only, however, to crush down the young hope by a mistaken reading of prophecy:—

"The arts are growing as if there was to be a new start and the world was to become young again. I hope God will finish with it; we have come already to the White Horse. Daniel's four empires, Babylon, Persia, Greece, and Rome, are gone. Another hundred years and all will be over. The gospel is despised. God's word will disappear for want of any to preach it. Mankind will turn into Epicureans and care for nothing. They will not believe that God exists. Then the voice will be heard, 'Behold the Bridegroom cometh.'

"Asia and Africa have no gospel. In Europe, Greeks, Italians, Spaniards, Hungarians, French, *English*, Poles, have no gospel. The small electorate of Saxony will not hinder the end," he replied to one who observed that when Christ came there would be no faith at all on the earth, and the gospel was still believed in that part of Germany.

Philip Schwarzerd or Melanchthon (1497–1560), gentle son of the locksmith of Heidelberg, was by temper and culture more akin to the missionary spirit than Luther. But neither in this, nor in toleration, was he above or before his age. The seventh article of the Augsburg Confession, which he wrote, defines the Church as an assembly of saints in which the gospel is truly taught and the sacraments are duly administered,—but has no reference to the Kingdom and the Church's duty thereto. Through one of the Greek students studying at Wittenberg, Melanchthon sent a Greek translation of this and of Luther's Small and Large Catechisms to Joasaph II., Patriarch of Constantinople, for an alliance of the Reformed with the Greek Church was longed for, as against Rome. But missionary considerations had no place in the scheme, then or afterwards. Melanchthon has been recognised by the Germans as forming a connecting link between Luther and Erasmus, whose admiration of "this boy's" attainments in Greek and Latin literature was great.

Desiderius (Gerhard) Erasmus (1467–1536), Netherlander of Rotterdam, and afterwards of Basel, was already sixteen years of age, and about to be condemned by his guardians to the misery of monastic life, from which he was delivered at twenty-three, when Luther was born. He was thus behind the Reformation, as it were, all his life, which he spent in the hope of a compromise through a general council and the forbearance of both sides. But he was before it in the clearness of his view and eloquence of his exposition of the duty of the Church to preach the gospel to heathen and Mohammedan. And his is the imperishable glory of having given to his age, in 1516, the New Testament in the original Greek, with a Latin translation of his own, which became the text of the great vernacular translation of Luther published in 1534. For the first time since apostolic days men had the Divine word placed in their hands in its original purity, and Jerome's Vulgate fell back, for Protestants, into its proper place of a mere translation. "I wish," he wrote in his preface, "that even the weakest woman should read the Gospels,—should read the Epistles of Paul; and I wish that they were translated into all languages, so that they might be read and understood not only by Scots and Irishmen, but also by Turks and Saracens. I long that the husbandman should sing portions of them to himself as he follows the plough, that the weaver should hum them to the tune of his shuttle, that the traveller should beguile with their stories the tedium of his journey." By his Commentaries or "Paraphrase" of the word, he brought its truths home to the people. To the complaint that women and cobblers conversed about the Holy Scriptures, he replied, "I would rather hear unlearned maidens talk of Christ than certain rabbins who pass for men of high attainments." The spirit and almost the words of Raimund Lull mark his references to the Turks, which are in striking contrast to those of his younger contemporaries. In his *Enchiridion*, or *Christian Soldier's Dagger*, he writes, "The most effectual way of conquering the Turks would be, if they were to see the spirit and teaching of Christ expressed in our lives; if they perceived that we were not aiming at empire over them, thirsting for their gold, coveting their possessions, or desiring anything whatever save their salvation and the glory of Christ." Again, in his "Paraphrase" of the New Testament: "The Scriptures ought to be read by clowns and mechanics and even by the Turks. . . . The Scriptures should be translated into all tongues."

The Missionary Treatise of Erasmus.—In the year before his death, Erasmus gave to the world a treatise *On the Art of Preaching*, which he had long promised to his friend the Bishop of Rochester, under the title *Ecclesiastes sive Concionator Evangelicus*. Of the four books of which it consists, the first has been more than once reprinted in England for the preparation of candidates for the ministry of the word. That book treats of the dignity, the responsibility, the piety, the purity, the prudence, and other virtues of the preacher. Passages of this treatise read like a modern missionary address, and might be placed side by side with the appeals of Alexander Duff three hundred years after. After pointing to the illustrious examples of Basil, Chrysostom, Augustine, and Gregory the Great, who, though burdened with the care of all the churches, and weakened by sickness and disease, gave themselves to continual preaching and sent forth missionaries to far distant regions, Erasmus continues :—

"We daily hear men deploring the decay of the Christian religion, who say that the gospel message which once extended over the whole earth is now confined to the narrow limits of this land. Let those, then, to whom this is an unfeigned cause of grief, beseech Christ earnestly and continuously to send labourers into His harvest, or, more correctly, sowers to scatter His seed. Everlasting God! how much ground there is in the world where the seed of the gospel has never yet been sown, or where there is a greater crop of tares than of wheat! Europe is the smallest quarter of the globe; Greece and Asia Minor the most fertile. Into these countries the gospel was first introduced from Judea with great success. But are they not now wholly in the hands of Mohammedans and men who do not know the name of Christ? What, I ask, do we now possess in Asia, which is the largest continent, when Palestine herself, whence first shone the gospel light, is ruled by heathens? In Africa what have we? There are surely in these vast tracts barbarous and simple tribes who could easily be attracted to Christ if we sent men among them to sow the good seed. Regions hitherto unknown are being daily discovered, and more there are, as we are told, into which the gospel has never yet been carried. I do not at present allude to the millions of Jews who live among us, nor to the very many Gentiles who are attached to Christ merely by name, nor yet do I refer to the schismatics and heretics who abound. Oh, how these would turn to Christ if noble and faithful workers were sent among them, who would sow good seed, remove tares, plant righteous trees, and root out those which are corrupt; who would build up God's house, and destroy all structures which do not stand on the Rock of Ages; who would reap the ripe fruit for Christ and not for themselves, and gather souls for their Master, and not riches for their own use. The King of Ethiopia, commonly known as the land of 'Prester John,' lately submitted himself to the Roman See; and he held no small controversy with the Pope, because the Ethiopians, although not alien from faith in Christ, had been so long neglected by the shepherd of the world. And some good men, who are anxious to extend religious knowledge, complain that the Pilapians, who live to the north of Scythia, and are wonderfully simple and uncultured, are enslaved by some Christian princes; but so hard pressed are they by the heavy yoke of man, that they cannot take upon them the easy yoke of Christ. The wealth of others, moreover, has so spoiled them that the riches of the gospel avail them nothing. But is it not well-pleasing and right in the sight of God to enrich rather than to spoil those whom we strive to win for Christ, and so to initiate them into our faith that they may rejoice to have become subservient to those under whose sway they may live more righteously than they were hitherto accustomed to do? We have known wild and horrible beasts to have been trained either for pleasure or for ordinary labour; but have we known men to have been so humanized as to serve Christ? Kings keep in their employment men whose duty it is to teach elephants to leap, lions to sport, and lynxes and leopards to hunt; but has the King of the Church ever found men ready to call their fellows to the service of His dear Son? I know there is no beast so difficult to tame as the stubborn and hardhearted Jew; but nevertheless even he can be brought into subjection by kindness and love. But now I speak of nations who stray as sheep without a shepherd, because they have never had any Christian teaching. So true is this, that if we can credit the account of travellers who visit these regions, the Christian princes themselves who rule them prevent any missionary of the gospel from visiting their domains, lest, gaining wisdom, their subjects should throw off the grievous yoke under which they labour. For these tyrants would rather rule asses than men.

"And what shall I say of those who sail round unknown shores, and plunder and lay waste whole States without provocation? What name is given to such deeds? They are called victories. The heathen would praise a victory gained over men against whom no war had been declared. But, they say, the Turks delight in such victories. This then is an excuse for razing cities to the ground! I do not know whether the advancement of the Christian faith would excuse the demolition of a city by a Turk. There is the greatest difference between robbery and Christian warfare, between preaching the kingdom of faith and setting tyrants with their interests in this world, between seeking the safety of souls and pursuing the spoil of mammon. Travellers bring home from distant lands gold and gems; but it is worthier to carry hence the wisdom of Christ, more precious than gold, and the pearl of the gospel, which would put to shame all earthly riches. We give too much attention to the things which debase our souls. Christ orders us to pray the Lord of the harvest to send forth labourers, because the harvest is plenteous and the labourers are few. Must we not then pray God to thrust forth labourers into such vast tracts? But all offer various excuses. Moreover there are thousands of the Franciscans who believe in Christ, and a large number of them in all probability burn with seraphic fire. And the Dominicans also abound in equal numbers, and it is admitted that very many of them have in them the spirit of cherubim. From among these let men be chosen who are indeed dead to the world and alive to Christ, to teach the word of God in truth to the heathen. Some excuse themselves on the ground that they are ignorant of foreign languages. Shall princes have no difficulty in finding men who, for the purposes of human diplomacy, are well acquainted with various tongues? Even Themistocles the Athenian in one year so mastered Persian, that he could dispense with an interpreter in his intercourse with the king. And shall we not show the same zeal in so noble an enterprize?

"Moreover, food and clothing were not wanting to the apostles among the savage and distant peoples visited. God also has promised to supply all the needs of those who seek to further His kingdom. But if missionaries labour among a people so ungrateful as to deny them bread, water, or shelter, let them follow the shining example of Paul, that strong pillar of the Church, who worked with his own hands that he might be independent of all. He, indeed, stitched together goat skins for those believers to whom he gave the Holy Spirit and consecrated the body and blood of the Lord. Neither will miracles be denied, if circumstances demand them, only believe with holy love. Or at least a mind free from earthly lusts, a life of unbroken sobriety, a zeal to serve all men, long-suffering, patience, becoming modesty, and a humble demeanour, will avail instead of miracles. For even the apostles did not everywhere work miracles, but they owed their success in preaching the gospel rather to those attributes which I have mentioned. For miracles, which show the Spirit of God working in men, are ascribed by many to magic.

"I have not dealt with the last excuse, that of the risk of death. Indeed, since men can die but once, what can be more glorious and blessed than to die for the gospel? Travellers go to the uttermost parts of the earth to see Jerusalem, and in so doing expose their lives to danger. Nor do all such return in safety from their journey. Yet crowds of men go every year to Jerusalem to see all sorts of places, and give no excuse for the risk they run of being killed. To see the ruins of Jerusalem! What, I ask, is great in that? But what a great achievement it is to build a human Jerusalem in the soul! How many soldiers there are who fearlessly rush into battle, counting their lives vile in comparison with human praise. And yet does the Lord of all, who has promised as a reward a crown of eternal glory, find soldiers endued with a like mind? How much better it is to die as Paul did, than to be wasted by consumption, to be tortured for many years by gout, to be racked by paralysis, or to suffer a thousand deaths by the disease of the stone? And let us remember also that death will not come before the time God has appointed. Death is not to be feared under the protection of Christ, who will not suffer a hair to fall to the ground without the will of the Father. Lastly, how does it happen that those who are called to the apostleship are deterred from their duties by the love of life? It is the first duty of an apostle to spend his life for the gospel. Why, what account of life was taken by Crates the Theban, Socrates the Athenian, Diogenes of Sinope, and all these other philosophers who never knew Christ nor the apostles?

"Bestir yourselves, then, ye heroic and illustrious leaders of the army of Christ; put on the helmet of salvation, the breastplate of righteousness; take to yourselves the shield of faith, and the sword of the Spirit, which is the word of God; have your loins girt with humility, your feet shod with holy affections; in a word, be clothed with the whole mystic armour for preaching the gospel of peace. Address yourselves with fearless minds to such a glorious work. Overturn, quench, destroy, not men, but ignorance, godlessness, and other sins. For to kill thus is only to preserve. Do not, however, make earthly gain the object of your labours, but strive to enrich the heathen with spiritual treasures. Count it great gain if you save for the Redeemer souls snatched from the tyranny of Satan, and lead thousands in triumph to Him in heaven. It is a hard work I call you to, but it is the noblest and highest of all. Would that God had accounted me worthy to die in such a holy work, rather than to be consumed by slow death in the tortures I endure! Yet no one is fit to preach the gospel to the heathen who has not made his mind superior to riches or pleasure, aye, even to life and death itself. The cross is never wanting to those who preach the word of the Lord in truth. To-day even there are kings, not unlike Herod, who mock at Christ and His doctrine. There are men like Annas and Caiaphas, there are scribes and Pharisees who would rather see heaven fall than allow any part of their power or authority to decline. There are craftsmen who rage, as Demetrius did of old at Ephesus against the apostles who endangered his trade by their preaching. There are still Jews who, when they see the friends of Christ, would sell Him, and give His body to whosoever desired it. There are still the crowds who cry with vindictive hate, Crucify Him! crucify Him!"

Gaspard de Coligny and John Calvin (1555-1556).—While yet in the stage of compromise which Erasmus represents, believing that the Church of Rome might be reformed from within, Gaspard de Chatillon, Admiral Coligny, who became leader of the Huguenots, and perished on the day of Bartholomew 1572, sent to Brazil missionaries chosen by Calvin. This was the first of two, and only two, Reformation missionary enterprises. France had sent a ship to Bahia in 1504, and had seen savages brought thence to Rouen in 1509. In the next forty years the famous shipbuilders Ango and his son traded with Brazil from Dieppe, Honfleur, Havre, and Rouen, and fought the Portuguese. The infamous adventurer Villegagnon, who for cleverly conducting the Scottish Queen Mary and her four attendants from Dumbarton to Brest, had been made Vice-Admiral of Brittany, obtained Admiral Coligny's support to a project for settling a French colony in Brazil. Like the English Puritans afterwards, Coligny dreamed of a happier France—La France Antartique—where God might be worshipped in freedom. Villegagnon, who had been at the University of Paris with Calvin, but had remained a Romanist, asked his old acquaintance, then in Geneva, to send him Protestants to minister to those of the religion in the new colony. Calvin selected **Richier** and **Chartier**, who were joined by twelve others, of whom **Jean de Léry** became the historian of the expedition. As the persecution went on in France, thousands of Huguenots desired to follow them. But Villegagnon basely betrayed his trust. All the Calvinists returned to France, save five, who were hurled by him from a precipice. The Portuguese completed the ruin of a colony of which Coligny himself would have made a land in South America like that soon to be settled by the Pilgrim Fathers in the North. As to missionary work in Villegagnon's Island in the Bay of Rio Janeiro, there were native auxiliaries, and the Calvinists were instant in preaching, so long as they were allowed, and there were "frequent conversions." But soon the Indians fled from oppression into the forests of the mainland, where the Protestants joined them for a time. Six years after, Coligny tried a second Protestant colony under Ribaut at Charlesfort in Florida, and again at Caroline. There the settlers were first thinned by famine, then slaughtered by the Spaniards. De Gourgues afterwards avenged France, but had to retire to England, where Queen Elizabeth protected the last survivor of the Huguenot missions to Brazil and Florida.

Gustavus Vasa of Sweden (1559) sent out the second of the

Reformation missions to the Lapps of Northern Europe, under one Michael Gustavus Adolphus; opened schools, and had Swedish books translated into the tongue of the people. In 1738 there was such enthusiasm in Sweden for the conversion of its Lapp subjects, that a national subscription was raised for a missionary college, and the Diet ordered the translation of the whole Bible. But neither in the Lappmarks of Sweden nor in the land to the north-west of Russia has the Christianity of this small Mongolian people ever been more than nominal. In modern times the evangelical people of Sweden find fields for their missionary activities among the Hindoos of Central India and the Mohammedan Gallas of Abyssinia.

Oxenstierna (1637), nearly a century after Gustavus Vasa, sent out a Swedish colony to the Delaware, but the work of evangelizing the Red Indians was carried out by the English and Scottish Puritans in Massachusetts, and by the Moravians in the States of New York and Pennsylvania.

CHAPTER XI.

THE DAWN OF MODERN MISSIONS—THE DANISH-HALLE AND MORAVIAN MISSIONS.

The Two Reformation Principles of Missions—Grotius—Walæus—Lutheran Orthodoxy and Missionary Pietism—Baron von Welz—Leibniz—The Danish-Halle Mission to India—First Foreign Mission Hymn by Bogatzky—Hans Egéde—Missions of the Unitas Fratrum—Comenius, Christian David, Count von Zinzendorf—Growth of the Moravian Missions—Franke's and Zinzendorf's Work.

The Two Reformation Principles of Missions.—The Reformation begun in the sixteenth century took two hundred years to spiritualize the Protestant churches of Christendom, and to extend them over the New World of North America. Reckoning from 1512, when Luther nailed his ninety-five theses against the abuse of indulgences on the door of the Castle Church at Wittenberg, it may be said that the Reformation took three centuries to bring the churches back to apostolic purity of doctrine, worship, and life; but, besides this, to make them missionary churches in a wider and even higher sense than either the Fathers or the Reformers knew. This the Reformation did by two principles especially. (1) Luther had been careful, as a citizen of the Holy Roman Empire, which was conterminous with Christendom all throughout the Middle Ages, to base his reforms on the Nicene Creed, which had been approved of by Pope Damasus and gradually departed from by that Pope's successors. Protestantism returned to that pure creed from which it has never since departed, and which in its missionary enterprises it presents to heathen, Mohammedan, and Jew alike. (2) The Reformation, under Erasmus, Luther, and Calvin, —all, however, following Wiclif,—had put into the hands of the learned the true text of the Greek Testament, and had not delayed to translate the whole Bible into the principal languages of Europe. Thus with the written source of all Divine truth in the mother tongue, and linked on historically and spiritually to the Apostolic Church, the poorest and otherwise most ignorant Christian knew more of the love of God in Christ to himself, and of the commission of Christ to preach that love to all nations, than the wisest of the pre-Reformation teachers who had sealed up the word of God. The vernacular Bible became a missionary book to Christendom itself; and when Christians had mastered it somewhat during two centuries, they began to send it to the rest of the world, with missionaries to translate and to preach it. The process of mastering it, after more than ten centuries of doctrinal corruption and spiritual darkness, was slow. But here and there noble souls arose, above their age, to remind their fellows that the missionary covenant stood fast, that, as in Abraham's case, none truly received the blessing till they so propagated it that it might bless all the families of the earth.

We shall note the almost parallel developments of the missionary spirit, first in the Lutheran and then in the English-speaking churches of the Reformation.

Grotius (1559).—The Dutch, being the first to come into personal contact with the peoples of the East, as they gradually drove the Portuguese out of the Malay Archipelago, South India, and Ceylon, began well, but have gradually passed through the successive stages of zeal, of indifference, of a compromise with heathenism, and of opposition to evangelical missions. The great scholar Grotius wrote his admirable Latin work on the *Evidences of Christianity* as a text-book for the Dutch missionaries in their preaching to and conferences with the heathen, and this work was afterwards translated into Arabic by our Pococke. Grotius, moreover, personally influenced seven priests of Lubeck to go out to the East as missionaries. **Peter Heyling** went to Abyssinia in 1632, and translated the New Testament into Amharic.

Walæus, professor in the University of Leyden, which had been founded under remarkable circumstances in 1575, was the first, so early as 1612, to establish a college for the training of missionaries. This was ten years before Pope Gregory XV. founded the Propaganda. **Hoornbeek**, his colleague, wrote at Utrecht his missionary treatise, *Summa Controversia cum Gentilibus, Judæis, Muhamidis, et Papistis*, in 1659. **Junius** in Formosa, and **Baldæus** in Ceylon, were Dutch teachers and writers. In Brazil, the Dutch West India Company had as their Governor-General at Pernambuco, **John Moritz** of Nassau-Siegen. At his desire, in 1637, eight missionaries were sent out. They translated the Catechism, baptized several Indians, and opened schools, but the mission soon ceased under his successors.

Lutheran Orthodoxy and Missionary Pietism.—The seeds of controversies left by the Reformers soon bore a harvest which would have been fatal to the spirituality of the Church but for the Pietists, who fed their faith and zeal on the person of "Christ the sum and substance of the Holy Scriptures," the title of Franke's principal work. The revolt against what has been well called by Dr. Warneck, the barren orthodoxy and dead dogmatic controversy of the seventeenth and eighteenth centuries in Germany, began with George Calixtus of Helmstädt and two other professors, who were silenced. The laity who sought evangelical preaching, which was denied in the Lutheran Church, were thus fed by such divines as John Arndt, John Gerhard, and Valentine Andrea. But the man of all others who brought about the Pietist revival, was **Philip James Spener**, at Frankfort, Dresden, Berlin, and Halle. He became the spiritual father of the Danish-Halle Mission to Madras, through the greatest of his followers, **August Herman Franke** (1663-1727), who in his turn influenced Zinzendorf and the Moravian Missions.

Baron von Welz (1664), or more fully Freiherr Justinianus Ernst von Welz, however, anticipated all other Germans in the boldness and vigour of his missionary projects, but he was a generation before the time when they could be responded to. In 1664 this noble precursor of Franke and Zinzendorf published two pamphlets in German, whose titles alone mark the advanced position of the writer. The first was, "A Christian and Loyal Reminder to all Right-Believing Christians of the Augsburg Confession regarding a Special Society, through which, with Divine Help, our Evangelical Religion could be extended." The other was termed, "Invitation for a Society (*Gesellschaft*) of Jesus to promote Christianity and the Conversion of Heathendom." He puts to the dead conscience of the Church such questions as these:—Is it right to keep the gospel to ourselves? Is it right that students of theology should be confined to home parishes? Is it right for Christians to spend so much on clothing, eating, and drinking, and to take no thought to spread the gospel? Von Welz wrote a third invitation and warning, after he appealed in vain to the Protestants of Regensburg or Ratisbon, where the fine Schotten-Kirche testifies to the heroism of those who had first carried the gospel to its people. He urged the establishment in every Protestant University of a missionary college of three professors,—of Oriental languages, of the methods of converting the heathen, and of geography, beginning with Paul's journeys; bursaries also to be founded. Finally he gave himself. Laying aside his title, he was consecrated by the fanatic Breckling, "an apostle to the heathen;" and taking with him 36,000 marks, he went to Dutch Guiana, where he found a lonely grave. The attitude of Lutheranism to missions, at the close of the seventeenth century, is well marked by the superintendent of Regensburg, Ursinus, a theologian who, "otherwise excellent," declared the heathen to be "dogs and swine," and the noble Welz to be a "dreamer." If he was, being before the time, how very far were the churches behind that of the first three centuries of which their reformed creeds were the boasted, and in other respects the precious outcome!

Leibniz (1646–1716).—It was left to a layman, a non-theologian and the thinker of his time, to rouse the Church to its duty. Led by a scientific interest, and influenced by the action of the Jesuit missionaries at Peking, the great philosopher proposed that German missionaries should be sent, by way of Russia, to China. In 1700, when the Berlin Academy of Sciences was founded, he caused the design to be inserted in its statutes. But, while we rejoice to record this alliance of the scientific with the missionary spirit, it is not of such stuff that pioneer missionaries are made. The spiritual must come first, and that was found about the same time in the Pietists, the Methodists of Germany, as Franke was their John Wesley.

The Danish-Halle Mission to India.—In Denmark, Lutheranism was as barren as in Germany till Pietism found its way there, and, in the first instance, to the court of King Friedrich IV. **Dr. Lütken,** one of the royal chaplains, and formerly in Berlin, was the first, in 1704, to represent to the Danish king the duty of seeking the conversion to Christ of those Hindoos who had been his subjects since the Danish East India Company had purchased the Tranquebar town and territory from the Raja of Tanjore in 1621. The good king at once empowered his chaplain to look out for men of piety, common sense, and ability, to learn the Oriental languages, and to reason with the heathen in a Christian spirit; he gave a royal subvention of 9000 marks. Lütken at once founded at Copenhagen a *Collegium de Cursu Evangelii Promovendo*, to train the missionaries of the future; and meanwhile applied to his friend Franke at Halle to select missionaries fit to be immediately sent out. **Bartholomew Ziegenbalg**, and **Henry Plütschau**, students first trained by Lange, of the same Pietist school, in the gymnasium at Berlin of which he was rector, were happily chosen. Sent forth from Copenhagen on 29th November 1705, by Dr. Bornemann, Bishop of Zealand, they did not reach Tranquebar till 9th July 1706. Having touched at the Cape, then under the blighting rule of the Dutch, they sent home such an account of the Hottentots, who were denied Christian instruction and baptism, as moved the Moravians to begin the first mission to South Africa. These, the first Protestant missionaries to India, which had been under British as well as Danish and Dutch influence for a century, sat down among the native children, writing on the sand with their fingers, to learn the Tamil language. In that and in Portuguese they opened Christian schools, and began to translate the Catechism and the New Testament. They found the Danish officials more hostile to them and their work than even the Brahmans. On the 12th May 1707, ten months after their arrival, they publicly baptized five adult heathen slaves of Danish masters; on the 14th August they opened their first church under the name of "New Jerusalem," and on 5th September they baptized nine adult Hindoos. Next year Ziegenbalg made his first preaching tour into the kingdom of Tanjore, and at Negapatam he held the first of those friendly conferences with the Brahmans, the publication of which—as of his letters to Lange and Franke—excited a widespread interest in Europe. The "open door" began to result in "open eyes." Even the English East India Company offered to help the mission, by conveying books and letters free of charge. On 17th October 1708, Ziegenbalg began his Tamil translation of the New Testament, the first attempt worthy of the name to give one of the peoples of India the word of God in their mother tongue. The English Propagation Society, established in 1701 rather for colonial than foreign missionary objects, sent out assistance in money and in books, and three German colleagues, one of whom was **Grundler**, joined them. The English Society for Promoting Christian Knowledge, established in 1699, undertook to receive funds for the mission.

Sent out originally on an engagement of three or four years, Ziegenbalg resolved to live and die in India; while Plütschau did not return till ill-health forced him to seek home in 1711, after the first Tamil Testament had been completed, the first dictionary was well advanced, and the first printing-press had reached them. Plütschau took with him to Halle, for education as a missionary, the convert Timothy, the first born Hindoo who had visited Europe. In 1715 Ziegenbalg also was sent home by the physicians. He was presented to **King George I.**, who wrote to the missionary on his return to Tranquebar, a letter dated "at our palace of Hampton Court, the 23rd August A.D. 1717," expressing satisfaction "not only because the work undertaken by you of converting the heathen to the Christian faith doth, by the grace of God, prosper; but also because that, in this our kingdom, such a laudable zeal for the promotion of the gospel prevails." Notwithstanding, a full century was to pass before the Church of England sent its own missionaries to the heathen. In 1719, at the early age of thirty-six, in the midst of labours too abundant, Ziegenbalg died, as at his request they sang to him, with the accompaniment of the violin, his favourite hymn, "*Jesus meine Zuversicht*" ("Jesus my Confidence"). In 1849 Dr. Duff visited the spot, the "new" church of 1718 which Ziegenbalg reared in place of the old one swept away by the sea; the house which he built, with the remains of the afterwards famous old library of the mission. "I mounted the pulpit, and, with no ordinary emotion, gazed around from the position from which Ziegenbalg, and Grundler, and Schwartz so often proclaimed free salvation to thousands, in Tamil, German, Danish, and Portuguese. At the end of one of the wings on either side of a plain altar, lie the mortal remains of Ziegenbalg and Grundler,—two such men of brief but brilliant and immortal career in the mighty work of Indian evangelization. Theirs was a lofty and indomitable spirit, breathing the most fervid piety." Ziegenbalg left 355 converts and numerous catechumens, a complete Tamil Bible, a dictionary, a mission seminary, and schools. "Certainly," is Duff's verdict, "he was a great missionary considering that he was the first; inferior to none, scarcely second to any that followed him."

Franke was the first to publish, after 1710, regular missionary reports, under the title of "History of Evangelical Missions in the East for the Conversion of the Heathen." At this time, too, there appeared the first foreign missionary hymn, by **Bogatzky**, known for his *Golden Treasury*,—

"*Wach auf du Geist der ersten Zeugen.*"

"Wake up, thou spirit of the first martyrs."

The orthodox Lutherans checked the attempt to make the Danish-Halle movement a Church Mission. When German rationalism undermined it at the close of the eighteenth century, the Church of England Missions rescued it for a time till the Dresden-Leipzig Lutheran Mission took it up. Franke's missionary zeal was to some extent directed by the proposal of Leibniz, whose China project he advocated in his *Pharos Missionis Evangelicæ, seu Concilium de Propaganda Fide, per Conversionem Ethnicorum Maxime Sinensium.*

Hans Egéde (1686–1758), a Norwegian pastor, was sent forth by the Copenhagen College to Greenland in 1721, which also sent Thomas von Westen (1716–1722) to Lapland. Moved at first by a desire to search out and preach the gospel to the descendants of the ancient Norse settlers in Greenland, Egéde and his like-minded wife, Gertrude Rask, soon burned with zeal to convert the Eskimos. With some forty settlers in 1721, he laid the foundation of the modern colony of Christian Eskimos, of which Godthaab, or God's haven, is the capital. The hardships and disappointments which he suffered resulted in the return of many of his associates, and in the order of the good King Friedrich's successor, Christian VI., to discontinue the settlement. There happened to be present at the coronation of that king, as representing the Saxon court, the Count von Zinzendorf. At Copenhagen, in 1731, he met with two Eskimos who had been baptized by Egéde, and heard with sorrow that the mission was to be broken up. His attendants also heard from a negro named Anthony of the oppression of the slaves in the West Indian island of St. Thomas, and of their readiness to receive the gospel, which there was no one to preach to them. That visit of Zinzendorf was the beginning of the Moravian Missions.

Missions of the Unitas Fratrum.—In 1457, sixty years before Luther nailed his theses on the door of the Wittenberg church, at Kunewalde, eighty miles from Prag, the persecuted followers of Huss formed themselves into the Church of the Brethren of the Love of Christ. By 1467, these Bohemians, certain Waldenses, and the Moravians united as the Unitas Fratrum. By their enemies, who drove them into dens and caves of the earth, they were called "pitmen" or "burrowers;" yet when the German Reformation woke, they numbered four hundred churches, they translated the Bible into the Bohemian tongue, and they spread it widely by means of the printing-press. On the accession of Ferdinand II. in 1617, the anti-reformation of the Jesuits nearly exterminated the martyr Church of Bohemia. Its last bishop, of the Moravian province, was the famous Kornensky, known to literature as the greatest of early educationists and philologists, **John Amos Comenius.** The vernacular Bible kept a few remnants of the Church of Huss alive till 1715. Then **Christian David**, an ignorant Romanist, was converted by it, and from the Moravian province of intolerant Austria, he led a company of godly emigrants into the neighbouring Saxon Silesia. There the steward of Count Zinzendorf, in his master's absence at Dresden, invited them to cut wood and build. The visitor who takes train from Dresden for fifty miles, past the Bautzen of the first Napoleon's wars and the Hochkirch of Friedrich the Great's, comes to Herrnhut, the "Lord's watch," and on a monument in a grove near the highway he reads this inscription: "On this spot was felled the first tree for the settlement of Herrnhut, June 17, 1722. 'Yea the sparrow hath found an house and the swallow a nest for herself where she may lay her young, even Thine altars, O Lord of hosts, my King and my God.'" Here settled the spiritual descendants of Huss and Wiclif, and here their little Presbyterian Church, with humble bishops like those of Columba's and Knox's time, became, in 1732, a missionary Church in the same sense in which, during apostolic times, every Christian was a missionary. The whole number was not larger than 600 a century and a half ago; now the members are about 100,000 in three provinces,—the Continental, English, and American,—each under a Synod. All are confederate under a General Synod, meeting at Herrnhut every decade; the last, or twenty-ninth meeting, was held in 1879.

Count von Zinzendorf (1700–1760) was grandson of an Austrian noble who, for conscience' sake, surrendered all his estates, and whose son became a minister of the Elector of Saxony at Dresden. If grace can be inherited, young Zinzendorf is a case in point. Spener was one of his sponsors; his grandmother and aunt, who trained him, were Pietists. At four years of age he made this covenant with Christ: "Be Thou mine, dear Saviour, and I will be Thine;" and from the window of his grandmother's castle he used to toss out letters to the Lord, telling Him all his heart. At ten he was made a pupil of Franke at Halle; there he formed circles for prayer, while he was foremost in his Greek and

Latin studies. Sent to Wittenberg that he might become worldly enough for the high position for which his uncle destined him, he became an ascetic for a time, and when only eighteen his mediation was accepted by the polemic theologians of Halle and Wittenberg. All the seductions of Paris and the other cities of Europe which he visited, did not draw him from Christ, nor did the temptations of Dresden, when he became Aulic counsellor there. But his saying ever was that which Tholuck adopted as a motto: "*Ich hab' eine Passion, und die est Er, nur Er*" ("I have one passion, and it is He, He alone!"). At school he had formed his fellows into "The Order of the Grain of Mustard Seed," which pledged them to seek the conversion of others, heathen and Jews. When he married Erdmuth Dorothea, sister of the twenty-ninth Count of Reuss, the two covenanted with the Lord to cast all ideas of rank away, and to be ready, pilgrim-staff in hand, to go to the heathen and preach the gospel to them. During the marriage tour they found Christian David's fugitives from Moravia in their new home at his estate of Bethelsdorf. These he regarded as "a parish destined for him from eternity." All his property he surrendered to the work, not of organizing a sect, but of forming circles of pious souls within the Lutheran Church, as Wesley—learning from him—sought to do in the Church of England.

Growth of the Moravian Missions (1732–1882).—The seal of the Unitas Fratrum, earlier and later, was on a crimson ground, a lamb bearing the resurrection cross, from which hangs a banner of triumph with the motto, "*Vicit Agnus Noster; Eum Sequamur*" ("Our Lamb has conquered; Him let us follow"). The same year saw **Dober**, a potter, and **Nitschmann**—21st August 1732, a festal day of the Moravians—set out for St. Thomas, willing, if need be, themselves to become slaves for Christ's sake; and the two cousins **Stach** and **Boemish** offered themselves for Greenland, where Egéde welcomed the former with Christian David, and they established the settlement of Ny or New Herrnhut. In 1734 a mission was begun to the Red Indians, especially of the States of New York and Pennsylvania. There in 1749 the Moravians were protected from the intolerance of some of the colonial and military authorities by an Act of the British Parliament, and **David Zeisberger** (1721–1808) became the apostle of the Delawares. Zinzendorf himself, and **Spangenberg**, his successor and biographer, visited the American missions, and formed the first Moravian

Church of converted Indians, in 1742, at Shekomeko. Near this the Scottish agent, David Brainerd, began his work the year after, at a place now known as Brainerd's Bridge, sixteen miles east of Albany. In 1735, a missionary was sent from Herrnhut to the Indians of South America. In 1736, **Georg Schmidt**, the Bohemian Bunyan, after six years' confinement for the truth, was sent forth to the Koi-Koin ("men") and Bushmen, the yellow race of South Africa, whom the Dutch contemptuously called Hottentots and treated as beasts, until the Moravian missionary and the English Government interfered. No fewer than eighteen separate missionaries went forth from the little village of the Lord's Watch within the quarter of a century after 1732. In 1850, when Joseph Latrobe, brother of the Moravian agent in London, was Governor of Port Phillip, two brethren began a mission to the still lower blacks of Australia, to the north and east of Melbourne. Most pathetic as well as heroic of all the Moravian missions, however, has been that which Gutzlaff urged, to the Tibetans (1856). Of thirty volunteers, two laymen were chosen, **Pagell** and **Hyde**, afterwards joined by **Dr. Jäschke**, the greatest Tibetan scholar. Refused a road by Russia, they were welcomed by the English in India, and settled at the two States of Kyelang in Lahoul and Poo in Kunawar. There, snowed up for three-fourths of the year, they and their devoted wives have lived and—in the Pagells' cases—died for the stolid lama-worshippers, from whom they have now some forty converts, while Dr. Jäschke, aided only by a lithographic press for a time, translated much of the Scriptures into Tibetan, and prepared Tibeto-German and Tibeto-English lexicons. Lord Lawrence, when Viceroy of India, and his court did many an act of kindness to them from Simla. At Poo, in the early days of 1883, first Mr. Pagell and then his wife died within a few days of each other, after a quarter of a century's labours, and were buried by a faithful catechist. For five months their colleague at Kyelang could not visit the spot, because the Himalayan passes were snowed up. In all missionary literature there is no story so pathetic as that told by the Buddhists themselves of the devotion, the sickness, the death, the burial of the heroic couple. We have stood by the now neglected graves of the Brethren in the Nicobar Islands, where many perished after even greater sufferings, with none, not even a solitary convert, to close their eyes.

In August 1882, the Moravian Church celebrated the 150th anniversary of its foreign missionary work. It began in 1732 with two missionaries, who had £1, 4s. between them, and it has thus grown. In 1782 there were 27 mission stations, served by 165 missionary brethren and sisters. In 1832 the work comprised 41 stations, with 40,000 persons in charge, served by 209 brethren and sisters; while during the first century 1199 persons (740 brethren and 459 sisters) had been sent as missionaries. In July 1881 there were 113 stations; 315 missionaries (165 brethren and 150 sisters), among these 30 native missionaries, and in addition 1471 native assistants; there were 211 schools with 16,437 pupils (in addition, 89 Sunday schools with 6651 children and 6219 adult scholars); while the number of persons under care of the missionaries was 74,440, of whom 25,298 were communicant members, the remainder being chiefly baptized children (26,836) and adult candidates for full membership (14,477). The total number of missionaries, brethren and sisters, who have been sent out by the Moravian Church during these 150 years, is upwards of 2170.

The cost of maintaining this foreign mission work, including the schools, is upwards of £52,000 per annum, raised from the contributions of the converts, the proceeds of trade and agriculture, government grants for schools, the interest of endowments; while £19,728 is the result of collections, contributions, donations, and legacies from members and friends of the Church. The cost of the administration is $3\frac{1}{2}$ per cent. of the total expenditure.

Character of Franke's and Zinzendorf's Work.—The Pietists did much, in aim and in result, to redeem Lutheranism and the evangelical Christianity of the seventeenth and eighteenth centuries from the reproach of unbroken spiritual barrenness. But, at the best, and in the light of Christendom and the Church's duty, of heathendom and Islam and the Church's knowledge of them, the Pietist missions were (1) small in themselves, (2) conducted by men generally uneducated and untrained, (3) directed to races and tribes too obscure, savage, or transient to influence the great centres and citadels of heathendom, the great non-Christian and anti-Christian systems and civilisations. The Church of the living God, as such, stood haughtily aloof, as the Pharisees had done when Christ consorted with publicans and sinners. *That* had to be won as a Church with numbers, resources, organization, independence, and the authority given by the Spirit to all its living members combined under the commission of its Head. The Moravian Brethren in Germany, the Puritans and Nonconformists in England, the Seceders and Societies in Scotland, added to the fact that they were the pioneer missionaries the really greater fact that they led the Church to become the federation of missions which has marked our nineteenth century. What the Moravians began in 1732, it was left to William Carey to develope in 1792.

CHAPTER XII.

THE DAWN OF MODERN MISSIONS—THE ENGLISH IN NORTH AMERICA AND IN INDIA.

The Open Door and the Open Eye—Scotland—England—The Pilgrim Fathers—The First Protestant Missionary Corporation—Cromwell—John Eliot—The Mayhews and Brainerds—The Wesleys—The East India Company—Schwartz—Kiernander—The Real Missionary Influence of the East India Company.

The open door gives the open eye, say the Germans. Rather, in the development of His kingdom and the building of His city, God opens both the doors of the world and the eyes of the faithful together. In the time of preparation, all through the eighteen Christian centuries, the open door generally came first. Waves of barbaric invasion swept down from north and east on the Church, the Turkish conquest of Constantinople spread the Renaissance over Europe, the Crusaders brought back some knowledge of the Eastern world, the New World was discovered, but only the Spaniards, the Portuguese, and the Dutch carried a Christianity of compromise to the heathen races. In this century the missionary has often been the first to open the door of discovery and commerce. It has been so altogether in North America, partly in India, very largely in Africa. With the opening of the seventeenth century the time came, in God's providence, for the English to take the lead in colonization and commerce. It was the open eye that led the English Puritans to New England. It was the English East India Company that opened India—often against its will—to Christ, when Portugal and the Netherlands had been rejected.

Scotland.—The missionary development of the Reformation was arrested in Scotland and England as it had been in Germany, so that only a few obscure and persecuted but spiritual and heroic Christians sought the conversion of the nations, and that by unorganized agencies outside of the Protestant Churches. We have seen that Lutheranism became fossilized into a stony orthodoxy and polemical dogmatism, leaving it to a few Pietists and United Brethren to preach and suffer for the kingdom of Christ. In Scotland, where the whole people, after successful struggling for civil freedom, carried out the Reformation in its most radical form, the self-seeking "Lords of the Congregation" plundered church and school and poor alike of the Abbey properties, and persecution followed in its most pitiless form. The **Covenanters** had enough to do in keeping the Presbyterian Church from being altogether consumed by the flames. In the Pictish and Saxon times, the Scots had been the missionaries of a free and spiritually independent Church, as opposed to the Romanism of Augustin of Canterbury and of Boniface. In the wars against English invasion, they had vindicated those principles of civil freedom which have become the life of the constitution. Now their contribution to the missionary cause was the triumphant assertion of the crown or kingly rights of Jesus Christ to the faith and obedience of every man, and to the loyal service of every Church, free from priestly interference or civil coercion. **John Knox** wrote in the first Confession (1560) of the Church of Scotland the old text of Chrysostom and Luther, but without their eschatological gloss, which destroyed the evangelic meaning of our Lord who spoke it: "And this glaid tydingis of the kyngdome sall be precheit through the haill warld for a witnes unto all natiouns and then sall the end cum." In 1647 the General Assembly recorded the gospel desire for "a more firm consociation for propagating it to those who are without, especially the Jews." In 1699 it enjoined the ministers whom it sent forth with the unhappy Darien expedition to labour among the heathen, and the year after it added: "The Lord, we hope, will yet honour you and this Church from which you are sent to carry His name among the heathen." Ten years after that, in 1709, the **Society in Scotland for Propagating Christian Knowledge** was founded, chiefly for the evangelization of the Highlands as a home mission; but it received endowments for foreign missions also, which it applied for a time in America, and, at a later period, in Africa and India, on a trifling scale.

England.—The Reformation which Wiclif, two centuries before, had begun to make by and for all the people, as in Scotland, became under the Tudors a twofold movement, which issued in a comprehensive but sacerdotal Church of England, and in those who were first called Puritans and afterwards Nonconformists. The evangelical refugees whom the intolerance of Mary drove to the Continent, learned at Frankfort, and especially at Geneva, a purer and hardier Protestantism than that of the Prayer-Book of Edward VI. Those who returned—the most pure in life as well as doctrine, and the most learned men of their day—found Elizabeth determined to mould a Church of her own, wide enough to contain Romanist and Genevan, while, under the Bishop of Peterborough, these noble witnesses to Christ's truth showed, at Northampton, that the Church in England might have been made truly catholic and purely evangelical, free and loyal. In 1572 the first presbytery was formed in England, by some who took warning from the massacre of St. Bartholomew which had just occurred. Elizabeth induced Parliament to launch the first Act of Uniformity. Under pain of death for "heresy," the attempt had been vainly made to compel all to think alike. From this time the still more fruitless effort was made to force all to worship God alike by conforming to Elizabeth's compromise, and Nonconformity became the watchword of all free Englishmen. It proved a missionary word, for it sent the Puritans to America, to succeed where the Huguenots and the Dutch, following the Spaniards and Portuguese, had failed.

The Pilgrim Fathers were the first Puritan missionaries. Fleeing from Lincolnshire to Amsterdam, under their pastor **John Robinson**, a congregation of "the Lord's free people" sailed, in 1620, in the *Mayflower*, landed at New Plymouth on the coast of Massachusetts. The hundred or two souls of that day have become fifty millions in the Republic of the United States, and four and a half in the British Dominion of Canada. The Red Indians have given place till they are under half a million at the present day, and often owing to causes the responsibility of which rests on churches slow to learn Christ's last and greatest law of toleration, and especially on civil rulers whose path has been marked by fraud and war. Even the venerable Robinson had reason to write to the Governor of New Plymouth: "O that you had converted some before you had killed any;" and the one stain bewailed by Americans since the extinction of slavery, is the official policy towards the Red Indians, a stain from which Canada is said to be free. But the Pilgrim Fathers did not lose time in caring for the natives,—one of their number was set apart "to promote the conversion of the Indians." In December 1621, an elder, **Robert Cushman,** appealed to England on behalf of "these poor heathen," and in 1636 the colony legislated for the "preaching of the gospel among them." Meanwhile the Scottish James, from whose training so much had been expected, had, in 1622, issued a proclamation, declaring zeal for the extension of the gospel to be the special motive for colonizing the New World; and in 1628, Charles I. gave Massachusetts colony its charter, asserting this as "the principal end of the plantation," that the colonists may "win and invite the natives of the country to the knowledge of the only true God and Saviour of mankind and the Christian faith." In 1646 the Colonial legislature accordingly passed an Act for the Propagation of the Gospel among the Indians.

The First Protestant Missionary Corporation was undoubtedly that created, not by a Church, but by the Long Parliament. In one sense **Cromwell** was a missionary. In 1644 some seventy English and Scottish pastors petitioned Parliament to encourage the sending of missionaries to America and the West Indies. In 1649 an ordinance was passed creating the "Corporation for the Propagation of the Gospel in New England," and ministers were enjoined to read it from the pulpit and make collections for it. The Universities of Oxford and Cambridge wrote to the ministers, urging them to stir up the people to the good enterprize. The army—an almost theocratic force at that time—helped with money, for the country was slow to respond. Still capital enough was raised to purchase lands yielding nearly £600 a year at that time. Thus the nation as such became the first missionary society, and the corporation was its executive. The Red Indians were the first heathen who had become British subjects, and Cromwell was not slow to send them the pure gospel, as we shall see, at the hands of Eliot and the Mayhews, of "Mistris Bland," the first English woman missionary, and others whose names are entered with full details in the accompt sent annually to the Corporation in London by the Commissioners of the United Colonies. It is significant that, on the restoration of Charles II., attempts were made to rob the Corporation, on the plea that it was dead in law. But in 1661 it was revived under a new charter, under the influence of another great lay missionary of the time, the famous son of the great Earl of Cork, **Robert Boyle.** For thirty years he was governor of the Corporation, and the constant correspondent of Eliot and the other missionaries. As a director of the East India

Company, he did even more for the early evangelization of India than of the Moheecan Indians. He learned Hebrew, Syriac, and Chaldee, that he might be as much a master of Biblical criticism as he proved to be of Baconian physics, when he founded the Royal Society. He had the Gospels and Acts translated into Malay, and he circulated these and the Arabic translations of his friend Pococke, at his own cost, in all countries where these tongues were spoken, besides Welsh and Irish Bibles at home. Nor should we part from Cromwell without mentioning his plan for converting old Chelsea College into the seat of a council for the Protestant religion, to train evangelists for the East and West Indies, for Turkey and Scandinavia, and for the enlightenment of the Romish Church which had caused the slaughter of the Vaudois bewailed in Milton's sonnet. Dr. Hyde proposed, in 1677, that Christ Church, Oxford, should be used for the purpose, and Boyle revived a project for India which Dean Prideaux submitted to William III. in 1694.

John Eliot (1604–1690) was the first Puritan missionary of renown. Born at Nasing in Essex, master of the Bible in the originals, and a distinguished student at Cambridge, he became a teacher and an earnest Christian, under Mr. John Hooker in the Grammar School of Little Baddow. At twenty-seven he followed the Pilgrim Fathers to freedom in New England, reached Boston a year after its foundation in 1630, was ordained Presbyterian minister of Roxbury, and gave up the remaining fifty-eight years of his life to the evangelization of the Pequot tribe of the Iroquois nation. Like William Carey, three centuries after, Eliot possessed the three gifts of grace, learning, and toil. His biographer Cotton Mather remarks that *Toile* is the anagram of his name, and he himself, the most modest of men like Carey, closed his grammar of the Indian language with the remark, "Prayer and pains, through faith in Jesus Christ, will do anything." It was in 1646, at the age of forty-two, when the legislatures, Colonial and English, were in accord on the subject, that Eliot felt himself fully equipped for the spiritual campaign. Not till 1660 was he convinced that he had trained his converts up to the high Puritan platform, and then he at once baptized and admitted to the Lord's Supper the first Red Indians, who formed a church at Natick, on Charles River, eighteen miles from Boston. In 1661–63, the Moheecan Bible, the first Bible printed in America, was printed by him at Cambridge, the now famous Boston suburb, and this was followed by a succession of original works and translations chiefly from Richard Baxter. The Bible, said to have been written with a single pen, was presented to Charles II., Clarendon, and the two Universities. At Cambridge, the seat of Harvard University, a small Indian college was erected to train twenty native pastors and teachers. Before he passed away, at eighty-six, with the words "Welcome, joy," on his lips, he saw 1100 Indian members in six churches, one under **John Hiacomes**, the first native minister, on the Island of Martha's Vineyard, and one his own successor at Natick, named Takawompbait. In the English and French and American wars that followed his death, the Moheeans became extinct; the story is well told by Cooper in his *Last of the Mohicans*. In 1836 only one hut with four inmates of mixed Indian and negro blood represented the work of John Eliot. Now we look with pathetic interest at the rare copies of a Bible which there is none to read. But did the great, the gracious, the learned evangelist's work perish? No more than did that of Abraham when he was laid in the cave at Hebron, in his only purchased possession in all the land of promise.

The Mayhews and Brainerds.—An example to the many colonists and captains of labour who still settle in India and among native races, **Thomas Mayhew**, Esq., Crown patentee of Martha's Vineyard, Nantucket and Elizabeth Isles, off the coast of New England, devoted his own profits and his sons' and grandsons' lives to the conversion of the Red Indians. In 1650 the first two "powaws" or wizards were converted, with the result that a great company became obedient to the faith. Not till 1806 did the last missionary Mayhew pass away, at the great age of eighty-nine,—an apostolic succession extending over a century and a half. On the mainland at Meshpee, fifty miles from Boston, **Mr. Bourne** worked along with Eliot and others representing the New Plymouth colony. In 1734–49, **Mr. John Sergeant** used past experience to devise plans for the conversion and civilisation of the Indians on the River Housatunnuk, not unlike those of the Free Scottish Mission to the Kafirs at Lovedale and Blythswood now. He was succeeded in 1751, at Stockbridge, by the great thinker and divine **Jonathan Edwards**, who in 1758 became president of the New Jersey College at Princeton. But Edwards is more closely still connected with early missionary enterprize, as the friend and biographer of the young and ardent **David**

Brainerd (1718–1747), who at the early age of thirty handed on his work among the Indians of the Delaware fork to his brother John. Both were agents of the Scottish Propagation Society,—the latter till the American War of Independence. David Brainerd's brief missionary career of three years, and his spiritual breathings, which, like Henry Martyn's half a century after, have made his name almost a household word, were influenced, like Edwards, by **Whitefield**, who, with **John and Charles Wesley**, was the outcome of the evangelical revival which succeeded Puritanism, and was the lineal descendant of the Pietists Franke and Zinzendorf, who again had sprung through Huss from the teaching of Wiclif. The first specially foreign missionary of Wesleyan Methodism was the intrepid and self-denying **Dr. Coke**, who worked from 1786 among the negro slaves in the West Indies, to 1814 in Ceylon, where he died. But the Methodism of the Wesleys and of Whitefield, of Fletcher, Coke, and Lady Huntingdon, like the Reformation from which it sprang, was rather directly a home than a foreign mission, till 1813, when the General Wesleyan Methodist Missionary Society was established. As a foreign mission, especially in Jamaica, the Methodists suffered hardships, even to the death, in their philanthropic efforts to ameliorate and abolish the horrors of slavery. Indirectly Whitefield did more than if he had himself been a foreign missionary, for the freedom of the slave and the extension of missions which mark the nineteenth century, by becoming the spiritual father of John Newton, and probably Cowper the poet; of Claudius Buchanan and William Wilberforce; of Thomas Scott and, through him, of William Carey; and of the rest of the band of evangelical fathers, lay and clerical, Episcopal and Nonconformist, who irradiate the closing years of the eighteenth century. The Methodist revival, arrested in the last quarter of the eighteenth century after forty years of vivifying influence, became, in the nineteenth century, the inheritance rather of the Church of England, and helped to create the Church Missionary Society.

The East India Company, in the 258 years of its existence, from Queen Elizabeth to the Queen-Empress Victoria, proved all unwillingly to be the most noteworthy servant of Jehovah since the empire of Cyrus the Great. On the last day of the year 1600, "The Governor and Company of Merchants of London trading with the East Indies" received their first charter from Queen Elizabeth. Gradually the traders, first at Surat in 1613, became territorial proprietors; then, at Madras in 1639, political rulers or virtual sovereigns, only subordinate to the imperial power at Delhi, on 12th August 1765, eight years after Clive's victory at Plassey; and then, on 1st November 1858, the Company gave place to the direct rule of the Crown and Parliament of Great Britain. That is, practically as well as constitutionally, the Christian people of England, Scotland, and Ireland became trustees for the good of the people of India, now 254 millions in number. Thus each citizen of Great Britain and Ireland is immediately and individually responsible to God for the discharge of that trust, the greatest in all history.

Edward VI. had issued instructions to the navigators whose success resulted in the establishment of the Company, to the effect, in the words of the chronicler of Sir Humphrey Gilbert, that "the sowing of Christianity must be the chief interest of such as shall make any attempt at foreign discovery, or else whatever is builded upon other foundation shall never obtain happy success or continuance." Sir Humphrey's step-brother, Sir Walter Raleigh, cared for the conversion of the natives in the first English colony, that of Virginia, and the first baptism of a native is recorded as having taken place on 13th August 1587. About the same time that Grotius wrote his treatise, *De Veritate Religionis Christianæ*, for a similar end, John Wood, D.D., in 1618 published *The True Honour of Navigation and Navigators*, dedicating it to Sir Thomas Smith, governor to the East India Company.

Like the royal and Puritan planters of the American colonies, the directors of the East India Company at first professed their desire to Christianize the natives of India. Each of their East Indiamen was provided with a chaplain, and also each of the central factories at Surat and Bombay, Madras, Hoogli, and Calcutta. **Henry Lord** is the first "preacher to the Honourable Company of Merchants," with whose name we meet so early as 1616. He joined Lescke, the chaplain at Surat, and proved himself at once a good missionary to the natives and the earliest Oriental scholar, by his now rare book on the Hindoos and Parsees, *A Display of Two Forraigne Sects in the East Indies*, 1630. The Company's representative at the imperial capital of Agra at the same time was **Joseph Saalbank**, a layman who urged the Company to send out "not only solid and sufficient divines that may be able to encounter with the arch-enemies of our religion, but also godly, zealous and devout persons, such as may, by their piety and purity of life, give good example to those with whom they live." One of Lord's successors was **Terry**, who was the chaplain of Sir Thomas Roe's embassy from James I. to the Great Moghul, and who reported that the natives said of the English, whom alone they knew: "Christian religion, devil religion; Christian much drunk; Christian much do wrong; much beat, much abuse others." Thus early are we introduced to what has proved to be one of the greatest obstacles to the acceptance, by heathen and Mohammedan, of pure Christianity in all lands. **Thomas Coryate** would hardly be called a missionary now; but this eccentric and indomitable traveller, who died at the seaport of Surat in 1617, was so roused by the usual call of a Moolla to prayer, that he ran to an eminence opposite the mosque, and shouted in Persian, "There is no god but God and the Lord Jesus the Son of God, and Mohammed is an impostor."

There were some excellent Christian men among the Company's early governors, such as Kerridge at Surat; Oxenden, who in 1681 raised money for the first church in which the English should worship, and the natives "observe the purity and gravity of our devotions;" Aungier, who looked forward to the time when "the merciful pleasure of God should touch the natives with a sense of the eternal welfare of their souls," and his friend **Streynsham Masters**, who in 1680 built St. Mary's Church, in Fort George, Madras, at his own cost. The last, when Governor of Madras for three years and a half from 1678, is described as having "strenuously endeavoured to instil a sense and remembrance of the true religion in the rising settlement committed to his charge," and as having been "highly conspicuous among the worshippers of the true religion of Jesus." Hence in the almost contemporary *Memoirs* of Asiaticus we find this well-deserved exclamation: "In British India be the name of Streynsham Masters immortal!" These were worthy predecessors of a long list of the civil and military servants of Government, who—in the succeeding two centuries, to John and Henry Lawrence, Herbert Edwardes, and Colin Mackenzie, and to men still living, like Sir William Muir and Sir Charles Aitchison—have ruled India in the fear of God. In the happy times when Cromwell guided England's foreign policy, the despatches of the Court of Directors contained passages not unlike modern missionary correspondence. Not less so in the good days of King William III., whose **Charter of 1698**—applied to the United East India Company in 1708—contained provisions for a missionary and an educational as well as an ecclesiastical establishment. A schoolmaster and minister were to be maintained in every garrison and central factory, to learn both Portuguese and the local vernacular, "the better to enable them to instruct the Gentoos in the Protestant religion." Soon after this the directors ordered the use of "a form of prayer, beseeching God that these Indian nations, amongst whom we dwell, seeing our sober and righteous conversation, may be induced to have a great esteem for our most holy profession of the gospel." But it was left to the Danish Government and the German Pietists to send the first avowed missionaries to India for the evangelization of the natives, in the persons of Ziegenbalg and Plütschau, as we have seen. Their work was practically confined to the Danish territory of Tranquebar,—not so that of the greatest of their successors.

Christian Friedrich Schwartz (1726–1798), Prussian of Sonnenburg, in Brandenburg, and dedicated by his mother from his birth to the service of God, studied under Franke at Halle. There he met Schultz, early colleague of Ziegenbalg, who had come home to pass through the press a new edition of the Tamil New Testament. In spite of all his friends and his widower-father, the eldest son went forth at twenty-three to a career which closed with these words: "I am now at the brink of eternity, but to this moment I declare that I do not repent of having spent forty-three years in the service of my Divine Master. Who knows but God may remove some of the great obstacles to the propagation of the gospel? Should a reformation take place among the Europeans, it would no doubt be the greatest blessing to the country." The East India Company, which gave him and his companions a free passage in their ship in 1750, turned out William Carey forty-three years after, and forced him and his colleagues to seek an asylum from little Denmark in its Bengal settlement of Serampore. But Schwartz owed the peace and protection which enabled him to lay the foundation of the Native Church of Southern India—now numbering half a million of souls—to the Company, first in Tanjore and then in Tinnevelli, and he returned the service by his influence with the Tanjore Raja and the Mohammedan Haidar Ali of Mysore. Schwartz, too, was the first to establish a scheme of Christian vernacular schools, supported by the Raja, his ward, and by the British Government, till stopped by the wars with Tipoo. He was the first to anticipate and provide for a three years' famine, after 1780, partly caused by these wars, by storing rice, and supplying not only the dying natives, but the English troops and Raja's dependents. His ward, Raja Serfojee, erected a Christian church and manse in his fort; and when the missionary died, in 1798, both this Hindoo and the East India Company erected noble monuments to his memory, the latter by Bacon, in St. Mary's Church, Madras. Of the Tanjore Fort Church and Flaxman's monument there, Dr. Duff wrote thus when he visited the spot in 1849: "I went to see this singular monument of the triumph of Protestant influence and ascendency at a heathen court, —the most remarkable visible monument of the sort, perhaps, in the whole realm of Gentilism. . . . The church is a neat edifice; at the west end is the marble monument. . . . I stood before it. I forgot time and space. I knew not where I was, for consciousness was gone. Call it a dream, or vision, or trance, or absorption, I care not. It was human nature, human feeling, human sympathy. Before me, in solid, well-grained marble, in bold but not obtrusive or glaring relief, was the couch of the dying saint; on it stretched lay the pale, bald, worn-out veteran apostolic man, whose assistance and mediation heathens, Hindoo and Mohammedan, as well as Christian governing powers, eagerly coveted, in the last gasp of expiring nature. Behind him, at his head, stood the affectionate, tender, sympathizing, loving fellow-labourer **Guericke**, who ever looked up to him as a father. . . . And there is the Raja Serfojee, in his full dress, standing by the couch, and holding the left hand of the dying father in his. . . . It is a simple, natural, and affecting scene, and the group who compose it possess an interest for the Christian mind beyond what mere words can express."

Kiernander, a Swede of the Danish-Halle Mission at Cuddalore, became the first Protestant missionary to Calcutta in 1758, the year after Plassey, on the invitation of Clive himself. During the next twenty-eight years he built the still well-known mission church there, and was the means of converting 209 heathens and 300 Romanists. **Charles Grant**, an Inverness-shire boy, born in 1746, went out to Bengal, first as an officer and then as a civilian. There he was converted at thirty, having met and married his sister to **Mr. William** Chambers, brother of the Chief Justice, and a friend of Schwartz. Mr. Grant had as his steward Mr. O'Beck, a pupil of Schwartz. He was succeeded by Mr. **George Udny** as Company's agent at Malda, where before the close of the century William Carey received employment while he learned

Bengalee, and began to translate the Scriptures. Mr. Chambers himself was the first to attempt a translation into Persian, of which he was the official interpreter in the Supreme Court. This Christian society, led by Grant, became the first centre of evangelical missionary effort in Northern India. They wrote home to Charles Simeon to look out for eight missionaries, of whom Grant was to support two; and Lord Cornwallis, when Governor-General the first time, promised not to oppose such a mission. After studying the languages three years at Benares, the eight were to begin the glorious work of giving light to the heathen with every probability of success. When Charles Grant went home, he did more for Christian missions to India than any other man; his elder son continued this as Baron Glenelg; and his second son, Sir Robert, as Governor of Bombay, friend of Dr. John Wilson, and author of some of our most beautiful hymns. In 1797 he wrote a work which did not see the light till Parliament published it in 1813, but which contained the germ of all subsequent spiritual and social reforms in India,—*Observations on the State of Society among the Asiatic Subjects of Great Britain*. Recalling the laudable zeal of the Company in earlier periods for extending the knowledge of the gospel to the pagan tribes among whom its factories were placed, the preface continued: "The duty therefore of the Company, as part of a Christian community, its peculiar superadded obligations, its enlarged means, and its continual dependence on the Divine favour, all call upon it to honour God by diffusing the knowledge of that revelation which He has vouchsafed to mankind." Alas! intoxicated or demented by the very political success which God had permitted to it, the East India Company had become the most intolerant enemy of Christian missions. Charles Grant wrote his treatise in 1792 to influence the new Charter then under discussion. In spite of all his efforts and those of **Wilberforce** in the Commons, his brother directors and proprietors caused Parliament to refuse to insert even this vague moral or "pious" clause, as it was called, in the Charter of 1793: "That it is the peculiar and bounden duty of the British Legislature to promote, by all just and prudent means, the interest and happiness of the inhabitants of the British dominions in India; and that for these ends such measures ought to be adopted as may gradually tend to their advancement in useful knowledge, and to their religious and moral comfort." This was not even formally adopted till the Charter of 1813, and not really carried out till that of 1833.

The Real Missionary Influence of the East India Company, exercised by Providence through it in spite of its frequent intolerance and continued professions of neutrality, till it was swept away in the blood of the Mutiny, was like that of the Roman Empire: (1) The Company rescued all Southern Asia from anarchy, and made possible the growth of law, order, property, and peace as a sort of moral police; (2) the Company introduced roads, commerce, wealth, and the physical preparation for the gospel during a time of transition; (3) the Company quickened the conscience of Great Britain and its churches as they awoke to their duty after the close of the eighteenth century, partly by its extreme opposition to missions, partly by the earnest civilians and officers, and in a very few cases merchants and chaplains, whom it sent home with knowledge and experience. The East India Company has hardly any higher praise than that of the pagan Roman Empire, but it is entitled to that,—it did for the southern nations of Asia what Rome had done for the northern nations of Europe.

All things are now ready for the rising of the sun of Christian missions. But we must first record the stages of the compromise made with heathenism by the Latin Church from the time of the Reformation.

CHAPTER XIII.

THE MISSIONARY COMPROMISE OF THE LATIN CHURCH WITH HEATHENISM.

Monachism and Missions—The Counter-Reformation—Francis Xavier—Xavier's Missionary Principles—Xavier's Missionary Methods—Propaganda Institutions—India, Results—The Madura Mission—Goa and the Present Organization of Indo-Romish Missions—Japan, China, and the Philippine Islands—Africa—Results.

Monachism and Missions.—Monachism, on its good side, was the missionary organization through which Christendom worked, up to Wiclif, Huss, and Luther. Begun unconsciously in 250, in the Lower Thebaid of Egypt, when one Paul fled from the Decian persecution to a cave; adopted by Anthony from choice; introduced into the West by Athanasius on his visit to Rome in 340, the "lonely" life, which the word signifies, became in Banchor, Iona, and Lindisfarne, in Lerins, Luxeuil, and the Benedictine Monte Casino, the best nurse of missionary zeal and activity in the centuries of savagery. These brotherhoods and sisterhoods were long the only missionary societies of the Church. What at the beginning of the thirteenth century the Dominicans and Franciscans began to be, we have seen. Almost every generation gave birth to a new monastic order, and as the Latin Church grew corrupt, these at first checked but soon fed the corruption. The very good of the early brotherhoods became evil, till how great was the darkness! The Christianity of West and East alike became an offence, a scandal, a stone of stumbling to Mohammedan, Jew, and idolator, as it is in the East to this day. In the fourteenth century (1302–1373) two Councils and three Popes approved of the *Revelations* of Bridget of Sweden, which confirm the worst charges against monasteries and convents of nuns. Luther's experience as a monk and his visit to Rome were powerful factors in the Reformation, preceded as it was by the wit of Erasmus and the satire of Ulrich von Hütten.

The Counter-Reformation.—What the Church of Rome lost in the Reformation she sought in the New World, of West and East, opened up by the "most Catholic" powers of Spain and Portugal. Her agents she found in the new Order of Jesus, founded by **Ignatius Loyola, Xavier,** and five others in 1534, in the crypt of St. Denis on the height of Montmartre which overlooks Paris. Xavier had been influenced by the Reformed doctrines of grace when under spiritual conviction, and the stronger nature of Ignatius fascinated him. Four years after the foundation, Pope Paul III. appointed a committee of the eight ablest cardinals, who reported in language that was too late, coming after Luther, that the religious orders should be "all abolished" as "a grave scandal to seculars, and doing the greatest harm by their example." In 1523, Cardinal Wolsey had the Pope's authority to suppress forty small monasteries and apply their revenues to education. The Council of Trent attempted to correct some superficial abuses. But Rome's answer to the Reformation from Wiclif to Luther was practically confined to the confirmatory Bulls of 1540 and 1543, the former of which is the charter of the Society of Jesus, but limited it to sixty members, so bitter was the opposition of the highest ecclesiastics, while the latter converted the brotherhood into a World Society, with powers which enabled it to defy the Popes themselves. By 1556, when Loyola died, the Jesuits had a hundred houses grouped in twelve provinces, not only in Europe but across the ocean. For the new order was not a monastic body, with stringent rules as to dress and ritual, but a Spanish *Compania* or body of fighting men under a captain, "the actual embodiment of the Church militant upon earth." The Sorbonne of Paris and the Gallican Church protested as well as the cardinals of Italy. "This is the finger of God," said Paul III. as he read and adopted Loyola's scheme. From that day to this the Jesuits have directed the policy of the Court of Rome, at home and abroad, but the Counter-Reformation has been above all a foreign missionary movement. For a century after Luther the Church of Rome and the Latin Powers of Europe "organized and sustained foreign missions on a magnificent scale," with results statistical, but above all spiritual and civilising, not only disproportionate to the effort, but in many cases the opposite of or hostile to pure and undefiled religion.

Francis Xavier, born in 1506 in the kingdom of Navarre, was in his youth surrounded by Protestant influences. Its brilliant court, over which the sister of Francis I. presided, was filled with Reformers from Germany and Switzerland. By 1533 so far had the spirit of toleration spread, that Calvin and Cop, Rector of the University of Paris, proclaimed the new doctrines in the face of the Sorbonne, which protested against the charter granted to the Society of Jesus not long after. Xavier was a reader in Aristotelian philosophy in the university at the very time Calvin was writing his *Institutes* in the same city. In the first of the 146 letters which form the reliable autobiography of Xavier, we find him, in 1535, writing to his brother that Ignatius Loyola had saved him from "the deplorable dangers arising from my familiarity with men breathing out heresy." At the age of thirty-six, in May 1542, Xavier landed at Goa, with the new viceroy, sent out by John III. of Portugal as head of the first Jesuit mission. Many Franciscans and others had been sent to the East from Mozambique in East Africa, and from Ormuz in the Persian Gulf to Ceylon, and the Spice Islands which fringe the Pacific. But the new order was in vogue, and a missionary college had been opened at Coimbra to train two hundred Jesuit associates for India. Xavier's first determination was to establish a similar institute in Goa for native preachers, when the viceroy sent him to the casteless and partially Christianized pearl-fishers on the Coromandel coast from Cape Comorin to Madras. The viceroy's object was purely political, to secure through them a monopoly of the lucrative fishery. For three years Xavier toiled in South India; for two and a half he was occupied in a visit to the Chinese Archipelago; the next four years he spent in superintending the Jesuit missions in India, and in a visit to Japan, where he resided two years and then returned to Goa. The last year of his life (1552) he spent in a disastrous attempt to enter China as he had done Japan. He died on the Island of Sancian (St. John), off Canton. A shrunken mummy, said to be his body, is still adored by pilgrims in the Goa Church of Bom Jesus, with two toes bitten off by a relic-hunting lady.

Xavier's Missionary Principles.—As a man, Xavier's early familiarity with the doctrines of grace which the Reformers preached in Navarre and Paris, in Germany and Geneva, in his days, made him saintly in experience and aim and life. As a missionary, under Loyola's influence his whole principles and modes of action were based on the Romish and idolatrous sacramentarian theory. He sought to secure in his converts, not an *opus operans*, a subjective change of nature working out into the life, but an *opus operatum*, an external work which required only the recitation of the Creed and a few prayers and baptism. He never met the natural difficulty which is the stumbling-block of every Asiatic, — that outward ceremonies cannot purge from sin. Romanism shares this error with all non-Christian religions; and hence, while its converts may be better than they were as heathens, we cannot expect that in the future any more than in the past its missions will be successful.

Xavier's Missionary Methods.— Such being his principles, his modes of action corresponded. He did not make the mistake of his successors, in living as a Hindoo and lowering the dignity of his soul to the degraded level of the idolator, like Robert de Nobili and the Abbé Dubois. Even when he despaired most of success, when he was most shocked at the vices of his converts and of the unbaptized, he never lost his affection for them. In the spirit of his Master, Xavier yearned for the people who were as sheep without a shepherd, and he did not spare himself for their sake. But he never mastered one Oriental language, and he was frequently without an interpreter. It is doubtful if the people understood the translation of the Creed into their own language. He tells us that they had mis-translated the very first word of the Creed, having substituted "I will" (*volo*) for "I believe" (*credo*). His expression always is, *I have made* Christians (*feci Christianos*). At the same time, he insisted, by a strict discipline, on at least an outward conformity to the Decalogue. His principal argument with his home friends to send more missionaries, was that souls will thus be delivered from the pains of purgatory. His zeal was of the impulsive order,—it demanded immediate fruit. Hence his restless journeys from place to place. Two years was sufficient to convince him that to Christianize the poor fishermen was hopeless, even with the help of "gold fanams," and he resolved to confine his attention to the "kings" of India and the East. As a director of the missions, his instructions and personal intercourse reveal the zealous proselytizer, the intelligent scholar, the wise ruler, and the courteous gentleman. If he left no abiding work behind him, let us be grateful that we have in his letters at once beacons to warn us from his mistakes, and the picture of a character which has had no late parallel in his Church, though he was excelled by Raimund Lull at an earlier date.

Xavier thus describes his missionary work among the pearl-fishers of Tuticorin:—

"In each village I leave one copy of the *Christian Instruction*. I appoint all to assemble on festival days, and to chaunt the rudiments of the Christian faith, and in each of the villages I appoint a fit person to preside. For their wages, the Viceroy, at my request, has assigned 4000 gold fanams. Multitudes in these parts are only not Christians because none are found to make them Christians." "Here I am, almost alone from the time that Anthony remained sick at Manapar, and I find it a most inconvenient position to be in the midst of a people of an unknown tongue, without the assistance of an interpreter. Roderick, indeed, who is now here, acts as an interpreter in the place of Anthony; but you know well how much they know of Portuguese. Conceive, therefore, what kind of life I live in this place, what kind of sermons I am able to address to the assemblies, when they who should repeat my address to the people do not understand me, nor I them. I ought to be an adept in dumb show. Yet I am not without work, for I want no interpreter to baptize infants just born, or those which their parents bring; nor to relieve the famished and the naked who come in my way. So I devote myself to these two kinds of good works, and do not regard my time as lost."

Propaganda Institutions. — From the first and throughout their career the Jesuits have sought to control education and to use it for the ends of the order. Gregory XV., the first Jesuit pupil who became Pope, founded at Rome on 21st June 1622, and richly endowed, the famous Congregation for the Propagation of the Faith. Consisting of thirteen cardinals, two priests, one monk, and a secretary, this papal missionary society was "designed to propagate and maintain the religion of Rome in all parts and corners of the world." Urban VIII. and many donors since have "prodigiously augmented" its revenues. Urban VIII. added to it, in 1627, the Collegio di Propaganda Fide, founded by a wealthy Spanish noble, who gave his all for the education and training of foreign missionaries. The two form the richest and best equipped missionary institution in the world, which supports extensive undertakings abroad as well as charitable enterprises at home, for the good of all who may have suffered from their zeal in the papal cause. The spirit spread to France, where in 1663 the royal authority was given to the Congregation of Priests for the Foreign Missions, and the bishops themselves founded the Parisian Seminary for the Missions Abroad. These French agencies supply the missions of Siam, Anam, Tongking, and Persia, and have generally been in conflict with the Jesuits. In 1644 the Congregation of the Holy Sacrament was founded in France, to supply the Pope with ecclesiastics for pagan nations. Thus in the seventeenth century "legions of missionaries covered in a manner the whole face of the globe, and converted to the profession of Christianity at least, if not to its temper and spirit, multitudes of persons in the fiercest and most barbarous nations," to use the language of Mosheim. Let us outline their results.

India—Results.—The Roman Catholic population of India is returned by the Census of 1882 as 963,058, or half the whole Christian population of 1,862,634. Yet on the death of Xavier three and one-third centuries before, the number of Romanist converts in the western portion of South India alone was taken at 300,000. The official Census supports the statement of Abbé Dubois, who was in India so late as 1815, that the number of converts had fallen off more than one-third after the middle of the eighteenth century. But if the accuracy of the Xavier estimate be assumed, it is the case that the Romish missions in India have increased only two-thirds since 1552, in 330 years, while a careful census shows the native Protestants alone to have increased from 103,000 in 1852 to 500,000 in thirty years, and to be increasing at the rate of 86 per cent. in the decade. This is quite irrespective of the character of the converts, and of the influence of the Christian communities formed.

The Madura Mission, which does not stand alone in its shame, is perhaps the greatest scandal of the Jesuit order. Fifty years after Xavier, about 1606, **Robert de Nobili**, nephew of Cardinal Bellarmine and grand-nephew or Pope Marcellus II., began in South India that system of conversion based on a lie, which lasted for a century and a half before it ended in the collapse of the mission and the suppression of the order. He, the martyred **Brito**, the learned **Beschi**, and many associates of like ability and culture, deliberately professed to be Brahmans, making solemn oath that they had sprung from Brahma. They lived as "Saniassies" or penitents, clad in orange-coloured dress, and sitting on a tiger-skin; and joining in idol worship alike impious and indecent. The object was to conceal their foreign origin, which they believed to be fatal to missionary success. Pope after Pope, except when of Jesuit training, denounced the lie and forbade the scandal—in vain. Cardinal de Tournon, sent out by Clement XI. to investigate this and a similar abomination in China, exposed and condemned the Malabar rites in 1704—in vain. Benedict XIV. in 1745 succeeded in dissevering the worship of Christ from the worship of devils by a Brief so stringent that disobedience became impossible. In the Karnatic wars between English and French, the deluded converts discovered the fraud and apostatized in thousands. Twenty years after, Fra Bartolomeo, who worked among the small remnant, described their vices and ignorance, especially of their native priests, in language too gross for transcription. In twenty-five years, he asserted, he had not met a single Christian among them. And later on, Abbé Dubois went the length of declaring the conversion of the natives to be impossible. In other parts of India the same policy was pursued. Xavier's nephew Geronimo wrote for the eclectic Emperor Akbar, one of whose wives was a Romish Christian, the *History of Peter*, a work full of legends so suggestive of indecency as to be blasphemous. Clement XIV. suppressed the order altogether, and Pio VII. restored it because of the danger of refusing "to employ the vigorous and experienced rowers, who volunteer their services in order to break the waves of a sea which threatens every moment shipwreck and death."

Goa and the Present Organization of Indo-Romish Missions.—If the Madura Mission has a century and a half's history of impious fraud, what shall we say of the cruelty of the Portuguese mission at Goa, under **Menezes** especially ; what of the Inquisition ? The horrible story of the independent and comparatively orthodox Syrian Church in Malabar, and its persecutions, is fairly told by Hough, the historian of Christianity in India, who was long a chaplain on the spot. The gradual and unsought supremacy of Protestant Britain saved the remnant of that Church, and enforced toleration over the whole empire, or was intolerant only to Protestant missions from ill-grounded political fears. The Portuguese had an archbishop at Goa, and suffragan bishops at Cranganore and St. Thomé. In 1662 their monopoly was first encroached on by the French, whose Société de Missions Étrangères sent a vicar-apostolic or missionary bishop to Siam, and in 1776 to Pondicheri. In 1882 an Irish vicar-apostolic was appointed at Madras. Against such intrusion the Portuguese Government long protested to the Pope. In 1861, after sending out two priests to investigate the matter, Pio Nono decided that, while the Archbishop of Goa shall retain the title and rank of Primate of India, the vicars-apostolic shall exercise jurisdiction as missionary bishops.

Japan, China, and the Philippine Islands.—Xavier's greatest success was in Japan, and that too ended in the ruin of the native Church, which lasted three generations. The disputes of the various orders of missionary priests, the avarice and wiles of the Jesuits, their compromise with the superstition and vice of the Japanese, and finally their political intrigues, revealed by their Dutch rivals, resulted in the persecution which began in 1586 and continued till 1637, when Japan was shut to foreigners. Into China **Matteo Ricci** and two associates found an entrance in 1579. As in Madura, though not to the same extent, Ricci introduced the policy of conniving at and even seeming to countenance heathen practices, that he might commend his order to the emperor and the government. He lived as a Bonze, and was taken into the imperial service at Nanking. He died in 1601, after making many converts and publishing Christian books at Peking. The arrival of their Dominican and Franciscan rivals in 1630 soon led to an exposure of the practices of the Jesuits. The Chinese rites became as notorious as the Malabar rites. But the Fathers were too useful to the emperor in surveying the country and in many industrial arts. In 1692 an edict of toleration was published, declaring Christianity to be good and salutary. Then came Cardinal Tournon, who, in China as in India, issued a decree denouncing the Jesuits, with this result that he perished in a Portuguese prison in Macao. The Bull of Clement XI. in 1715 at last secured apparent obedience. When **Father Ripa** went out in 1710 from the Propaganda, he found that 500 missionaries in all had been sent out since 1580, and that "they could not produce any satisfactory results in consequence of the formidable barrier of the language, which up to my time none had been able to surmount so as to make himself understood by the people at large." After thirteen years he left, and took three Chinese pupils with him, the nucleus of the Chinese College at Naples. In 1870 there were 254 European and 138 Chinese priests, claiming a community of 404,530 Christians.

Colbert, who gave to the reign of Louis XIV. the only true and abiding glory which can be ascribed to it, devised the project of extending French influence by sending to China and other lands missionaries skilled in the mathematical sciences. After his death six Jesuits were sent out to China in 1685. We have an account of their mission from the pen of one of them, Louis le Comte. His English edition in 1699 published what is really a contemporary account of the arts by which the Jesuits came to be hated in and ultimately expelled from China. Le Comte states that in his time there were in the whole country above two hundred churches, in the three dioceses of Peking, Nanking, and Macao, under Goa, and under three vicars-apostolic who were Franciscans or doctors of the Sorbonne. There were several Spanish Dominicans and Augustinians from Manila, and forty Jesuits.

On the death of the tolerant emperor in 1722, a violent persecution arose. In 1810 the Bishop of Macao claimed six bishops, two coadjutors, twenty-three missionaries, eighty native agents, and 215,000 native Christians in all China. Since that time the Romanist methods of proselytizing have led to frequent revolts, and have proved to be a political danger to foreigners. The Spaniards, who have held the Philippine Islands since 1565, now with an area of 65,100 square miles and population of four and a half millions, have treated them ecclesiastically as the Jesuits did **Paraguay**. Monks of the Augustinian, Franciscan, and Dominican orders rule over the people, divided in parishes, and virtually control the whole administration, which is represented by authorities like General Colin Mackenzie, C.B., and even the Austrian officers of the "Novara" Expedition, as a disgrace to Spain. Here, say the latter, the Roman Catholic ritual has become mingled in the most extraordinary manner with ceremonies borrowed from Paganism.

Africa.—From the earliest voyages of her navigators Portugal attempted small mission stations at various points on the coasts of Africa. Since the French conquest of Algeria in 1830, that military settlement has been the base of several missions by French priests. In 1846 Cairo became the starting-point of an exploratory mission which professed to include Nubia from Khartoum, Kordofan, and the whole Soudan. In 1878 almost the first act of the present Pope Leo XIII. was to issue a rescript to the Algerian missionaries, directing them to evangelize the whole breadth of Central Africa from Zanzibar to the Congo mouths, which the King of the Belgian International Association is exploring for future settlers. Lake Nyassa, Lake Tanganyika, Kabebe, and the North Congo were fixed on as missionary centres. At Mtesa's court, on the Victoria Nyanza, the Algerian missionaries have simply checked the progress made by the Church Missionary Society. The Jesuits have made similar attempts on the Upper Zambesi, in all cases at a terrible expense of life and money. Thus far Romanist missions have failed in Africa, in spite of heroism though ill directed, and zeal though without knowledge.

Results.—The whole Romish Propaganda is said to have raised £244,200 from all parts of the world in 1878, and £11,500 from Great Britain in 1882–83; Protestant missions raised £2,275,000 in 1882–83.

The following list[1] states roughly the principal Romanist and Greek missionary agencies outside of Christendom at the present time :—

1. The Augustinians.—Labouring in the Eastern Churches and Australia.
2. Anglican Benedictines.—Labouring in the English Colonies and Oceania.
3. The Capuchins.—Head-centre at Rome. Missions in Brazil, Chili, Levant, Mesopotamia, Tunis, and the Seychelles.
4. The Carmelites.—Many bishops in India, vicar-apostolic in Baghdad.
5. Dominicans.—Missions in Canada, Constantinople, Chili, Brazil, Peru, Tongking, and the United States.
6. Eudists.—Missions in many of the Antilles.
7. Franciscans.—Centre in Rome. Missions in various countries.
8. Jesuits.—Head-centre, Florence. Missions in Algeria, Australia, Bombay, Calcutta, Guatemala, Guiana, Java, La Plata, Madagascar, Syria, United States ; more than 700 missionaries.
9. Maristes.—Missions in New Zealand, New Caledonia, Oceania, Sydney.
10. Missions Étrangères, or Lazarists.—Missions in China, Cochin China, America (North and South), India, Japan, and Tongking.
11. Missions Africaines.—Head-centre, Lyons. Missions in Dahomey.
12. Missions Étrangères de Bruxelles.—Missions in Mongolia.
13. Missions Étrangères de Dublin.—Missions in various countries.
14. Missions Étrangères de Genes.—In Brazil, Constantinople, Jerusalem, and the United States.
15. Missions Étrangères de Milan.—Missions in India and Oceania.
16. Oblates of the Immaculate Conception.—In Natal and Polar North America.
17. Oratories of England.—Missions in Ceylon.
18. Passionists.—Bulgaria, Wallachia, North America.
19. Patriarchate of Jerusalem.—Establishments of Palestine and Delegation of Lebanon.
20. Priests of the Sacred Heart of Jesus, Mary or Pietas.
21. Salvatoristes.—Missions in America and Bengal.
22. Saint Esprit, St. Cœur de Marie.—Negroes in Africa, America, and Asia.
23. Propaganda.—Head-centre, Lyons. In all the world.
24. Propaganda de Foi.—Income, 500,000 francs from weekly sou collections.
25. Spanish Benedictines.—In Archipelago of the Pacific.
26. Grand Society of the Russian Church.—Missions in China, Japan, and Central Asia.

---

[1] *The Missionary Review*, Princeton, United States of America.

PART III.

ENGLISH-SPEAKING UNIVERSAL EVANGELIZATION, 1784-1884.

CHAPTER XIV.

FOUNDATION OF ENGLISH MISSIONS—WILLIAM CAREY THE FIRST ENGLISH MISSIONARY, 1761-1834.

Prayer the Origin of Modern Missions—William Carey the first Englishman who was a Foreign Missionary—Foundation of the Baptist Society—Carey's Six Years of Preparation in Dinajpore—Abraham and Carey——Carey, Marshman, and Ward in Serampore—Financial—Spiritual—Results of the Serampore Mission—Death of William Carey—Progress of the Baptist Missionary Societies.

Prayer, Hearty and Persevering, the Origin of Modern Missions.—Evangelical religion seemed to be dead in all the churches in the second half of last century. The Reformation had spent its power, for the time, in Germany and Holland, where it was checked by rationalism; in France, where it had been extinguished by the blood or the expulsion of the Huguenots; in England, where it was smitten by the blight of Arianism or Socinianism in the Established Church, and by that of Antinomianism and false Calvinism among the Dissenters; and in Scotland, where the Union and the Revolution Settlement of Queen Anne had handed the Church over to the Moderates for a century or more. The faith preached by Luther and the free grace set forth by Calvin survived only in the then small pietistic communities outside the churches, in Moravians and Methodists, in Puritans and Baptists. The honour of making England the missionary, or in some sense the Fifth Empire of history, that of the Little Stone of Daniel, was given to the last.

In 1784, at a periodical meeting of the Northamptonshire Association of Baptist Ministers, **John Sutcliff**, minister of Olney,—Cowper's, Newton's, Thomas Scott's Olney,—made a motion "to the ministers and messengers of the Associate Baptist Churches assembled at Nottingham respecting meetings for prayer, to bewail the low estate of religion, and earnestly implore a revival of our churches and of the general cause of our Redeemer, and for that end to wrestle with God for the effusion of His Holy Spirit, which alone can produce the blessed effect." It was unanimously agreed to solemnly exhort all their churches to engage "heartily and perseveringly" in prayer to God on the first Monday of every calendar month, and at the same hour. **John Ryland**, jun., of Northampton, drew up the plan which, with the italics, thus concluded :—

> "The grand object in prayer is to be, that the Holy Spirit may be poured down on our ministers and churches, that sinners may be converted, the saints edified, and the name of God glorified. At the same time remember, we trust you will not confine your requests to your own societies, or to our own immediate connection ; let the whole interest of the Redeemer be affectionately remembered, and *the spread of the gospel to the most distant parts of the habitable globe, be the object of your most fervent requests.* We shall rejoice if *any other Christian societies* of our own or other denominations will unite with us, and we do now invite them to join most cordially heart and hand in the attempt. Who can tell what the consequences of such a united effort in prayer may be ! Let us plead with God the many gracious promises of His word, which relate to the future success of His gospel. He has said, ' I will yet for this be enquired of by the house of Israel, to do it for them ; I will increase them with men like a flock ' (Ezek. xxxvi. 37). Surely we have love enough to learn to set apart *one hour* at a time, twelve times in a year, to seek her welfare."

On this occasion **Andrew Fuller** preached his first printed sermon on *Walking by Faith,* and soon after Sutcliff republished the work of Jonathan Edwards, *Humble Attempt to promote Explicit Agreement and Visible Union of God's People in Extraordinary Prayer for the Revival of Religion.* Two years after that meeting at Nottingham, a Church of England clerical society, in London, began to discuss, "How might the gospel be carried to the heathen?" Three years before the Nottingham meeting, a journeyman shoemaker, joined with eight others to form what is now the Baptist Church in the hamlet of Hackleton, took to himself a wife, and there preached his first sermon. A year before, he had been baptized by Ryland in the Nen, and in 1787 he was ordained by Andrew Fuller to the ministry at Moulton village. From the hour of his conversion and his reading Cook's *Voyages*

Round the World, he was ever pondering the state of the heathen, and longing to go as a missionary to Otaheite. That shoemaker was **William Carey**. His meditation and self-dedication, running parallel with the people's praying and Fuller's preaching and writing on *The Gospel worthy of all Acceptation*, resulted in Modern Missions. In 1792 the Baptist Missionary Society was formed at Kettering, of which Carey became the first missionary and Fuller the first secretary; Sutcliff, Ryland, and Reynold Hogg (treasurer), formed with these two the first committee. **Samuel Pearce** of Birmingham was one of the first twelve subscribers of £13, 2s. 6d. at Kettering in 1792; he too had been pondering the subject like Carey, and he desired to dedicate himself to the work of the mission, but a premature death removed his seraphic spirit from earth. But even Andrew Fuller, in 1787, replied to Carey's urgency for immediate action:—"If the Lord should make windows in heaven, then might this thing be." The fact, published by his contemporaries in 1793, and verified by all the history since, is thus expressed by Dr. Ryland, another unbeliever in immediate duty like Fuller:—"I believe God Himself infused into the mind of Carey that solicitude for the salvation of the heathen which cannot be fairly traced to any other source."

William Carey, the First Englishman who was a Foreign Missionary (1761-1834), was born on 17th August, in the long Northamptonshire village of Paulerspury—Pery of the Paveleys; was apprenticed to a shoemaker at Hackleton when fourteen years of age; was converted to Christ, and became a Dissenter at eighteen; was ordained Baptist minister at Moulton when twenty-six; was called to the Harvey Lane Church at Leicester, in which he was afterwards succeeded by the great Robert Hall, and went out to Bengal as a missionary in 1793, where, at Serampore, he died at the age of seventy-three, honoured all over India, Great Britain, and America, but the humblest of the servants of the Lord Jesus Christ. He was called from his youth, by the Spirit of God, to supply the actively spiritual side to that revolution in thought and morals, in politics and society, which, introduced by the French terror and Napoleonic despotism, has made the contrast between the English-speaking world of to-day and that of the last century. His grandfather was the village schoolmaster, and, after working as a weaver for a time, his father succeeded to the office both of schoolmaster and parish clerk, with its small official cottage and garden. He was a man of high character, who survived till 1816. William Carey, eldest child, with three sisters and one brother, was studious, and was especially observant of insects and birds, of plants and animals. He was a favourite of his childless uncle, a gardener; and this fact, with the scope which the schoolmaster's garden gave him, made him the botanist and agricultural improver which he became in Bengal. He was tenderly watched by his grandmother, a woman of force of character, and he knew his Bible well if only from his responses in the parish church. He afterwards bewailed that he was addicted to lying, swearing, filthy talk, dishonesty, and bell-ringing, like John Bunyan in the neighbouring county not very long before, but his contemporaries tell us nothing of this. Under the difficulties of his lot he mastered Latin, Greek, French, Dutch, and Hebrew, with a plodding perseverance which, in the days of his renown, was all he would allow that he possessed beyond others. He was fond of arguing as a proud Churchman, till the influence of a godly fellow-journeyman, and the preaching of Chater of Olney in 1799, led him to prefer the reproach of the evangelical Dissenters. A little book by the father of Robert Hall, and the preaching of Scott the commentator, so enlarged his views to the breadth of evangelical theology, that Andrew Fuller was attracted to him by one of his occasional sermons. From 1781, privately and in meetings with his brethren, he did not cease to press for an immediate attempt to send the gospel to the heathen. When meditating his village sermons, when teaching geography to the school by which he attempted to eke out a living, and when cobbling the old or making the new shoes to which dire necessity drove him, like the tentmaker Paul, he was consumed with the one thought. *That* was the object of all his reading, which was wide for the time. Scott, who first knew him when visiting his master, and used to pass his shop at Hackleton in his frequent journeys from Olney to Northampton, spoke of the humble shed—still standing—as Carey's College. Fuller found him on his stall at Moulton with a map of the world pasted up, and on it the statistics, religious and political, of every country so far as then known. In 1792 Carey published his "*Enquiry into the Obligations of Christians to use Means for the Conversion of the Heathens;* in which the Religious State of the Different Nations of the World, the Success of Former Undertakings, and the Practicability of Further Undertakings, are considered." But one copy of the original work, or its reprint in

1826, exists so far as we know. It is a marvellous compendium of accurate information, wide generalization, and impassioned appeal. It marks a distinct point of departure in the history of Christianity. In the same year, on 30th May, he preached at Nottingham, where the prayer-covenant had been agreed on, a sermon which was so pathetic and irresistible in its home-thrusts, that the formerly unbelieving Dr. Ryland confessed—"If all the people had lifted up their voices and wept, as the children of Israel did at Bochim, I should not have wondered at the effect; it would only have seemed proportionate to the cause, so clearly did he prove the criminality of our supineness in the cause of God." Yet the ministerial meeting was about to separate, although nine years had passed since the prayer began, when Carey, taking Fuller by the arm, said beseechingly, "And are you, after all, going again to do nothing?" It was resolved to do what was accomplished at the next meeting on 2nd October at Kettering. Carey had preached his two since famous mottoes, "Expect great things from God: attempt great things for God," from the verses in Isa. liv. 2, 3, which follow the picture of the Face and Form marred more than any man, Who was to sprinkle many nations; of Him whose soul was made an offering for sin, that He might see His seed and might prolong His days, and that the pleasure of the Lord might prosper in His hands. The two verses in which was that day laid the foundation of Modern Missions, thus run: "Enlarge the place of thy tent, and let them stretch forth the curtains of thine habitations: spare not, lengthen thy cords and strengthen thy stakes; for thou shalt break forth on the right hand and on the left; and thy seed shall inherit the Gentiles, and make the desolate cities to be inhabited."

Foundation of the Baptist Society.—Retiring to "the little parlour" of the widow Beeby Wallis, in a white house still visible from the Midland Railway, twelve ministers contributed £13, 2s. 6d., and passed these resolutions:—

"Desirous of making an effort for the propagation of the gospel among the heathen, agreeably to what is recommended in Brother Carey's late publication on that subject, we whose names appear to the subsequent subscription, do solemnly agree to act in society for that purpose.

"As in the present divided state of Christendom it seems that each denomination, by exerting itself separately, is most likely to accomplish the great ends of a mission, it is agreed that this society be called 'The Particular [Calvinistic] Baptist Society for Propagating the Gospel among the Heathen.'

"As such an undertaking must needs be attended with expense, we agree immediately to open a subscription for the above purpose, and to recommend it to others.

"Every person who shall subscribe ten pounds at once, or ten shillings and sixpence annually, shall be considered a member of the society."

Here are all the marks of the old missionary covenant, after eight years of "hearty and persevering" prayer, obedience and faith, such that even their fellows ridiculed such "great things" as £13, 2s. 6d. and twelve obscure Northamptonshire ministers attempting "the propagation of the gospel among the heathen." The solemn agreement to act was as catholic in the recognition of the duty of others as it was shrewd in the organizing of their own. Nor should we omit to observe that it was Calvinism—the doctrines of grace of Paul and Augustine, of Columba and Wiclif—acting against the false or anti-Calvinism which had emasculated the churches, that led the van in the great missionary crusade to which Christendom was summoned by a higher reading of the cry which Peter the Hermit adopted as his watchword: "God wills it." The very next year saw William Carey not at Otaheite but in Bengal, with Thomas, surgeon of an East Indiaman, who had happily led the new society to the one field for which God had specially prepared Carey. The two landed at Calcutta on the 10th November 1793, from a Danish ship, in spite of the opposition of the East India Company. Contrary to all human expectation, and even the Company's repeated desire, India had become virtually a British empire under Lord Cornwallis at that time. Even so, it was to become the dominion of Christ, although for other twenty years the Company reserved the power, and more than once used it, to persecute Christianity alone, while encouraging Hindooism and Mohammedanism for political ends, a policy which exploded in the Mutiny of 1857 and in its own destruction.

Carey's Six Years of Preparation in Dinajpore.—The Moravian brotherhood of self-support and community of goods, was the only missionary system practically known to Carey when he planned the conversion of the whole world. Once landed in India and started in a station, he told his society that he would require no more money from them, but that they should send missionaries to other lands, which they unsuccessfully did to West Africa. But before he could reach the position of self-support in a country hostile to English labour like tropical India, he and his family literally starved. At Bandel, on the Hoogli, at Calcutta itself, and amid the tiger swamps of the Soondarban tracts to the east of Calcutta, he made three attempts to preach and toil with his hands at the same time. After seven months of hardships unknown to any other missionary in India before or since, he became an indigo manufacturer at Mudnabatty, in the county of Dinajpore, to the south of Bhootan and Tibet, which he twice visited. There for five years he perfected his knowledge of Bengalee, wrote a grammar of that vernacular, translated the New Testament into it, learned Sanskrit, mastered the botany of the region, corresponded with Schwartz and Guericke in the far south, set up a printing-press, and planned new missions, all at his own cost. Of a few converts, Bengalee and European officials, he formed a church. His appeals for more missionaries, answered at first by sending out only Mr. Fountain whose democratic opinions and imprudence caused trouble, and his success lighted up what he described in 1799 as "the hitherto inextinguishable flame in England and all the Western World." Four colleagues arrived, of whom **Marshman** and **Ward** became only less famous than himself, and he found them under the protection of the Danish Government represented by Governor Bie, the friend of Schwartz, at the pretty little settlement of Serampore, on the right bank of the Hoogli, fourteen miles above Calcutta. Thence the gospel sounded forth over Northern India and all Southern Asia, during the time of transition until Duff, the apostolic successor of Carey, began the full era of the destruction of Brahmanism and the Christianization of Asia, from the metropolis of Calcutta itself.

Abraham and Carey.—Unconsciously Carey served himself heir to Abraham, with whom God had made the universal missionary covenant. In the sadness and bewilderment and trial of faith which marked his first years in India, the founder of Modern Missions turned ever to the words with which Isaiah (li. 2-6) was sent to comfort the captive Jews: "Look unto Abraham your father, . . . for I called him alone and blessed him and increased him." "It has been a great consolation to me," wrote Carey, "that Abraham was alone when God called him." At a later time, fourteen years after his arrival in Bengal, he wrote with more assured faith: "We have no security but in God. I feel a confidence, however, in Him, especially as it respects the concerns of His Church. The example of His increasing Abraham, who was alone when God called him, and this being held up to encourage the hope that He will comfort, repair, beautify, and fill His *Church* with gladness, is a support to me." Had not Paul, in his letter to the Romans, and the writer of that to the Hebrews, declared the first missionary to be the father of many nations, because he looked for the City which hath the foundations?

Carey, Marshman, and Ward in Serampore—Financial.—Carey joined his new colleagues at Serampore on the 7th January 1800. The three missionaries purchased and enlarged a house and grounds, to be at once church, home, and press; opened boarding-schools for boys and girls of the mixed class called Eurasians, to yield an income for the mission, and Carey himself was appointed by Lord Wellesley, the Governor-General, first Bengalee and then Sanskrit and Marathee professor in the College of Fort William, wisely established for the training of the young English civilians who were to be the rulers of the people. The three families formed a brotherhood, who lived at the same table, at a total cost of little more than £100 a year. When Ward died, **Mr. John Marshman**, afterwards C.S.I., the son, joined the missionary partnership, and **Mack**, a young Scotsman from Edinburgh University, was afterwards united with them as a "beloved associate." From the first Scotland was the most liberal and sympathetic supporter of what came to be known as the Serampore Mission. This brotherhood contributed, from first to last, in the half-century ending 1854, when Mr. John Marshman returned from India, close upon £90,000 to the mission in various forms. It held all property, created by itself, in trust on behalf of the Society at home. Till the death of Andrew Fuller, the secretary, in 1815, the arrangement worked well. The Baptist Society was enabled to devote all the resources, which the success of Serampore chiefly enabled it to raise, to other missions. But when Carey was left sole survivor of the five who had founded the Society, their successors would not work an arrangement, which is the purest, the loftiest, the most Christlike since the days of the early Christians. The Serampore missionaries separated from the Society in its second generation, and, aided by the Christians of England, Scotland, America, and India, who appreciated their self-denying toil, extended their work in these three directions: of Bible translation, new evangelizing stations, and the creation of a magnificent college to train missionaries on the spot and educate Brahmans and Mohammedans in a Christian spirit. The financial burden, increased by the failure of the great Calcutta firms just before Carey's death, proved too much for them. But Mr. John Marshman nobly redeemed all the pledges of the brotherhood. He made over to the Society the property which the missionaries had created with the countenance and help of the King of Denmark, and then bought it back,—thus paying for it twice. He till 1854, and his two successors till 1875, made it the centre of all those civilising and Christianizing influences which were identified with the weekly newspaper known as *The Friend of India.* "Three things seem to be necessary to perpetuate in this station the great facilities already acquired to the evangelizing of India,—talents and energy, union, and an unwavering attachment to the plan of devoting the whole proceeds of the united labours of the family to the cause of God." That, written in 1816, is the keynote of the administrative side of the Serampore Mission.

Carey, Marshman, and Ward in Serampore—Spiritual.— The spiritual covenant into which these missionary heroes and their families entered, and to which they adhered till death, is not less remarkable even in the history of Christian missions. On Monday, October 7, 1805, they drew up and signed a "Form of Agreement respecting the Great Principles upon which the Brethren of the Mission at Serampore think it their duty to act in the Work of Instructing the Heathen." This agreement was read publicly at every station, at the three annual meetings on the first Lord's day in January, in May, and in October. The unique document, which covers twelve printed octavo pages, expounds in lofty and catholic language these points, upon which "we think it right to fix our serious and abiding attention :"—

"(1) It is absolutely necessary that we set an infinite value upon immortal souls; (2) That we gain all information of the snares and delusions in which these heathen are held; (3) That we abstain from those things which would increase their prejudices against the gospel; (4) That we watch all opportunities of doing good; (5) That we keep to the example of Paul, and make the great subject of our preaching, Christ the Crucified; (6) That the natives should have an entire confidence in us and feel quite at home in our company; (7) That we build up and watch over the souls that may be gathered; (8) That we form our native brethren to usefulness, fostering every kind of genius and cherishing every gift and grace in them, especially advising the native churches to choose their pastors and deacons from amongst their own countrymen; (9) That we labour with all our might in forwarding translations of the sacred Scriptures in the languages of India, and that we establish native free schools and recommend these establishments to other Europeans; (10) That we be constant in prayer and the cultivation of personal religion, to fit us for the discharge of these laborious and unutterably important labours; let us often look at Brainerd, in the woods of America, pouring out his very soul before God for the perishing heathen without whose salvation nothing could make him happy; (11) That we give ourselves up unreservedly to this glorious cause. Let us never think that our time, our gifts, our strength, our families, or even the clothes we wear, are our own. Let us sanctify them all to God and His cause. Oh that He may sanctify us for His work! No private family ever enjoyed a greater portion of happiness than we have done since we resolved to have all things in common. If we are enabled to persevere, we may hope that multitudes of converted souls will have reason to bless God to all eternity for sending His gospel into this country."

That agreement embodies the divine principles of all Protestant scriptural missions. It is still a manual to be daily pondered by every missionary, and every Church and Society which may send one forth.

Results of the Serampore Mission.—In the first third of the nineteenth century, during which this mission was the model and stimulus of almost all others, we have these direct spiritual and indirect or civilised results:—The first complete or partial translations of the Bible, printed in forty languages and dialects of India, China, Central Asia, and neighbouring lands, at a cost of £80,143; the first prose work and vernacular newspaper in Bengalee, the language of seventy millions of human beings; the first printing-press on an organized scale, paper-mill, and steam-engine seen in India; the first Christian primary school in North India; the first efforts to educate native girls and women; the first college to train native ministers and Christianize educated Hindoos; the first Hindoo Protestant convert, Krishna Chundra Pal, baptized in 1800; the first medical mission of which that convert was to some extent the fruit; the establishment and maintenance of at least thirty separate large mission stations, besides Judson's great work in Burma, which resulted in the foundation of the American Baptist Missionary Society; the first Botanic Garden, and Society for the Improvement of Native and European Agriculture and Horticulture in India; the first Public Library in India; the first translations into English of the great Sanskrit epics, the *Ramayan* and *Mahabharat*, and the first translation of the Bible into Sanskrit, both as means of bringing the learned classes of India and the gospel into sympathetic accord. The indirect results of the work of Carey and his beloved associates, can best be expressed as the *Præparatio Evangelica*, which, fifty years only after Carey's death, has increased the Protestant native Church of India to a community of half a million of souls, who have more ordained pastors of their own than foreign missionaries, and who increase at the rate of eighty-six per cent. every decade.

Carey died seventy-three years old, and after forty-one of these spent in Bengal without a break, at sunrise on the 9th June 1834. The graveyard where the immortal three of Serampore rest from their labours is not the old Danish cemetery, but a spot selected by themselves for the native Christians, near the present railway station. In the whole history of Christian missions we know no chapter so grand as this of Serampore, whether we look at the *personnel*, or the relation of the mission to what went before and to what has sprung from the labours of the first English missionary.

Progress of the Baptist Missionary Society.—Beyond occasional grants to the Serampore Brotherhood, the Baptist Missionary Society opened and supported new missions. Its annual income, which was only £3421 by 1810, is now upwards of £70,000, including the Zanana and Bible Translation work. This Society has of late greatly extended its work in West Africa, where it has undertaken the Congo Mission.

The General Baptist Missionary Society, founded at Derby in 1816 by the **Rev. J. G. Pike,** author of *Persuasives to Early Piety,* has an income of £9000. Its missions are chiefly in Orissa and Ganjam, India, where it has created a Christian community of 3000, and has done much to lead to the mitigation of the cruelties and obscenity of the Krishna-worship of Jugganath. Its first missionaries, **W. Bampton** and **James Peggs,** took up the work of Carey in Orissa.

CHAPTER XV.

THE GREAT MISSIONARY AND BIBLE SOCIETIES, 1792.

England and Scotland.

The London Missionary Society—The Scottish and Glasgow Missionary Society—Robert Haldane's Proposed India Mission—The Church Missionary Society—Bible and Pure Literature Societies—Christian Missions to the Jews by Societies—The Wesleyan Methodist Missionary Society—The Society for the Propagation of the Gospel in Foreign Parts—The Society of Friends—Medical Missions—Women's Missions.

The United States of America.

The Board of Commissioners for Foreign Missions—The Baptist Missionary Union—The Methodist Episcopal Society—The American Bible and Tract Societies.

The Continent of Europe.

The Netherlands Missionary Society—The German Protestant Societies—The Paris Society for Evangelical Missions—The Norwegian, Swedish, and Swiss Societies.

England and Scotland.

The London Missionary Society, founded in 1795, was the immediate result of the Bengal Mission of William Carey. When Dr. Ryland, of the Baptist College, Bristol, received the first letters from Carey and Thomas, he invited two friends who happened to be on a visit to that city to come and hear the intelligence. These were the **Rev. Dr. David Bogue**, Presbyterian minister of Gosport, and Mr. Stephen. After reading the letters, the three knelt down and prayed for a blessing on the Baptist Mission. Dr. Bogue and Mr. Stephen then called on Mr. Hay, a man of wealth, and received a promise of his support if they organized a Missionary Society for non-Baptists. Dr. Bogue then sent to the *Evangelical Magazine* the "Address to Professors of the Gospel," which appeared in September 1794, calling upon all to subscribe "annually" to maintain "at least twenty or thirty missionaries among the heathen," and to pray, converse, and consult with one another. In England and in Scotland the effect on spiritual men was instantaneous. On 4th November the first formal meeting of evangelical ministers of all sects was held; in January 1795 they issued an address and letter to many, which resulted in the foundation of the Society at the "Castle and Falcon," Aldersgate Street, London, on 21st September 1795. The "evangelical ministers and lay brethren of all denominations" elected twenty-five directors. The "difficulties" which "occurred in the election of a secretary, on account of the great diversity of abilities requisite to the advantageous fulfilment of the complex and various duties," were most happily solved, by the choice of the **Rev. Dr. John Love**, and Mr. William Shrubsole, "to each of whom distinct departments were assigned." Joseph Hardcastle, Esq., was the first treasurer. Dr. Love was then Presbyterian minister of Hoxton. Born at Paisley in 1756, he died minister of Anderston Church, Glasgow, in 1825. Sorrowful at "the awful withdrawing of that majestic energy of the gospel at home, which would give life and impulse to the attempt of darting beams of saving light into the darkest habitations of cruelty throughout this evil world," he threw himself at once into the missionary enterprise. He sought the concurrence of Scotland especially, because he looked to it for missionaries of "more regular education" and "more solid and durable piety" than had yet been found in England, which nevertheless had just sent forth the greatest missionary since Paul.

Catholic in its constitution from first to last, and largely assisted at the outset by Presbyterians and Episcopalians in the true spirit of evangelical unity, "The Missionary Society," as it was at first called, has come to be identified with the Independents or Congregationalists, as other churches have learned to take their place in the missionary host. As Carey had been influenced by the narrative of Captain Cook's *Voyages* to desire the South Sea Islands for the scene of his mission, while God prepared him for the more important work in Southern Asia, the directors were led by the same narrative to the great Pacific Ocean. The first volunteer missionary who offered himself was **Captain James Wilson**, officially described as "a worthy gentleman who had retired to affluence and ease from the East India service." So many as thirty men, of whom six were married, with their children, formed the first missionary party; four of these were ordained, and one was a surgeon, the others were artisans. On 10th August 1796, they sailed down the Thames in the ship *Duff*, with a crew of twenty two, to join the East India convoy at Spithead, singing as they went the hymn, "Jesus, at Thy command we launch into the deep," while their friends waved adieux from the banks, and some of the directors prayed and preached. So began the second missionary expedition sent out by English Nonconformists, like the first. Its annual income, which had risen to only £5298 in 1810, is now £128,000. It has seen the islands of all but the Western Pacific turned to Christ, and its missions have spread out from Polynesia to India, China, Africa, Madagascar, and the West Indies. The one medical and four ordained missionaries of 1795 have increased to upwards of 150 now, with some 400 ordained natives, 4500 native preachers, 90,000 communicants, native adherents to the number of the third of a million, and 110,000 boys and girls at school, all contributing £13,000 locally for spiritual and educational purposes.

The Scottish Missionary Society, at first under the name of the Edinburgh Missionary Society, was the next to spring into action, in February 1796. The **Rev. Greville Ewing**, at that time assistant to Dr. Jones of Lady Glenorchy's Chapel, Edinburgh, was secretary. His address to the Christian public, dated 18th March 1796, is the most eloquent appeal which had appeared up to that time. The Society counted ministers and members of the Established and Secession Churches, **Dr. Erskine** representing the former, and Mr. Peddie the latter. The other directors for the first year were the Rev. Sir Henry Moncreiff, Dr. Johnston, Dr. Hunter, Mr. Hall, Mr. Black, Mr. Colquhoun (Leith), Mr. Struthers, and Mr. Banks; Messrs. Alexander Bonar, James Bonar, C. Mowbray, **James Haldane**, John Pitcairn, W. Pateson, J. Scott, **John Campbell**, and W. Ellis. Mr. John Tawse, W.S., was treasurer, and Mr. William Dymock clerk. The influence of the London Missionary Society, guided by **Zachary Macaulay**, the West India overseer of slaves, whom Christ had drawn to become their friend, and governor of the Sierra Leone Company's settlement at Freetown, led the Society to send their first missionaries to the Susoos, 120 miles in the interior. **Peter Greig** and Henry Brunton were the two first Scottish missionaries. The former was the first missionary martyr of modern times. Like Robert Moffat in later times, Peter Greig was a godly gardener of Donibristle, Inverkeithing, who worshipped in the Secession Church of the Rev. Ebenezer Brown there. Moved by love for the perishing heathen, but modest with the humility of Carey, whom in some respects he resembled, he used to ask Mr. Brown to accompany him to the church, after the toil of the day, that there, as Dr. John Brown puts it, "amid the darkness and solitude he might speak more freely the thoughts of his heart." Peter Greig was murdered and robbed by native traders of Foulah, to whom he had shown kindness, after he had been only a year in the country. Mr. Brunton returned soon after, and sailed with Mr. A. Paterson on a mission to the Mohammedan Tartars of Russia at Karass, between the Black and Caspian Seas. There he translated the New Testament into their language. Russian intolerance led ultimately to the extinction of this and the subsequent London Society's mission under **Mr. Swan**, but it has been revived by **Mr. Gilmour** among the Mongols from Peking. The Scottish Missionary Society's energies were transferred to India, where, in August 1822, a mission was begun by the **Rev. Donald Mitchell**, a "son of the manse," who had been converted to Christ when a lieutenant in the Company's army at Surat. This mission became remarkable for the labours of the Rev. James Mitchell, the **Rev. Robert Nesbit**, and **John Wilson, D.D.**, who in 1835 transferred their services to the Church of Scotland, by which they and their colleagues had been ordained. This Society became finally absorbed in the missionary work of the churches in 1847, when it transferred its second Jamaica mission, established in 1824 by the Rev. George Blyth and Hope M. Waddell, chiefly to the United Presbyterian Church. This Jamaica Mission had been undertaken with the help of such proprietors as A. Stirling, Esq. of Keir, and W. Stothert, Esq. of Cargen, for the instruction of the slaves. The Jamaica congregations are now almost self-supporting.

The Glasgow Missionary Society was established at the same time as that of Edinburgh, and on the same catholic basis. Of twenty-two ministers who organized it, some of the names are perpetuated in the mission stations, as Dr. Burns of the Barony Parish, A. Pirrie of the "New Light Burgher Connection," and Dr. Kidston of the same body, Dr. Macfarlan of Greenock, and Dr. Love, who in 1800 became minister of Anderston, Glasgow, where one of his successors has been **Dr. A. N. Somerville**, who has travelled much as an evangelist all over the world. Its two first young missionaries, a weaver and a tailor, accompanied Greig and Brunton to Sierra Leone. They were unworthy of their office, and their two immediate successors soon yielded to the climate. But in February 1821 this Society began in Kafraria, the mission which has since prospered greatly under the Free and United Presbyterian Churches of Scotland, and is again being united into the Presbyterian Church of South Africa. The Rev. W. R. Thomson and Mr. J. Bennie were the first missionaries. In 1823 the **Rev. John Ross** began his Kafir apostolate, which ceased only with his death in 1878, and is continued by his sons Richard and Bryce Ross. The "Voluntary" controversy so divided the Society in 1837, that the mission separated into two presbyteries, one of which in 1844 came under the Free, and one in 1847 under the United Presbyterian Church.

Robert Haldane, proprietor of the beautiful estate of Airthrey, on the Stirling slope of the Ochils, had not long found Christ for himself, when his friend the **Rev. Dr. Innes** of Stirling sent him the first number of the *Periodical Accounts* of the Baptist Mission. At once he resolved to sacrifice himself and his all to found a mission, and he selected Benares as the spot, being the very centre of Brahmanical idolatry. One of the first and largest subscribers to the London Missionary Society, he naturally turned to Dr. Bogue and Dr. Innes to help him. These men, one in the vigour of forty-seven, and the other not thirty, with Greville Ewing, the brother-in-law of Innes, and also a young Presbyterian minister, and Mr. Ritchie, a printer and devoted home missionary, were all engaged by Mr. Haldane. After providing for their salaries, he resolved to give £35,000 more, from the sale of Airthrey to Lord Abercromby, to endow the mission in the case of his own death. A more heroic sacrifice had not been made since the days of Barnabas of Cyprus. But Haldane's own friends Pitt and Dundas, the dictator of Scotland and of the East India Company, refused the Scottish gentlemen and ministers permission to land in India. Mr. Dundas offered the living of St. Cuthbert's, Edinburgh, to Dr. Bogue, which on his refusal fell to Sir Henry Moncreiff. As to the Company's directors, one of them said he would rather see a band of devils in India than a band of missionaries. What India lost at that time—and who shall estimate the loss?—Scotland gained in the home mission work of Robert and James Haldane. It had been proposed that Mr. John Campbell, afterwards of the London Mission, should be a catechist of Haldane's mission, but he was opposed by the Rev. John Newton, while fifteen members of the evangelical Eclectic Society discouraged the whole mission. This want of faith and duty was about to be nobly atoned for.

The Church Missionary Society.

The Church Missionary Society was founded in 1799, under the name of the Society for Missions to Africa and the East. Evangelical in its origin, it has ever expressed all that is noblest and most catholic in the Church of England, the Propagation Society representing rather the sacramentarian side. In 1783 the Eclectic Society had been instituted by ministers like Newton and Cecil, for the discussion of religious questions by evangelical members of the Church of England, and also by a few Dissenters. Charles Grant, Wilberforce, and Simeon had done more than any other men for missions up to the time of Carey and Fuller, and it was Carey's experience that sent **Henry Martyn** out to India. But, as Charles Grant afterwards said, "Many years ago I had formed the design of a mission to Bengal, and used my humble endeavours to promote the design. Providence reserved that honour for the Baptists." If later in the field, the Church Missionary Society has become the greatest of all by God's blessing. It sprang from the discussions of the Eclectic Society on the 12th April 1799, when sixteen clergymen met at the "Castle and Falcon." Admiral Gambier, the first president, was in 1835 succeeded by the Earl of Chichester, who still lives. The most remarkable of the founders were the successive secretaries, **Thomas Scott**, the commentator; **Josiah Pratt**, father of the learned Archdeacon of Calcutta; and **Henry Venn**. For fifteen years the crown bishops restrained their sanction, and have generally been rather hurtful than helpful to the cause, even in recent days. Till 1815 none but German Lutherans could be secured as missionaries. The revenue has steadily risen from £911 to £2467 in 1810, and, chiefly by local associations, to upwards of £220,000 a year now. This Society's missions, which began in West Africa in 1804, in Madras in 1814, and in Calcutta in 1820, now extend "all round the world" and prosper. In Africa they occupy Sierra Leone, Yoruba, the Niger, the Victoria Nyanza country, the coast east of it, and Cairo. In Asia they work in Palestine and Persia, all over India, Ceylon, Mauritius, China, and Japan. They have done much to Christianize the Maories of New Zealand. They light up North-West America and the North Pacific. The number of European missionaries and teachers is upwards of 220, of ordained natives more than 200. The native Christian adherents exceed 130,000, of whom one-fourth are communicants. Some 60,000 pupils attend the Society's mission schools. The Society is now in its eighty-sixth year.

Bible and Pure Literature Societies.—The **Religious Tract Society** also was instituted in 1799, for the circulation of religious books and treatises throughout the British dominions and in foreign countries. It spreads the gospel in 166 languages. Its purely missionary income in 1882–83 was £26,227; the expenditure amounted to £51,801, the excess being supplied from the trade funds, which also bear the cost of management. The Society's help to missions consists in its grants of money, paper, electrotypes, and publications to missionaries, and in its circulation of a pure and Biblical literature. **The British and Foreign Bible Society,** founded in 1804, is even more closely allied with foreign missions. We have seen what, unaided, Carey and his colleagues did for Bible translation and circulation in India. It was the need for the Holy Scriptures in Wales which first suggested the idea of this Society to the **Rev. Joseph Hughes**, who became one of its secretaries. Mr. Steinkopff, of the Lutheran Church in the Savoy, represented the foreign element, Charles Grant that of India, and Wilberforce and **Samuel Mills** helped; the last drew up the plan. **Rev. J. Owen** represented the Church of England, as Mr. Hughes did the Nonconformists, and Mr. Steinkopff the foreign Protestants. **Lord Teignmouth**, the retired Governor-General of India, was appropriately the first president; the **Earl of Shaftesbury** has long held the office. The Society granted £13,500 in all for the Serampore translations, which subsequent scholars like **Yates** and **Wenger** perfected. But a controversy regarding the rendering of the words for "baptism" severed the connection between this Society and Serampore. The translation, printing, or distribution of the whole or part of the Bible has been promoted by this noble Society directly in 196 languages or dialects, and indirectly in 59, or 255 in all. The number of versions, including the chief revisions, is 354. The home organization consists of 1042 auxiliaries, 364 branches, and 3625 associations, or 3031 in all, besides 492 sections of the Hibernian Bible Society. Up to the present year, 1883–84, the British and Foreign Bible Society has issued a hundred million copies of the word of God, from London, from agencies in the principal centres of Europe, from nine societies in British India and Ceylon, and through foreign societies like that of the Basel Bible Society, established in the same year 1804. In 1882–83 the free income was £112,428, and the receipts from the sales of Scriptures were £98,068. In 1883 the income from all sources was £228,000.

In the words of Earl Cairns, late Lord Chancellor:—

"Where would the Missionary Societies have been without the Bible Society and without the Religious Tract Society? The preacher and the teacher might have used their voices within a very limited circle; they could do little with their voices alone in comparison with that which they could do with the aid of such literature as the Tract Society supplies."

In a paper recently published by the British and Foreign Bible Society, it is stated that "about 210,000,000 copies of the Holy Scriptures have now been provided in a printed form, more than three-fourths of the number having been issued by the Bible Societies. But of these copies Protestant nations have received upwards of one-half, — 90,000,000 being in the languages spoken in Great Britain and its dependencies; while among the thousand millions of heathens, Jews, and Mohammedans, not more than ten million copies of the Sacred Volume have been circulated." Some portion of the Scriptures is now to be found in 330 languages, but the whole Bible is not yet translated into one-third of that number, while there are said to be 600 languages in which no part of Scripture has yet been issued.

The **National Bible Society of Scotland** is composed of the Edinburgh Bible Society established in 1809, the Glasgow Bible Society in 1812, the Glasgow Auxiliary to the British and Foreign Society in 1821, and the National in 1859, all united in 1860. This vigorous Society circulates only the Authorized Version of the English Bible, without the "Apocrypha," and diffuses the Bible in all European languages, and in China, Japan, India and the Netherlands India, Africa, and Armenia. Its total issues of the Bible, complete and in portions, are about half a million a year. This Society's rupture of 1826 with the British and Foreign Bible Society was healed in 1882.

"Since 1861 the Auxiliaries have increased from 50 to 313, embracing 620 parishes; and their contributions from £931 to £8418. The total annual revenue has grown from £7887 in 1861 to £31,343 in 1882; and the annual issue of Scriptures from 103,610 to 481,166 copies or portions. The development of the Society's foreign mission work is specially worthy of notice. The amount annually expended on it has grown from £731 to £15,073; the foreign circulation from 11,248 to 320,214, and that over an immensely wider area. The report for 1882 refers to the labours of 160 colporteurs wholly maintained by the Society, beside 120 other workers who are partially subsidized by it, in almost every European State, in Syria, India, China, Japan, and Brazil; so that sixty-six per cent. of the issues of the year were in foreign lands,—a larger proportionate foreign circulation than is effected, it is believed, by any other Bible Society. Previous to the union of 1861, no Scottish Bible Society had published a new version of the Scriptures. Since then this Society has printed, for the first time, the entire Bible in Efik, the New Testament in a dialect of the Dutch East Indies, one or two portions in other Eastern tongues, and, together with the British and Foreign and the American Bible Societies, it is now engaged in the production of the Scriptures in Japanese. The Society has assisted in the publication of two Gospels in Corean.

"The Society has circulated since 1861 upwards of seven million copies or portions of the Word of Life, and it is now counted third among the Bible Societies of the world. Last year it issued 1318 copies every day, and each £1 expended put into circulation eighteen Bibles or Testaments (or an equivalent number of portions)."

The Christian Vernacular Education Society for India, established in 1858, when the Sepoy Mutiny quickened the conscience of England, does a unique work for the people of India, providing Christian education for them in their mother tongues, by three great normal schools, by improving and Christianizing indigenous schools, and by preparing and circulating school-books and a general Christian literature for native homes. With an annual expenditure of £11,500, the Society has trained 735 native teachers and mission agents, has brought 100,000 children under Christian instruction, has printed 1027 publications in 18 languages, of which ten million of copies have been sold, and employs 500 colporteurs in India and Ceylon. The founder and manager is **Dr. John Murdoch**, a Scotsman, who was a teacher in Ceylon.

Christian Missions to the Jews by Societies.—After an attempt in 1801 by **G. C. Frey**, a Christian Israelite, to work among his brethren according to the flesh through the London Missionary Society, **The London Society for Promoting Christianity among the Jews** was established in 1809, on a catholic basis at first, but in 1815 in connection with the Church of England. The Rev. Andrew Fuller helped the work at its beginning among the Jews in London, and Claudius Buchanan, who had visited the communities of Jews in South India, induced it to prepare a translation of the New Testament in Biblical Hebrew, of which the standard edition is that of 1838. In 1825, **Michael Solomon Alexander**, reader of the synagogue in Plymouth, was baptized, and became first Protestant Bishop of Jerusalem. He was succeeded by Bishop Gobat, of the Church Missionary Society. Of all converted Jews the most remarkable missionary has been **Joseph Wolff**, whose travels through the most barbarous parts of Central Asia and Abyssinia are rich in adventure, between 1826 and 1866; he called himself the Protestant Xavier. This Society has worked with the best results in Poland (Posen) and Palestine, with the co-operation for a time of the late King of Prussia. **The British Society for the Propagation of the Gospel among the Jews**, formed in 1842, has twenty-five paid and upwards of one hundred workers in all, in the principal cities of England, and in Germany, Italy, and Russia.

The **Wesleyan Methodist Missionary Society** dates its organization from 1813, on the last day of which Dr. Coke (see page 138) sailed for Ceylon with six missionaries, who were welcomed by the authorities, and laid the foundation of a prosperous mission at Jaffna and in the north of the island. Soon after, the Society began its South African Mission at Namaqualand and in Kafraria. In 1882, from Australia, it commenced operations in the Friendly Islands, since spread over Fiji with remarkable results. Besides these, this Society has extended its efforts in India, South China, Natal and Western Africa, and the West Indies. For these purely foreign missions, and for its work in Europe, Ireland, and Canada, it annually raises £152,000.

The **Calvinistic Methodists**, formed as the result of George Whitefield's preaching, in the two branches of the Welsh Calvinistic Methodists and Countess of Huntingdon's Connection, devote £6000 a year to missions, chiefly in Assam. The **Primitive Methodist Society** was formed in 1843, up to which time from 1810 some of the circuits had their own missions. The foreign work of the Society is in South Africa and Fernando Po. The **United Methodist Free Churches** raise £17,600 a year for home and foreign missions.

The **Society for the Propagation of the Gospel in Foreign Parts** became a distinctly missionary agency in 1821, after India had been opened to the gospel in 1813, and Bishop Middleton had built Bishop's College, nearly opposite Calcutta. But it had given assistance to missions, after its incorporation by royal charter in 1701 "for the religious instruction of the Queen's subjects beyond the seas; for the maintenance of clergymen in the plantations, colonies, and factories of Great Britain, and for the propagation of the gospel in those parts." Its income was £1537 in 1701, and £12,858 in 1821. It rose to £109,000 in 1883. Its ordained missionaries number 327, of whom 161 are in Asia, which has 14 dioceses; 129 in Africa, which has 14 dioceses, including Madagascar and Mauritius; 20 in Australia and the Pacific, which has 20 dioceses; 216 in America and the West Indies, and 1 in Europe. There are 1404 catechists and lay teachers, mostly natives, and 300 students in colleges. Of this Society's missions the most remarkable is in India, under **Dr. Caldwell**, Bishop of Tinnevelli, with headquarters at Tuticorin port. **The Universities Mission to Central Africa**, established in 1861 on the proposal of Dr. Livingstone to the Universities of Oxford and Cambridge, is conducted on the principles of this Society. Its first bishops were **Mackenzie**, Tozer, and **Steere**. This Society raises £13,000 a year for work from Zanzibar along the east coast of Africa, and into the interior as far as the east coast of Lake Nyassa. It has 16 ordained and 11 lay missionaries, besides ladies and native catechists.

The Society of Friends, like the Moravian Church, has always been remarkable for the devotion of almost every member to the missionary as well as other philanthropic causes. The Quakers, as they are popularly called, number 18,000 only at home, and 500 abroad, besides 6000 adherents. They work individually in Madagascar, India, Syria, and elsewhere, and assist all evangelical missions.

Medical Missions.—The teaching and the example of our Lord, and the union with Paul of Luke, the beloved physician, form the special warrant for the medical form of missionary work, which is fully justified by the words of the final Missionary Charge. It was through a physician, Gabriel Boughton, that the British obtained from the Delhi Emperor their first settlements in India, especially Calcutta. The first medical missionary of modern times was William Carey's colleague, **John Thomas**, who was the means of bringing to Christ the first caste convert of Northern India, Krishna Pal, a carpenter whom he healed. Thereafter a few medical men occasionally went out as missionaries from both England and America. It was one of these, **Rev. Peter Parker, M.D.**, an American missionary of China, who, when on a visit to Edinburgh in 1841, led the good and great physician **Dr. John Abercrombie** to establish the **Edinburgh Medical Missionary Society**. This is still the only medical missionary society or training institution in existence. **Dr. John Coldstream** and **Mr. Benjamin Bell, F.R.C.S.E.**, were its first secretaries, and the **Rev. G. D. Cullen, M.A.**, still survives as one of its founders. In 1822, Mr. Douglas of Cavers had, in his *Hints on Missions*, urged the advantages of medical missions. The Edinburgh Society gradually extended both its plans and its agency, until it has become, first and mainly, a home institute for training specially medical students, on graduation, for mission work; a Society conducting model medical missions at Nazareth, Japan (Niigata), and Damascus, and giving aid to the missions of Churches and Societies. Its Institute, named in memory of Livingstone, is held in the Cowgate of Edinburgh, and partly in the famous Magdalene Chapel, in which the first General Assembly met, and the body of the martyred Marquis of Argyle was placed after his execution. After fifteen years' service in Madras, as the missionary of the Free Church and Edinburgh Society jointly, **Mr. David Paterson, F.R.C.S.E.**, became the first house superintendent of the Institute. In it there are now, every year, about 16 resident students, while some 50 volunteer students attend the dispensary. Upwards of 11,000 patients are annually treated at the dispensary, and 10,000 at their own homes. The income of the Society is above £7000, of which one-half is from annual subscriptions. The various Churches and Societies receive medical missionaries also direct from the universities and colleges. There are at least 150 British qualified medical missionaries abroad, and nearly as many American; of the latter several are women, like the late **Miss Mary Seelye, M.D.**, who died in Calcutta. The Free and United Presbyterian Churches, and some of the English Societies, are training medical women missionaries at the Henrietta Home, London.

Women's Missions.—In all non-Christian countries, but especially in those which seclude women in the hareem as Islam does, and those with a caste civilisation and **zanana** system like the Brahmanical peoples, Christian missions have begun to evangelize the women only after the first or second generation of their fathers, husbands, and brothers have been brought within the kingdom. Hence Christian women's work for native women did not begin in an organized form till about 1854, when a demand for Christian education began to show itself. Up to that time the labours of **Mrs. Marshman** in Serampore (1800), **Mrs. Wilson** in Calcutta (1822), **Mrs. Margaret Wilson** in Bombay (1830), and **Mrs. Anderson** and **Mrs. Braidwood** in Madras (1838), had been confined to day schools and orphanages, and the Eurasian community, who yielded admirable assistants. Since that time the work has taken the form of the normal school, higher school for the native Christian community, and schools in the zanana or women's apartments. The societies which have done most in India are these:—Society for Promoting Female Education in the East, Indian Normal School and Female Instruction Society, Church of England Zenana Missionary Society, Propagation Society's Ladies' Association, Baptist Zenana Mission, and American Women's Union Zenana Mission.

The United States of America.

The American Board of Commissioners for Foreign Missions was formed in 1810. In the land of Eliot and Brainerd, the latter of whom had died in 1747, the movement which resulted in the Baptist and London Missionary Societies found a sympathetic response. Massachusetts and New York had their societies for local effort from 1787, and the Presbyterian Church had contemplated a mission to Africa in 1774. But it was two divinity students of New England, of Williams and Andover Colleges, who stirred up the churches to send forth the first American missionary. These were **Adoniram Judson** and **Samuel J. Mills**. The former was the first missionary, whom Carey sent to Burma; of the latter his mother said, "I have consecrated this child to the service of God as a missionary." Mills and four other students of Williams College drew up, in cypher—"public opinion then being opposed to us"—in 1808 the constitution of a Society of Brethren, who bound themselves to go forth as missionaries. In 1810 Judson wrote a paper, signed by himself, Samuel Nott, jun., Samuel J. Mills, and Samuel Newell, asking the General Association of Independent Ministers, which met at Bradford, "whether they may expect patronage and support from a missionary society in this country, or must commit themselves to the direction of a European society?" The result was the institution of the American Board of Foreign Missions, which in 1812 sent forth Judson and four other ordained missionaries to India. The Charter of 1813 was about to open the country when they arrived, but Dr. Judson was too early for that, and in God's good providence settled in the then independent State of Burma. Messrs. Hall and Nott were driven round to Bombay, where, after some temporizing, the Governor permitted them to land. There they followed up the pioneer work of Carey among the Marathas. Since that time this Board has been enabled by the annually increasing population of the United States to throw its organization over many parts of the world, and notably the corrupt Christian churches and races of Turkey. In 1883 (to October) it had a revenue of 590,995 dollars, or £120,000, to which the income had risen from 13,611 dollars in 1812. The Board's 134 ordained missionaries and 433 male and female labourers sent from America, with 144 native pastors and 360 preachers and catechists, work in twenty separate mission fields,

—in Natal, West Central Africa (Bihé), Turkey, India, Ceylon, China, Japan, Micronesia, Mexico, Spain, and Prag.

The **American Baptist Missionary Union** was founded in 1814, owing to the fact that, during the voyage to India, Dr. Judson and Mr. Rice became Baptists. Hence this Society has had its greatest triumphs among the Burman and Kareng hill tribes, the British authorities having greatly encouraged their missionaries, from the time when Sir Henry Durand was the friend of **Judson**, and Sir Arthur Phayre the friend of **Mason**, **Mrs. Ingalls**, and their colleagues. In Burma the Society has 99 missionaries; in Assam, 15; among the Telugoos of Madras, 37; in China, 25; in Japan, 12; and in Africa, 2, or 190 in all; besides missions in Sweden, Germany, France, Spain, and Greece. The Society's income in 1882–83 was 327,880 dollars, or £65,600. In Burma there are 479 churches, with 24,210 members; in that year 1681 were baptized. Among the Telugoos, where a great work has been done since the famine of 1878, there were 39 churches with 1685 members.

The **Methodist Episcopal Society** began in 1819 with 828 dollars, and in 1881 had an income of 625,668 dollars, or £125,000. Its foreign operations are carried on in Africa, South America, China, Japan, India, Mexico, and several countries of Europe. In India it has met with much success, chiefly in Oudh since the Mutiny of 1857, where it was established by **Dr. Butler**. The number of foreign missionaries is 99, and of assistants 70; there are 218 native ordained preachers.

The **Church Society for Promoting Christianity** among the **Jews**, in the United States chiefly, was founded in New York in 1878.

The **American Bible Society** has an annual income of £100,000. The **Tract Society** was, in 1825, developed from the Boston into the National American Tract Society, New York, chiefly by the **Rev. W. Allen** Hallock, **D.D.**, who guided it till 1880, creating an issue and circulation of 450 millions of books, tracts, and papers. Its whole annual receipts are £76,000, of which £54,000 are from sales. It is largely a home agency for the increasing population of the States, among whom it employs 200 colporteurs; but it assists mission work in Turkey, India, China, Japan, and Africa. An American writer remarks:—

"This employment of the periodical press as a religious instructor is pre-eminently *American*. Figures show that, of the world's 30,000 periodicals, more than a proportionate number are American. Our people *must* read newspapers, other peoples *may*. There is therefore the more need to make them religious in the best sense. The 962 daily journals of our country have an aggregate circulation of 1,127,337,355. Ah, if every one of them bore some message for Christ and Christian principles! This would create a current to carry religion into the shops and marts and hearts and homes of our masses of population. Consider the 15,000,000 of outlying non-churchgoers among our people, and the polyglot possibilities of the press with which to bridge our differences of race and language. Here is given *the* opportunity to try the experiment of a fully-developed religio-secular press."

The Continent of Europe.

We have already traced the action of Denmark so early as 1705, which is still represented in Southern India by the **Danish Lutheran Missionary Society** of Copenhagen.

The Netherlands Missionary Society was founded in 1797, as a result of the first address of the London Missionary Society, and under the influence of **Dr. Van der Kemp**. That great missionary, the first to the Kafirs, was born at Rotterdam in 1747; he became a cavalry officer, and then a physician, after studying at the University of Edinburgh. The drowning of his wife and child, and his own narrow escape, roused him from a life of bold scepticism, and he answered the first call of the London Society to go out to Africa. There he settled on the Keiskamma till war drove him south to work among the Hottentots; and he died as he had lived, protesting against his countrymen's oppression of the native races. This Society, after the superficial and temporary Christianization of Ceylon, confined itself to the Dutch East India Colonies left to the country by the treaty of 1824. In the Minnahassa or north peninsula of Celebes, **Riedel** and **Schwarr** were the means, after 1829, of turning to Christ more than half the population of 114,000. But the rationalism of the Church at home, and the purely materialistic polity and culture system of the Java authorities, have strangled the mission, which never raised more than £6750 annually to Christianize a population yielding vast tribute to the Netherlands, and have encouraged the spread of Malay Mohammedanism. The Rhenish Society of Germany, which does much for Dutch India, reports that there are fifty Dutch missionaries belonging to eight societies scattered over the whole Archipelago, "but

GERMAN PROTESTANT MISSIONARY SOCIETIES.

there are only a few places where their results are remarkable." The very considerable congregations formed long ago in the Amboyna, Kei, and Aru Islands, and in Timor and Wetter, are fast being lost to Islam. So true is it that nothing but evangelical faith and motives will make Christians aggressive.

The German Protestant Missionary Societies continue, as from the first, to prevent the Church or Churches, as such, from sharing in the great enterprise. In this respect, Lutheranism, like Episcopacy in England, is still in that missionary infancy from which the Free Churches in Scotland and America have grown. But the German mission organizations are far in advance of all others in the justice which they do to the enterprise on its literary side. Whether in order to rouse the churches, or to inform the world, the press must be the servant of missions, as it has never yet been in the English language. We take from Dr. Warneck statistics of the German Societies.

Founded.	Name.	Headquarters.	Countries.	Missionaries, 1881.	Native Christian Communicants, 1881.	Native Christian Community, 1881.	Income, 1881.
							£
1732	Moravian	Herrnhut in Saxony	Greenland, Labrador, West Indies, Central South America, S. Africa, Australia, West Himalaya	141	25,963	76,646	19,728
1815	Basel	Basel	South-West India, W. Africa, China	104	7,028	14,561	36,222
1823	Berlin	Berlin	South Africa, China	60	5,262	11,775	14,269
1829	Rhenish	Elberfeld-Barmen	South Africa, Dutch India, China	69	8,000	23,000	15,893
1836	North-German	Bremen	West Africa, New Zealand	11	250	700	4,194
1819	Leipzig	Leipzig	South India	21	5,000	12,273	12,254
1836	Gossner	Berlin	Central Bengal, among the Kols	19	10,614	32,000	7,866
1849	Hermannsburg	Hermannsburg	South-East Africa, India, Australia, New Zealand	90	3,000	7,828	13,011
1877	Schleswig-Holstein	Breeklum	South India	2	..	..	1,750
				517	65,062	178,783	125,737

To the annual revenue of £125,757, he would add considerable sums to represent the trading profits of the artisan missions of the

Moravian, Basel, and Rhenish Societies. The **Basel Society**, which is really not Swiss but German, was originally founded only to train missionaries, but it now maintains vigorous missions in South-Western India and elsewhere. Its students, who are non-university men, pass through a six years' course of Latin, Greek, Hebrew, English, and Theology; those who begin well educated have only a two years' course. There are generally eighty in residence in the pleasant and busy hive outside of Basel. The missionaries are ordained, but may not act as ministers at home. Their wives are generally reckoned in the statistics as missionaries, and unmarried women missionaries are rarely sent out.

The "Knaks Woman's Mission Union for China" (1850) has a Foundling and Orphanage at Hong-Kong. The "Woman's Union for the Christian Education of Females in the East" (1842) supports a few woman missionaries in India, Palestine, and South Africa. The "Kaiserswert Deaconesses Institute" has sent at least fifty sisters to the East.

The Paris Society for Evangelical Missions began in 1825 to help the missionary efforts of other Continental churches, but in 1829 it was led by Dr. Philip of the London Missionary Society to send MM. Rolland, Lemue, and Bisseux to South Africa, just as Duff was set apart for India. They were received by descendants of Huguenots who had in 1698 settled near Cape Town, and finally in 1833 by Moshesh, chief of the Basutos. There the French missionaries have done a great work, broken only by war for a time, but now likely to extend greatly under the imperial protection of Great Britain up to the Zambesi, which M. Coillard has surveyed for a mission. **Major Malan** gave up all for missions in South Africa, and he helped greatly this mission of his father's Church.

The Norwegian Mission Society of Evangelical Lutherans, founded in 1842 at Stavanger, where it has a Missionary College, has workers in Zululand, where some were martyred recently, and in Madagascar. **The Swedish Evangelical Lutheran Mission** works in the Central Province of India and among the Mohammedan Gallas of Abyssinia. **The Free Swiss Church**, Canton de Vaud, began mission work in 1875, at Valdezia, South Africa, among a mixed race of Basuto and Amatonga Kafirs.

CHAPTER XVI.

THE CHURCHES BECOME MISSIONARY, 1830.

Scotland, Ireland, and England.

The Church *versus* a Society as a Missionary Organization—Alexander Duff—The Free Church of Scotland's Foreign Missions—The Established Church of Scotland—The United Presbyterian Church of Scotland—The Presbyterian Church of Ireland—The Presbyterian Church of England—The Presbyterian Churches of the Colonies, Canada, Australasia, South Africa.

The United States of America.

The Presbyterian Church, North and South—The Protestant Episcopal Church—The United Presbyterian Church—The Reformed (Dutch) Church and the Reformed Presbyterian Church—The Evangelical Lutheran Church.

General Results of Foreign Missionary Churches and Societies.

Scotland, Ireland, and England.

The Church *v.* a Society as a Missionary Organization.—By its institution, constitution, object, and early history, the Church alone is and should always be a directly aggressive missionary power. It was so till the Reformation, up to which the Iro-Scottish brotherhoods and Greek and Latin monastic orders may be considered committees through which the churches, as such, directly worked. Since the sixteenth century the Romish orders, notably the Jesuits, have been societies often practically independent of their Church, and fighting against it both in its Divine principles of truth and charity, and in its ecclesiastical courts. The Lutheran Church drove its pietist members into the Moravian Brotherhood and Danish-Halle organizations. The Church of England similarly treated the Nonconformists and Methodists, acting on its Erastian civil basis; to this day the noble and extensive missions, conducted by its evangelical and sacramentarian members through two societies, are hampered and injured by the interference of bishops with sacerdotal and lordly rights. The Nonconformist Christians of Great Britain and America, or the Baptists and Independents, having no fitting church organization, as such, for mission purposes, are driven to form societies which act outside of the congregations. But Presbyterianism supplies now, as in the time of the Acts of the Apostles, just the agency and machinery wanted for Foreign as well as for Home Missions. The gradation of courts, in which the laity are equally represented, from the kirk - session to the General Assembly, which appoints the Foreign and other Mission committees annually, and annually reviews their proceedings, enables the whole Church to act directly on the mission fields, while it summons every member personally to pray and give, and secures missionaries from the front ranks of the divinity students and ministers. In the foreign field itself, as converts become formed into congregations, Presbyterianism—if honestly worked—enables them to "call" their own pastor, support their own machinery, and extend it around them as self-governing and self-developing communities. As the missionary enterprise of Christendom grows, it must tend to work less through societies, and more through churches.

Alexander Duff (1806-1878).—The Church of Scotland was the first Church, as such, since the Reformation, to send forth a missionary, and that under the influence of two men, **Thomas Chalmers** and **Dr. Inglis**. The former, while still minister of Kilmany, in 1812 published his sermon, preached before the Dundee Missionary Society, on Missionaries and the Bible, as "the two great instruments appointed for the propagation of the gospel." Again, in 1814, he preached the annual sermon for the Scottish Propagation Society, on "the Utility of Missions ascertained by experience," in which he showed the supercilious wit like Sydney Smith, and scoffer, that "what the man of liberal philosophy is in sentiment, the missionary is in practice." These two sermons, followed by the personal influence of Chalmers at St. Andrews, sent **Alexander Duff** to India in 1829. Born in 1806 (25th April) of peasant parents of deep godliness near Moulin, in the Grampians, he was early called in a vision to be a missionary; he passed through the University course of St. Andrews as the best student of his year; and when fully ripe for action, he responded, in 1829, to the appeal which Dr. Inglis had made to the people of

Scotland, in the name of the Church, in 1825. When he and his wife landed at Calcutta, after having twice suffered shipwreck, on the 27th May 1830, he began a career of devotion to the people of India, which ended only with his life, on the 12th February 1878. He served himself apostolic heir to Carey, as Carey had done to Schwartz. But more than either of these, he was led by the Spirit of God to institute the educational method of evangelizing the Brahmanical defenders of the very citadel of idolatry in Asia, which is still working, and will go on working, as Luther's Reformation in Germany and Knox's in Scotland. He founded the India, New Hebrides, and Syria Missions; he extended the African Mission; he organized the whole missionary agency at home, and his eloquent experience was the means of sending hundreds of missionaries from all the churches to the heathen abroad.

When, in 1843, the Disruption of the Church of Scotland took place, Dr. Duff and all the Indian missionaries,—then fourteen in number,—and all the missionaries to the Jews, with the converts and students, joined the Church of Scotland Free, leaving behind them only the property which they had created.

The Free Church of Scotland's Foreign Missions are now consolidated in six well-defined fields, and are extended among certain great races of marked individuality and influence, in the two continents of Asia and Africa. In and to the south of *Asia* the fields are—(1) India, and there specially the educated Brahmanical Hindoos, numbering seventeen millions, and the simple aboriginal demon-worshippers, numbering seven millions; (2) the New Hebrides group of thirty islands in the Pacific Ocean to the south of Eastern Asia, containing a hundred thousand cannibals of the Malay or Polynesian and Negrillo or Papuan races; (3) Syria, where, on Lebanon, twenty miles to the northeast of Beiroot, there is a medical and educational mission to the quasi-Mohammedan Druses, and to the ignorant Christians of the Greek and Latin Churches. In *Africa* the missions are at work among the three principal varieties of the great Bantu race of fetish-worshippers, termed by their Mohammedan oppressors Kafirs. These varieties are—(1) the Kafirs of Cape Colony, with whom we have fought seven cruel wars, but who are now peaceful, because largely Christianized and civilised around the provincial capital of King William's Town. In this great work the United Presbyterian and Free Churches are practically, and soon will be corporately, united. (2) The Zulus of Natal are evangelized from

Maritzburg, the capital; from Impolweni estate, where an institution is about to be built like Lovedale for Kafraria proper; and from Gordon, on the borders of purely native Zululand. (3) The Kafir-Zulu tribes of Lake Nyassa region, farther north, are cared for by the Livingstonia Mission, under the Rev. R. Laws, M.B., C.M., who again illustrates the blessedness of union, being a United Presbyterian missionary in the service of the Free Church of Scotland.

In the year ending 31st March 1884, above £80,000 was raised for and spent upon these missions, independently of that contributed for missions to the Jews, the Continent of Europe, and the Colonies, which made the whole missionary revenue of the Free Church for Christ's cause abroad about £100,000. The total cost of administering the £80,000 was under £1000, which is believed to be the lowest percentage of charge in the history of missions, not a little voluntary service being done for the Master's sake and the Church's good. Three of the sources of this revenue of £80,000 are of peculiar interest. (1) The natives themselves contributed £13,184 of it, partly for church and missionary purposes, and more largely as fees for school and college education; Europeans on the spot contributed £3771 besides. (2) The Free Church having left the voluntary question open, and its missions being educational as well as preaching, its missionary teachers and professors qualify for grants-in-aid, as at home, and in this shape £12,000 was received from the various Governments of India and South Africa. (3) The most important single source of revenue, spiritually and financially, is the congregational, created by Dr. Duff before the Disruption of 1843, and amounting last year to £15,954. Dr. Duff's ideal was an association of all the communicants in every congregation for prayer and giving on behalf of Foreign Missions, and Dr. Chalmers tells us he himself was led by this plan to devise the organization of the Sustentation Fund. About three-fourths of the 1060 congregations and stations of the Church have such quarterly associations, the other fourth still adheres to the annual collection at the church door. These associations are the sheet-anchor of the Church's missions, not only financially but spiritually. Through them the whole Church becomes missionary; without them there is a fear that the missions may be cared for by what will be virtually a society within the Church. This congregational revenue has steadily risen from £4374 nearly four-fold, and at the rate of £304 a year during the past six years. But not more than one-third of the whole communicants give for Foreign Missions, while, allowing for families and the very poor, the proportion should be two-thirds. The whole sum raised in Scotland alone by the Free Church for its Foreign Missions since 1843 is not short of a million sterling. But this is still the day of small things to the prayer of faith and labour of love. Like the other evangelical churches of Protestant Christendom, the Free Church has only begun to play its part in the world enterprise for which our Lord prayed the Father (John xvii. 20-22), and which He committed to every disciple in all ages.

The plan of Zanana Missions was first suggested by Prof. T. Smith, and carried out in 1854 by the Rev. John Fordyce of the Free Church, which raised £6118 for native women's education in India and South Africa last year. The Ladies' Society, charged by the Church with this since 1837, has recently so re-organized its system, that every congregation is asked to form an association of women only, separate from that for Foreign Missions and all represented in presbyterial auxiliaries. Zanana Missions must form only a small part of the agency which, as hitherto, must be largely devoted to Christian schools,—dropping the orphanages, however, as no longer necessary, and developing normal schools for the supply of indigenous Zanana teachers; high schools at which the native Christian community, growing in wealth, intelligence, and political and social influence, may receive a suitable Bible education; and Medical Missions by both Scottish and native practitioners fully qualified. From the Calcutta School of the Free Church there has gone up to the University one Bengalee Christian young lady, who received the degree of Master of Arts (with honours), amid the applause of her countrymen and the eulogies of members of the Government. If even so many of the women of India were Christ's, or under Christian influence, as the men, how much nearer would the time of India's redemption be!

The mean annual increment of adult converts to the Free Church Missions is 400, or more than an average congregation in Scotland. Its whole staff of Christian agents is 530 strong, at 28 central and 105 branch stations. It has 52 ordained missionaries, of whom 13 are natives, 11 native licentiates, 9 medical missionaries, 32 missionary teachers, of whom one-half are ladies exclusive of missionaries' wives, 18 evangelists and artisans, 282 native teachers, male and female; 111 catechists and colporteurs, and 25 Bible-women. When the writer landed in Calcutta thirty years ago, the number of Protestant native Christians in all India was hardly above 100,000; it is now 600,000, who contribute annually for the gospel among themselves and their heathen fellows a quarter of a million sterling. They have 750 ministers and missionaries of their own race, or more than the whole number of foreign missionaries sent out by forty-six churches and societies. There are two millions of Christians of all kinds in India to-day, and about three-quarters of a million in South Africa. "He shall see His seed, He shall prolong His days, and the pleasure of the Lord shall prosper in His hand."

The Established Church of Scotland did not respond to the appeal of Dr. Duff to begin new missions in the great cities of Northern India, and to make an equitable arrangement regarding the property. In 1845 it began the same kind of missions at Calcutta, in the Institution and house left by Dr. Duff, under the Rev. Dr. Ogilvie and Dr. Herdman; in Bombay, in the Institution built by Dr. Wilson, but which he had not had time to enter, and also in Madras. It has since added a mission at Goojrat and Chamba in the Panjab, and a prosperous mission among the Buddhist Lepchas of Darjeeling; also in China and at Blantyre, East Central Africa. It has a Jewish Mission in Egypt, Beiroot, Smyrna, Salonica, and Constantinople. The foreign expenditure is £25,000, and that in the Jewish Mission is £5400 annually. In 1878, **Dr. Norman Macleod**, of the Barony Parish, Glasgow, visited the missions, and on his return did much to stir up the Church to do its duty by his eloquence and his work as convener of its Foreign Mission Committee. This Church had one missionary martyr during the Mutiny of 1857, **Thomas Hunter** of Sialkot, who was shot with his wife and infant child.

The United Presbyterian Church of Scotland has the honour of having kept evangelical truth alive by the Secession of **1733**, so that the first Scottish missionary who went to the heathen, Peter Greig, was of this Church, although a society sent him. In 1835 the Church sent out to Jamaica the Rev. J. Paterson and W. Niven; in 1847 it took over the stations there of the Scottish Missionary Society. In 1846, sent forth by the Jamaica negroes to their race in Africa, the Rev. H. M. Waddell, a teacher, and two negroes, began the Old Calabar Mission and the study of the Efik language. The events of the Mutiny led this Church to open the first mission among the millions of Rajpootana and its feudatory states in the heart of North-Western India, acting on the advice of Dr. John Wilson of Bombay. The **Rev. Dr. Shoolbred**, an able student of Edinburgh University, founded the mission at Beawar in 1860, and it has greatly prospered. The origin of this Church's Kafir Mission we have already mentioned. Besides a mission in Spain, its other fields are China and Japan, where it has been greatly blessed in its medical and Bible translation as well as other work. The annual expenditure on the missions is £40,000. In these eight mission fields, including Jamaica, which is largely colonial and self-supporting, there are 71 congregations, with 11,000 members, and 10,000 children at the Sabbath schools. There are 199 day schools, providing Christian education for 12,524 pupils. To carry on this work there is a staff of 73 trained agents, 50 of whom are ordained missionaries sent from this country, 6 are medical missionaries, and 17 are ordained native pastors. Besides these, 15 other agents have been sent from this country, 7 of whom are Zanana missionaries, 5 are female teachers in Calabar and Kafraria, and 5 are male teachers. Native agents not pastors number 393, of whom 83 are evangelists or catechists. Altogether the educated agency numbers 481.

The Presbyterian Church of Ireland, in 1840, then known as the Synod of Ulster, was led by Dr. Duff's eloquence, and by a missionary survey which Dr. John Wilson had made of the feudatory states of Kathiawar, to begin a mission to Goojarat or North Bombay. The Rev. J. Glasgow and A. Kerr were sent out. This Church raises £10,000 a year for the mission, and has 11 ordained, 3 medical, and 6 women missionaries in 18 stations, with 13 native congregations, consisting of 1800 members. There are 41 native Christian agents. Its eloquent convener, Dr. W. Fleming Stevenson of Dublin, has visited the province, and made a missionary tour of the world.

The Presbyterian Church of England was virtually founded in 1570, when Cartwright opposed Episcopal intolerance, and it promised, during the period to the Civil War, to colour the religious life of England, where it was the legal form of worship and doctrine in 1641. After Cromwell it gradually became the mere representative of the divided Presbyterian Church in Scotland till 1876, when the congregations in England of the Free and United Presbyterian Churches there formed the Presbyterian

Church of England. Its ten presbyteries, 280 congregations with 60,000 members, contribute £17,000 a year for a China Mission, and £900 for Jewish Missions. The **Rev. William C. Burns** was sent out as the first missionary in 1847, and Dr. James Young was his medical colleague at Amoy. A Scottish branch of the mission, which raises a fifth of the income, sent out the **Rev. Carstairs Douglas, LL.D.**, and Rev. David Sandeman. These men were greatly blessed, as evangelists and scholars, before death stopped them in the fulness of their career. The Chinese Christian communicants now number about 3000, at 28 stations in Amoy, 23 in Swatow, and 31 in Formosa. A new mission has been opened at Singapore. The 23 European missionaries, of whom 7 are medical, have been trained chiefly in the Free Church of Scotland's Colleges. There are 4 women missionaries and 80 native evangelists.

The Presbyterian Church of Wales has 6 missionaries in Northern India. **The United Original Secession Church of Scotland** has a missionary in the Central Province of India.

The Presbyterian Churches of the Colonies.—As in England and Ireland, so in Canada, Australasia, and South Africa, the divided churches of Scottish Presbyterianism, freed from legal and historical obstructions, have united as Free Churches, and so have become missionary organizations. **The Presbyterian Church of Canada** has since 1845 been honoured to produce martyrs like the **Gordons** in Eromanga, New Hebrides, where it forms part of the United Mission Synod. Its other missions are at Trinidad, in Formosa, and in the great Hindoo state of Central India, of which Holkar is the intolerant Maharaja. This Church has 15 ordained missionaries, and an annual income for missions of £29,000. **The Australasian Presbyterian Churches** of New South Wales, Victoria, South Australia, Tasmania, and New Zealand are also represented in the United New Hebrides Mission, and have workers among the aborigines of their own lands and the Chinese immigrants. **The Dutch Reformed Church of South Africa**, offspring of the Reformation in Holland, is now a free and evangelical Church; there are also the churches of the Doppers and of the Transvaal, connected with the Church in Holland. The first has eleven missions and stations among the natives of South Africa. The Presbyterian Church of South Africa should one day include them all, and become more than hitherto a living Missionary Church.

The United States of America.

The **Presbyterian Church of the United States of America** formed its first presbytery in 1704, and held its first General Assembly in 1789, both at Philadelphia. It supplied the Scottish Propagation Society with the one missionary to the Red Indians, at its first station on Long Island, then David Brainerd in New Jersey and Pennsylvania, especially at Crosweeksung. John Brainerd, on his brother's death in 1747, became the first missionary paid (£30 a year) by his own church, which employed a native, Sampson Occum, among his Oneida Indian countrymen and others. After the War of Independence, which arrested this slight missionary work, in 1796 the New York Missionary Society was formed, under the impulse which had created the London Missionary Society, and in 1797 the Northern Missionary Society. But the General Assembly in 1803 sent Mr. Blackburn to the Cherokee Indians. In a United Foreign Missionary Society this Church worked along with the Reformed Dutch and Associated Churches among the Indians from 1818. In 1831 the always missionary Synod of Pittsburgh formed the Western Foreign Missionary Society, which sent forth agents to Liberia and North India, where the Lodiana Mission was soon established on what was then the frontier of British India. In 1837 the Society became merged in a Board of the whole Church. It has now an annual revenue of £130,000 from all sources, and 159 ordained missionaries among the American Indians in Mexico and South America, in China, Japan, Siam, India, Persia, Syria, and Africa. It has 265 women missionaries, 92 ordained natives, and 135 native licentiates.

The **Presbyterian Church, South,** formed in 1861, has 23 ordained and 28 women missionaries among the local Indians, in Mexico, Brazil, and China. Its income is £14,000.

The **Protestant Episcopal Church** comes next, with an income of £38,000. It has been a missionary Church since 1846.

The **United** Presbyterian **Church of North America** has been a missionary Church since 1843. It has consolidated its energies in vigorous missions in Egypt and India, and among the Chinese in California. With an income of £21,000, there are 17 ordained and 30 women missionaries. Of these the Rev. Dr. Hogg (of Scotland)

and Rev. Dr. Lansing are well known for their work at Asyoot and Cairo, as well as at Alexandria, notwithstanding repeated commotions and opposition from the Mohammedan authorities.

The Reformed (Dutch) Church was founded on Manhattan Island (New York) in 1628 by **Jonas Michaelius**, and did missionary work among the aborigines before John Eliot. In 1832 it sent missionaries to Arcot and South India. There and in China and Japan it has 18 ordained and 23 assistant missionaries. Its income is £13,000.

The Reformed Presbyterian Church of the United States became missionary in 1855, has eight ordained agents in Syria, and an income of £3300. The **Evangelical Lutherans**, in three branches, have agents in India and Africa. The Associate Reformed Synod of the South does Foreign Mission work through the United Presbyterian Church; and the General Synod of the Reformed Presbyterian Church through the Presbyterian Board. The Presbyterian divisions which emigrants have thus far perpetuated in America weaken both Home and Foreign Mission enterprise, but the vastness of the country and of the population (53 millions) must be remembered.

Total Results of Foreign Missionary Churches and Societies.—The latest statistics, for 1882-83, most of which we have verified, enable us to be certain that the Hundred Missionary Societies and Churches of Protestant Christendom—reckoning each which has a separate financial organization, though there may be more than one in each Church—raise every year more than $2\frac{1}{4}$ millions sterling from all sources, or £2,275,000, in the following proportions:—

Great Britain,	£1,530,000
America,	600,000
Continent of Europe,	145,000

These hundred organizations send out 2900 ordained missionaries, or 3120 altogether, including medical missionaries who have a full professional qualification. Including women missionaries and native preachers not ordained after a lengthened theological training, in the Presbyterian sense, we may accept the following figures as within the truth. They justify us in estimating the strength of the missionary host in the year 1884, a century after **the** Father of Modern Missions began his praying and preaching and writing for the conversion of the heathen, as five thousand European and American, and thirty thousand Asiatic, African and Polynesian missionaries of Christ.

GENERAL STATISTICS OF FOREIGN MISSION SOCIETIES.

Societies.	Missionaries of all kinds.	Native Helpers.	Communicants.	Scholars.
British, . . .	2,757	20,532	352,196	285,237
American, . .	1,395	6,498	198,587	80,395
Continental, . .	767	2,441	71,794	27,548
	4,919	29,471	622,577	393,180

CHAPTER XVII.

EVANGELICAL MISSIONS AND MANKIND.

Christians and Non-Christians in 1884—Native Christians (Reformed) in 1884—Communicants—British Asia—India and Ceylon—Straits Settlements and Mauritius—Russian Asia—Portuguese, French, Spanish, and Dutch Asia—China and Corea—Japan—Turkey—Persia—Arabia—**Australasia and South Seas**—**The Two Americas**—**Africa and Madagascar**—The Position—The Future.

Christians and Non-Christians in 1884.—When Carey wrote his *Enquiry*, which was the beginning of Modern Missions, the human race was estimated at 731 millions. In the only copy of that precious book known to exist, we find the young shoemaker and village teacher of Hackleton giving these figures as the result of his detailed missionary survey of the whole world as known to Christendom a century ago: Pagans, 420 millions; Mohammedans, 130 millions; Jews, 7 millions; Christians, 174 millions, of whom 44 were Reformed, 30 were Greek and Armenian, and 100 were Romanists. A century's progress in population, colonization, science, and evangelization has changed all that, which was wonderfully accurate for the time. To-day, 1884, the race, in its religious aspect, stands thus statistically, as the result of hardly a century of evangelical missionary effort; and the spiritual conquests of the non-Christian world by the Christ of the Gospels, the Epistles, and the Apocalypse, are going on at an almost geometrical and not merely arithmetical rate of progression. In India the scientific census reveals the fact that Christians increased at the rate, every ten years, of 53 per cent. to 1861, at 61 per cent. to 1871, and at 86 per cent. to 1881, while the normal rate of increase of all non-Christians there has been $6\frac{1}{2}$ per cent. in each ten years.

IN THE YEAR OF CHRIST 1884.

Christians,		440 millions.
Reformed,	160 millions.	
Greek and Eastern,	85 ⎫ 280 ,,	
Romanist,	195 ⎭	
Non-Christians,		1000 ,,
Jews,	8 millions.	
Mohammedans,	172 ,,	
Pagans and Heathens,	820 ,,	
The Human Race,		1440 ,,

EVANGELICAL NATIVE CHRISTIANS IN 1884. 195

We have made due allowance for the increase revealed in the latest census of the British and Russian Empires and of the United States Republic, but that is more than counterbalanced by the reduced estimate of the population of China, now fixed by the best authorities, missionary and scientific, at less than that of India, or 240 millions. The 315 millions of the British Empire alone increase at the rate of 25 millions every decade. The whole race grows in number 75 millions every ten years. Before the next decennial census of the British Empire comes round, at the beginning of 1891, the race will be 1500 millions strong. The problem which it presents to Evangelical Christendom, as represented by each professing member of the body of Christ, is shown vividly, if roughly, in this diagram. Of the twelve squares the pure white represents Evangelical or Reformed Christianity, and the two next to it, the Greek and Latin Churches.

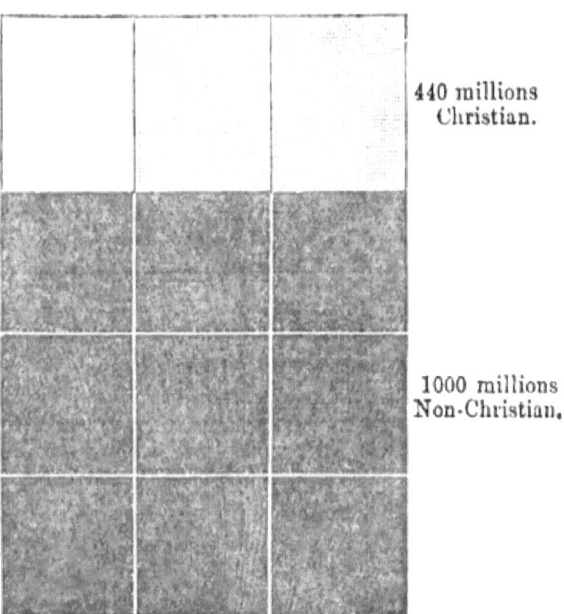

440 millions Christian.

1000 millions Non-Christian.

Evangelical Native Christians in 1884.—A view of the missionary growth of Christianity, at epochs widely separated from the ascension of Christ and from each other, enables us to show the comparatively rapid progress made in the present century, and especially in the last thirty years which have given the Christ the first-fruits of harvest.

	Christians.
Three centuries after Christ, Council of Nicæa,	5 millions.
Eight centuries after Christ, Scoto-Irish,	30 ,,
Ten centuries after Christ, Saxon and Romanist,	50 ,,
Fifteen centuries after Christ, Wiclif,	100 ,,
Eighteen centuries after Christ, William Carey,	174 ,,
Eighteen and a half centuries after Christ's ascension,	440 ,,

If we exclude all Christendom, we shall find, as we proceed to survey continent by continent and empire by empire, that the native converts who form the Missionary Church outside of Christendom, as the fruit of only half a century's really earnest effort by the evangelical churches, altogether apart from the native communities formed by Romanist and Eastern Churches, are:—

Asia.

	Native Christians (Reformed).
British,	710,000
Russian,	...
Portuguese,	...
French and Spanish,	...
Dutch,	150,000
China and Corea,	73,500
Japan,	13,000
Siam,	2,000
Turkey (Palestine),	100,000
Persia,	5,000
Arabia,	...

Australasia and South Seas.

Australia,	2,000
New Zealand,	30,000
Polynesia,	260,000
Micronesia,	8,000
Melanesia,	16,000

The Americas.

	Native Christians (Reformed).
Greenland and Labrador,	10,500
Red Indians in Canada and United States,	150,000
West Indies,	410,000
Central and South America,	140,000

Africa.

Egypt and North Africa,	8,000
West Africa,	110,000
South Africa,	200,000
East and Central Africa,	2,000
Madagascar and other Islands,	300,000
Grand total of Native Christian Communities,	2,700,000

Communicants.—The statistics[1] of seventy-five churches and societies, on pages 198 and 199, refer to the close of 1882, and show communicants only along with foreign and native missionaries at that time. Adding the increase of the year 1883 and the returns of the omitted societies, and multiplying the number of communicants by four, we arrive at a total Christian community somewhat larger than our own result of $2\frac{3}{4}$ millions.

[1] From Year Book of *Gospel in All Lands.*

ASIA.

British Asia.—The British Governments of the Empire of **India** and the Crown colonies of Ceylon, the Straits Settlements, and Mauritius profess neutrality towards all religions alike, and protect all. If, on the one hand, the practical effect of the Government of **India**, as an educator in its own schools and colleges, is secularist, on the other, its officials ever since the Mutiny of 1857 have been unmolested in their active proselytism as private Christians. The civil law, which follows the religion of each subject, protects Hindoo, Mohammedan, and other endowments of temples and mosques, which are of enormous extent and value, and these may some day be available for the vernacular education of the people. On the same principle the State spends about a quarter of a million sterling annually on an establishment of chaplains, Anglican and Presbyterian, Wesleyan and Romanist, for its own servants and white troops. Legislation has gradually withdrawn every inequitable or intolerant provision affecting religion, save on the question of the conscientious rights of minors converted to Christ. Christian missions have thus fuller scope in India, since the Mutiny, than in any other land outside of Christendom. Except in the great cities like Calcutta, with a million of inhabitants, where there is room for all, the evangelical churches and societies have tacitly divided the twelve provinces and 153 native states of India among them, so as not to waste their energies, while co-operating with each other in a brotherly manner unknown in Christendom itself. To this Christlike action there is only one exception, that of the Anglicans of the Propagation Society. Of the 100 Protestant churches and societies, 55 are at work in India, or 8 Presbyterian, 5 Episcopalian, 7 Lutheran, 8 Baptist, 3 Methodist, 2 Congregational, 1 Moravian, 1 of Friends, and 9 isolated. There are 7 women's agencies, and the two catholic Edinburgh Medical Missionary and Christian Vernacular Education Societies.

Looked at geographically, outside of the great English cities, the Free Church of Scotland holds the districts around Calcutta, Bombay, Poona, Madras, and Nagpoor, densely peopled by Bengalees, Marathas, and Tamuls, and has Gond and Santal missions among the simpler aborigines of the hills. The Established Church works successfully also among the Lepchas from Darjeeling and at Sialkot in the Panjab. The United Presbyterian Church is covering Hindee-speaking Rajpootana, from Ajmer,

British Foreign Missionary Societies.	Organized.	Foreign Missionaries.			Native Helpers.		Native Communicants.
		Ordinary.	Lay.	Women.	Ordinary.	Others.	
Society for the Propagation of the Gospel,	1701	463	13	42	64	1,349	26,678
Moravians,	1732	150	50	84	31	1,585	26,901
Baptist Missionary Society,	1792	70	12	13	56	477	40,247
London Missionary Society,	1795	142	10	124	383	4,436	86,422
Church Missionary Society,	1799	230	32	10	230	3,030	36,326
London Society for the Jews,	1808	36	27	43		83	
Wesleyan Methodist Missionary Society,	1814	270	31	228	267	1,720	91,486
General Baptist Missionary Society,	1816	8		10	22		1,193
Bible Christian Missionary Society,	1821	60					4,095
Colonial and Continental Church Society,	1823	150	50		87	325	
Established Church of Scotland,	1843	12	11		3	32	415
Free Church of Scotland,	1829	37	33	14	13	425	4,443
Presbyterian Church of Ireland,	1840	13	4	5	8	35	360
Welsh Presbyterian,	1841	8			12		467
British Society for the Jews,	1842	11	10	3		8	1,500
Primitive Methodist,	1843	6		6	2	4	387
South American Missionary Society,	1844	11	12	7		5	220
Presbyterian Church of England,	1847	19	8	5	19	60	2,768
United Presbyterian Church of Scotland,	1847	50	11	12	17	293	10,803
United Free Methodist,	1857	53				274	8,094
Methodist New Connexion,	1860	5		4	10	42	1,161
The Universities' Mission,	1860	18	9	12	1	28	220
Friends Foreign Mission Association,	1865	14		11	8	30	3,754
China Inland Mission,	1865	20	50	61		102	1,080
Indian Home Mission to the Santals,	1868		3	1	46	109	3,216
Total,		1863	378	695	1279	14,552	352,196
Foreign Missionary Societies of America.							
American Board,	1810	146	7	252	512	1,812	19,354
Baptist Missionary Union,	1814	75	2	116	174	511	102,261
Methodist Episcopal,	1819	105	38	122	246	1,599	29,095
Methodist Church in Canada,	1824	5		5	7	2	834
Reformed Church in America,	1832	20	1	23	20	115	2,843
Protestant Episcopal,	1835	16	6	26	38	107	1,190
Free Baptist,	1836	6		14		14	551
Presbyterian, North,	1837	160	21	265	92	718	18,656
Evangelical Lutheran, General Synod,	1839	5		7	3	157	2,537
Seventh-Day Baptist,	1842	2		2	1	4	33
African Methodist Episcopal,	1844	2	7	1			80
Presbyterian Church in Canada,	1844	17		22	1	6	1,262
Southern Baptist Convention,	1845	19		21		26	1,022
Methodist Episcopal, South,	1845	27		27		104	2,796

STATISTICS OF FOREIGN MISSION SOCIETIES.

Society	Year						
United Brethren in Christ,	1853	5	..	4	29	3	862
United Presbyterian,	1858	19	..	33	11	200	1,906
Reformed Presbyterian,	1859	3	1	5	..	43	120
Presbyterian, South,	1862	23	2	28	15	37	1,700
Baptist Church of Canada,	1866	5	..	2	5	12	925
Evangelical Lutheran General Council,	1869	4	..	3	2	43	300
Friends' Executive Committee, Indiana,	1875	3	13	12	..	..	189
Foreign Christian Missionary Society,	1875	18	..	5	..	..	1,255
Cumberland Presbyterian,	1876	2	..	5	3	9	35
Evangelical Association,	1876	60	1	2	..	9	8,646
Reformed Church in the United States,	1878	9	..	1	..	..	..
Associate Reformed Synod of the South,	1878	1	..	3	..	2	50
Methodist Protestant,	1878	1	..	1	..	..	..
German Evangelical Missionary Association,	..	2	..	..	..	6	175
Total,		**760**	**99**	**1907**	**1159**	**5,026**	**198,857**

Continental Foreign Missionary Societies.

Society	Year						
Netherlands Missionary Society,	1797	11	7	4	215	30	12,000
Basel Missionary Society,	1815	82	34	73	95	317	7,225
Danish Evangelical Lutheran Society,	1821	8	..	3	..	27	93
Evangelical Missionary Society of Paris,	1822	25	6	26	2	130	6,820
Rhenish Missionary Society,	1828	70	5	60	2	180	9,000
Leipzig Missionary Society,	1836	21	2	22	9	200	13,201
Gossner Missionary Union,	1836	12	1	19	7	261	10,786
Berlin Missionary Society,	1836	43	5	..	..	244	5,724
North German Missionary Society,	1836	9	10	7	1	10	110
Norwegian Missionary Society,	1842	38	..	13	..	200	1,080
Lund's Missionary Society,	1845	7	2	3	..	12	30
Jerusalem Missionary Society,	1845	4	..	..	..	2	177
Hermannsburg Missionary Society,	1849	40	55	55	21	186	3,800
Java Committee,	1855	6	3	6	..	13	350
Ermelo Missionary Society,	1856	6	..	4	..	14	50
Netherlands Missionary Union,	1858	8	8	8	..	5	150
Utrecht Missionary Society,	1859	10	..	10	..	12	100
Dutch Reformed Missionary Society,	1860	3	3	11	..	5	150
Christian Reformed Church,	1865	3	..	..	..	4	40
Finnish Missionary Society,	1869	5	..	2	..	5	6
Free Church of Canton de Vaud,	1880	3	3	3	..	5	60
Mennonite,	..	3	..	3	..	12	100

Continental	..	417	142	314	73	1,883	71,734
Great Britain and Ireland,	..	1863	378	695	1279	14,552	352,196
American,	..	760	99	1907	1159	5,036	198,857
Total,		**3040**	**619**	**2916**	**2511**	**21,471**	**622,537**

with a network of agencies. The Irish Presbyterian Church has charge of the Goojaratee country north of Bombay to Kathiawar. The American Presbyterians, in two bands, are evangelizing the valley of the Ganges from Allahabad up to that of the Indus at Lahore and Rawal Pindi. The Welsh Calvinists are in Assam, and the Canadian Presbyterians in the native state of Indore. The Church Missionary Society has the most extensive jurisdiction of all, having vigorous stations especially in the Panjab and Kashmeer, and in Tinnevelli in the far south. The Propagation Society shares Tinnevelli with it, Travancore with the London Missionary Society, and Burma with the Baptists. The English Baptists maintain the work begun by Carey in Bengal and up to Delhi. The General Baptists are most successful in Orissa. The American Baptists have, since Judson's time, done a work among the Karengs of Burma which has extorted the admiration of the coldest officials. The Lutheran and the Basel Missions are chiefly in West, South, and Central India. The English Wesleyans have made Mysore their own, and the Episcopal Methodists of America have taken possession of Oudh. The two great Congregational Societies, of England (London) and America, have spread their enlightening influence over great centres of population, the former especially in Travancore and the latter at Ahmednugger and Western India. The Moravian Mission, true to the old instinct, attempts apparently hopeless work amid the Himalayan snows on the borders of Tibet.

If we look at results, and include **Ceylon**, where the Wesleyan Baptist and Church of England Societies and American Board divide the field, we find that there are this year 660,000 native Christians at 720 stations, with 700 ordained native and 670 foreign and Eurasian missionaries, besides 3000 native lay agents, and contributing for the gospel at the rate of nearly 2 rupees or florins a year per head. The fees from schools and colleges, and the Government grants for efficient secular education, besides, meet all educational expenses except the foreign salaries. If we allow for the **Straits Settlements** where the Presbyterian Church of England is at work, and **Mauritius** where the Church Mission has long had representatives, we arrive at 710,000 as the number of evangelical native Christians in British Asia.

As Duff began the evangelization of the influential Brahmanical castes in 1830, now numbering 17 millions, with marvellous results, India missions have recently entered on the next essential stage of development, that of Christianizing the 120 **millions of women**,

of whom 21 millions are widows. There are now some 500
Foreign and Eurasian women missionaries in India, and 2000
native Christian helpers. They teach 70,000 girls, of whom 10,000
are ladies of caste confined to the **zanana**. In normal and higher
schools the girls of the rising native Christian community receive
an accomplished education, so that one has taken the M.A. degree
of the Calcutta University with honours, and several are studying
for a medical degree. In 1881 the creed and caste census brought
out results in favour of Christianity which startled purely secular
observers and critics, but only confirmed the assertions of Christian
experts :—

Christians (of all Sects) in 1881,		1,862,634.
Sikhs,	1,853,426	Buddhists, . . 3,418,884
Hindus,	187,937,460	Jains, . . . 1,221,896
Demonolaters,	6,426,511	Mohammedans, . 50,121,586

Russian Asia.—By the submission of the Toorkomans of Merv,
just accomplished as the result of steady aggression southwards,
Russia has become the neighbour of British India with only the
protected State of Afghanistan between. From her basis on the
Caspian Sea, at Michaelovsk, Russia has now an easy and uninterrupted road to the Afghan frontier post of Herat, to preserve
which from aggressors we have fought two wars. A railway is
open for 147 English miles from the Caspian to Kizil Arvat, the
line is being made thence for 135 miles to Askabad, and it has
been surveyed thence 185 miles to Saraks and 202 farther to
Herat, which is only 669 from Michaelovsk. For good or evil
Russia dominates the weak power of Persia, and marches with
Afghanistan. Since Vladimir's baptism was completed by Peter
the Great's autocracy, the Russian Romanoffs have been absolute in
the State and intolerant in the Church. But God uses such powers
to prepare the way for His Son. Even Russia must awake or break
up when there will be spiritual as well as political life from the
dead. Her Church cannot itself be said to evangelize while it
stops all others. In Japan one Greek Mission has 13 priests and
1255 converts. The Society of Orthodox Missions works in
Siberia, where, in 1882, it had 3801 converts from Islam and
Paganism. The Moscow Society raised £27,000 last year.

In 1882, the Russian Empire, in 63 governments and 11 territories, had a population of 91,118,514, now increased to 93
millions, against the 315 millions of the British Empire, while the
area of both was much the same, or 8 millions of square miles.

But the Church of Columba and Wiclif is missionary, while that of Constantine and Chrysostom needs to have missionaries sent to it. Meanwhile Russian Asia must still be included in the comparatively small list of lands shut to the gospel.

Portuguese Asia is now confined to small portions of Western India at Goa, of the Malay Archipelago at Timor, and of China at Macao. Where it boasted its compulsory or superficial converts by thousands all over Southern Asia, it now cannot reckon its whole Asiatic subjects at more than a million. Its hierarchy, shorn of the old proportions, counts many caste Christians even among that million, descendants of the nominal converts of Xavier. But practically there is no toleration for others.

French Asia has 2 millions of subjects in Cochin China and Anam, chiefly, and also at Pondicheri in South-east India, but though the rule be republican it is not favourable to evangelical freedom. Still less so is **Spanish** rule in the Philippine Islands, and it affects $4\frac{1}{2}$ millions of subjects.

Dutch Asia includes $23\frac{1}{2}$ millions in the glorious archipelago of the Spice Islands, which Carey's missionaries were evangelizing under Sir Stamford Raffles when Java was given back to Holland after Lord Minto's conquest. We cannot reckon more of these millions than 150,000 as even nominal Christians of the Reformed Church.

China was turned to Buddhism by missionaries from India, and it awaits regeneration to some extent from the same source. China proper consists of 18 provinces, each nearly as large as Great Britain, and all practically open to the Protestant missionary. With Tibet, in which a few Romanist missionaries alone manage to exist in partial disguise, and Manchuria and Inner Mongolia, the empire is as large as Europe with Russia.

These conditions are peculiarly favourable to missionary work as contrasted with India, where they are absent,—There is one written language intelligible wherever Chinamen dwell; there is no caste or hareem exclusiveness such as marks Brahmanical and Mohammedan peoples; the climate and products are those of both temperate and tropical lands; China sends swarms of men all over the surrounding lands and seas from Calcutta to Australia and California, and even South America, who are the busiest and cheapest but most dangerous labourers of the whole East, because of their secret societies and the fact that they leave their wives at home. Once Christianized, the Chinese should become the missionary race of Eastern Asia, as the English-speaking peoples have been made from the West. In the forty years since twelve missionaries and six converts of the London and American Societies met in conference, the year after the cession of the island of Hong-Kong (1842), the evangelical missions have produced these results all over the eighteen provinces. There are 500 foreign missionaries, men and women, sent forth by 13 British and Continental and 11 American Churches and Societies, and working at about a hundred central and 600 out-stations, with 350 native churches, some of them self-supporting and having 100 native pastors of their own. Medical missions have been especially successful, and the time has come for such Christian colleges for the higher education of both the Christian and the non-Christian communities as India has long enjoyed. In 1878 **Dr. Legge** estimated the professedly Christian community at 50,000, and it may now be taken as not less than 73,500, especially since a great famine has in North China as in India given an impetus to the success of evangelical missionaries, who endeared themselves not only to the suffering people but to the officials of the Government.

The Presbyterians at least have formed, by an organic union, a purely Chinese Church, known as the **Ta-hoey** (Classis or Presbytery) of Amoy. The word literally means the Great Assembly; that adopted by the congregations of the London Missionary Society is the **Ho-hoey**, or Harmonious Assembly, and it is to be hoped both will become one. From the apparent absence of obstacles to conversion which exist elsewhere, the progress of Christian missions in China should be more rapid than during the same period in India. But the fall of Brahmanism would seem to be a preliminary to the extension of Christianity all over Southern and Eastern Asia. **Corea** is only this year opened up to the gospel, by treaty, after long intolerance. A Corean noble educated in Japan, where he found Christ, has devoted himself to the enterprise of evangelizing his native land with its estimated 12 millions of people, and he is translating the Scriptures into the language. The United Presbyterian Church of Scotland has a mission there. Already there are converts, besides those made by the Roman Catholic Church.

Japan is as large as four-fifths of France, with nearly the same population, or 35 millions. The religions are Shintoism, the worship of famous ancestors as the incarnations of the Supreme Spirit, and Buddhism. The empire consists geographically of the four islands, of Yezo; Nippon, the central and most important, with Tokiyo (formerly Yedo), the capital, as large as Calcutta or Bombay; Kiushiu, the south-western island; and Shikoku, the southern island. The whole is divided into thirty-five ken or provinces, under the absolute ruler the Mikado, who governs through a great council, after the model of the third French Empire. America surprised the country into forming a treaty in 1854, and in 1859 sent the first Protestant missionaries to its people. For thirteen years till 1872 the "vile Jesus doctrine" was prohibited on pain of death, but the missionaries taught in Government schools and privately, and there was a growing hope of toleration as foreign influence and trade prevailed. In 1854 there was not one Japanese who had justifying faith in Jesus Christ. Soon after, when a gentleman of rank found an English New Testament floating in the Bay of Yedo after one of the English or American ships had left, this led him to send to Shanghai for a Chinese copy. He applied, for its interpretation, to one of the American missionaries, **Rev. Dr. G. F. Verbeck**, being "filled with admiration, overwhelmed with emotion, and taken captive by the nature and life of Jesus Christ." This gentleman of fifty and two friends were the first Japanese to receive true Christian baptism. After 1872, hundreds of Japanese youths were allowed to study in Europe and America, where many became Christians. A week of prayer resulted in the formation of the first Japanese Christian Church, which was organized at Yokohama with eleven members.

The American Reformed, American Presbyterian, and Scottish United Presbyterian missionaries joined to form one indigenous Presbyterian Church, as in China, on the establishment of a church in Tokiyo, the capital, but failed, in 1874, to effect a union with the Congregational Mission at Kobe and Osaka. **This Union Church of Christ in Japan** (Nip'pon Kirisuto It'chi Kiyo Kuwai) was fully constituted in 1877, under the consent of the home churches, with its own Presbyterian form of government, based on the Synod of Dort, Westminster Assembly and Heidelberg Catechism, its directory for worship and book of discipline. It has a theological school, and indigenous presbyteries in which foreign missionaries sit by virtue of their office, but the missionaries as such are not there recognised, having their own council. Presbyterian polity has been eagerly adopted by the Japanese

Christians. This Japanese Church consisted at the end of 1883 of a synod and 3 presbyteries, having 31 organized churches, 89 preaching places, 20 ordained and 4 non-ordained foreign missionaries, 16 single women missionaries, 21 ordained and 14 licensed native ministers, 33 students at various stages, and 2500 members, of whom 859 are women, who contributed 961 dollars for the gospel. Some of the native churches are self-supporting. The New Testament has been translated, chiefly by the **Rev. Dr. Hepburn** of this Church, and the Old Testament version is about to be completed. The United Church plans a mission to Corea. From its insular character and the early huddling of the foreigners together at Yokohama, and from its people having only one language and being able to read and write, union of this kind was from the first more easy than elsewhere. In all there are some 75 foreign and 50 native ordained missionaries in Japan, representing the three churches thus united, the American Episcopal, the Methodist and Baptist Churches, and the Church of England. Each mission has schools. Christian literature is being supplied largely by educated natives in defence of the gospel. In the ten years since the missionaries were allowed fairly to influence the people, some 5000 converts have been gathered to Christ, and there is now a community 13,000 strong. There is a prospect and a need of rapid growth if the secular progress of the people under foreign influences is to be pure and elevating. The Buddhist priests are fighting for their faith, studying even the Bible for controversial purposes; but the struggle there, as in Christendom itself, will more and more be with secularism, sensuality, and philosophical scepticism.

Siam, with 6 millions, is being evangelized by the American Presbyterians and Baptists.

Turkey, shorn of territory both Christian and Mohammedan in Europe and Asia by the Treaty of Berlin, still unhappily consists directly of $20\frac{1}{2}$ millions, covering $1\frac{1}{5}$ millions of square miles of the lands which were first Christianized and sent forth missionaries until the Mohammedan apostasy began. Of the population $4\frac{1}{2}$ millions are still in Europe, in 4 vilayets or provinces, and 16 millions are in Asia in 12 vilayets. In 1839 and in 1856 after the Crimean War, the Sultan was compelled to concede religious freedom to his Christian subjects and the right to hold land, along with other rights never really enforced. In 1878 the "Convention of Defensive Alliance between Great Britain and Turkey" placed Asiatic Turkey under British protection and leased Cyprus to us, the terms being that we defend Turkey "by force of arms" if necessary, while the Sultan is pledged to reforms chiefly for protection of the Christians. Thus far the Convention has been a dead letter. After the massacres of 1860, Lord Dufferin secured a special administrative system for the Lebanon under a Christian Governor-General. Practically no Mussulman may become a Christian under pain of death, and Christian work is confined to the followers of the corrupt Eastern churches, Greek, Armenian, Nestorian, and Coptic. Dr. Claudius Buchanan led the Church Missionary Society to begin the evangelization of the East from Malta as a centre in 1811; its efforts are now directed to the Arabic-speaking population in the **Holy Land**, and to the Turkish-speaking population of **Constantinople** (700,000 population). The American Presbyterian Board conducts the Syrian Protestant College at **Beiroot** (70,000 population), and has as stations besides, Abeih, Sidon, Tripoli, and Zahleh. The American Board (Congregational) has done even greater work in Constantinople; it has colleges there (Robert) at Smyrna (150,000 population), Aintab, and Harpoot, with seminaries for women at Samokov, Broosa (37,000 population), Mavisa, Marsovan, Marash (35,000 population), and Mardin. The Bible has been translated into Arabic and Osmanli-Turkish, and much pure literature. Medical missions have been planted not only there, but by the Edinburgh Society in great centres like **Nazareth** and **Damascus**. The base of the Lebanon Missions of the Free Church of Scotland and Lebanon Schools Society, under the Rev. Dr. Carslaw, a medical missionary, is Beiroot, and their centre is **Shweir**. A Syrian Evangelical Church has been formed, chiefly by the Americans, with several presbyteries. **Jerusalem** (28,000 population) has been a field worked by many agents since the first Anglican bishop, Gobat, was appointed in 1846. The quasi-Mohammedan Druses, and the Maronites, Metawallees, Badaween, and Gypsies, have all been influenced. There are churches also at **Salt** (Ramoth-Gilead) and **Gaza** and in the **Hauran**. Besides these principal agencies, there are many others directed to the Jews at **Safet** and Hebron, and many schools, which lead to the conviction that brotherly organization would at once save wasted labour and produce better results. There are 200 foreign missionaries in Palestine and Syria. We assume the number of evangelical native Christians in the Turkish Empire as, at most, 100,000. Of these, very few indeed were Jews and Mohammedans by birth; Mohammedan converts have to flee to Great Britain, not only from Turkey but from Egypt. The political changes begun by the Crimean War and hastened by the Treaty of Berlin and the Egyptian War, are more rapidly preparing the way of the Lord in our day than in any since the Crusades.

Persia has been gradually reduced by Russian aggression and Mohammedan misrule to a desert, with a population variously estimated at from $4\frac{1}{2}$ to $7\frac{1}{2}$ millions, covering a country the size of half Europe. The majority of these are *Shiite* Mohammedans, or the dissenting followers of the fourth Kaliph Ali, who hold that he ought immediately to have succeeded his father-in-law Mohammed, and who worship his son Husain as a martyr. Almost all the rest of Islam are *Soonnees* who follow the first three Kaliphs and the traditions. A few Parsees are still left, and, with the Jews, are oppressed. The Armenian and Nestorian Christians, numbering 66,000, are better treated. Among these chiefly the American Presbyterian Board conduct successful missions at Ooroomiah and Tabreez in the west, at Tehran, Hamadan, and Resht in the east; the Church Mission is at Julfa, the Armenian suburb of Ispahan. There Dr. Bruce has amended Henry Martyn's Persian translation of the New Testament. In 1747 two Moravians made the first and unsuccessful attempt to reach the Parsees of Kerman, and the Greek Church of Russia drove out the Scottish and Basel missionaries who, from Sheeshab in the Caucasus, sought to influence Persia. Of these one was the learned controversialist **Dr. Pfander**, who removed to India.

Arabia, which was the scene of Christian kingdoms and churches in the north and in the south-west corner, has, since the *Hejra* of Mohammed 1301 years ago, been not only itself the headquarters of Mohammedan intolerance and sensuality at Mecca, but the fruitful source of Antichristian error to the West, as Indian Buddhism has been for the same time to the East of Asia. The area is somewhat larger and the population less than that of Persia. The Mohammedan *Haj* or pilgrimage to Mecca annually spreads the fanaticism. No missionary or Christian dare enter the city, or even travel in the country, save in disguise, as the travellers Burton and Palgrave have done. At **Aden** only, as a British possession, is there Christian worship, and from that centre much might be done for the Jews, as Dr. Wilson of Bombay long ago urged.

AUSTRALASIA AND THE SOUTH SEAS.

Australasia in all its vastness, from being a land of savage blacks, has, like America, been made by the British a great Christian Dominion, the seven colonies of which are soon to be federated. In half a century, over an area of nearly three Europes, the English-speaking population has grown to be above 3 millions, and is likely to equal the 50 millions of the United States, for only one-twentieth of the land has yet been taken up. Except in New Zealand, the few blacks have almost disappeared, but these, numbering 40,000, have not been neglected by missionaries. The Maories of **New Zealand** were early Christianized, passed through a time of national revolt provoked by the seizure of their lands and the *Hau-Hau* superstition, and now form a Christian community of 30,000.

South Sea Islands.—In the third of the globe covered by the Pacific Ocean, between Asia and the Americas, there are 17 groups of islands, 9 of which have been altogether and the others partially converted to Christ practically in fifty years. The Eastern groups, or Polynesia proper, are inhabited by a tall brown race called *Sawaioris* from the principal island; and the Western groups next Asia by a small black *Papuan* race. The *Tarapons* are, as to colour, size, and position, between these two classes. The vices carried by foreign ships and the demands of the labour traffic for Australia are doing much to reduce in numbers the somewhat small populations of these islands, on which Christianity has won some of its greatest triumphs over cannibalism, idolatry, and sensuality. The Hawaians, first evangelized by the American Congregational Board, have long been missionaries to others. The London, Wesleyan, Presbyterian, and Propagation Societies have divided with it the whole field. **New Guinea** is fast being opened up by missionary pioneers like Mr. Macfarlane.

The Two Americas.—The diminishing native races of North and South are evangelized not only by the evangelical churches beside them, but by the Church Missionary Society in the North away to British Columbia on the Pacific, and by the South American Mission in the forbidding region around Cape Horn, in Patagonia and in Uruguay. The negroes of **Jamaica** and the West Indies under English-speaking influences have been Christianized since the Moravians and Wesley began the work a century and a half ago. Many coolies from India have taken to the sugar colonies their idolatry, and missionaries are grappling with that.

AFRICA AND MADAGASCAR.

With an area of 11 millions of square miles, or eight Indias, Africa presents a population of some 200 millions. Mr. Cust classifies these in 6 families, as Semitic, Hamitic, Nuba-Fulah, Negro, Bantu or Kafir-Zulu, and Hottentot, speaking, so far as is known, 438 languages and 153 dialects, or 591 in all. Next to the Negro the Kafir class contains the largest number, or 168 languages and 55 dialects. The Bible, in whole or portions, has been translated into 5 Semitic, 8 Hamitic, 4 Nuba-Fulah, 20 Negro, and 18 Bantu or Kafir-Zulu languages, and also into the one Khoi-Khoi Nama tongue of the Hottentots. As yet the good work is only beginning, except in the case of the Arabic, Coptic, Zulu, and Kafir Bibles. Among the savage races of Africa, even more than in the case of Wiclif-Tyndale's and Luther's translations in England and Germany, the Bible has a combined literary and spiritual power.

There are now 35 Protestant Missionary Churches and Societies at work in Africa. The earliest attempts made to convert the Bushmen of the South by the Moravians, and the Negroes of the West by the Scottish missionaries, were abandoned from Dutch opposition and from ignorance of the malarial climates of the coast. But in the past sixty years 600,000 natives of Africa have been added to Christendom.

Egypt is the scene of the triumphs of the United Presbyterian Church of America. At Cairo, Asyoot, and the Thebaid, El Fayoom, Monsoora, and Alexandria, and many smaller stations, the dead Coptic Church has yielded an evangelical community of 8000 in 23 churches, and some Mohammedans have received courage to confess Christ. The Church Missionary Society has resumed its labours there. Confined to the Nile delta and the Red Sea littoral, under British influence the kingdom of Egypt should pass out of the wars and confusion of centuries into the light and peace of gospel lands. Amid all the tumult the native churches have remained stedfast. **Abyssinia** will share in this near future after past vain efforts by **Krapf** and others to quicken its Church. The Jewish and Swedish missionaries have made some converts. In Tripoli, Tunis, Algeria, and Morocco the Jews are cared for by the London Society.

West Africa is dotted with successful mission stations from Sierra Leone, if not Senegal, by the Gold and Slave Coasts and the Congo or Livingstone delta down to Cape Town. A Negro bishop, Dr. Crowther, once a slave boy, and republican Liberia point to the future of the indigenous Negro race. Here there are at least 110,000 native Christians.

South Africa is, however, the scene of the most prosperous missionary effort, whether we look at spiritual or secondary results, owing to British influence and the work of men like Dr. J. Stewart of Lovedale. Among Kafirs chiefly, but also Hottentots, who number in all $1\frac{1}{4}$ millions, we find at the present time a Christian community numbering a sixth of the whole, or 200,000.

East and Central Africa.—Rising to the lake and plateau region above the unhealthy coast, we have seen, since Dr. Livingstone's death, the Scottish, London, and Episcopal Missions from the East Coast, and the English Baptist and American Congregationalists from the West Coast approaching each other by the Zambesi, Congo, and Nile, till highways of the gospel, from east to west and south to north, are being tracked out. For years these missions must be in the pioneering stage; but already vigorous native churches have been formed by some of them, and the first-fruits may be reckoned at 2000.

Madagascar, coming next to Australia and Borneo in size, has four times the area of England and Wales, and a Malay population estimated at $4\frac{1}{2}$ millions. Whether we look at the history of the reception of Christianity especially by the dominant Hovas, to their constancy in persecution lasting for a quarter of a century, or to the progress of the gospel and of civilisation since that ceased in 1862, we may claim Madagascar as the most remarkable illustration of the rapid efficacy of the gospel among savage races. The Christians number upwards of a quarter of a million, and the attempts of France to destroy Hova independence have thus far only called out Christian virtues while consolidating national patriotism.

The Position.—Christendom, consisting of 440 millions, stands marshalled against or scattered among the rest of the human race, or 1000 millions. If Christendom were itself pure or in earnest, Christ's work would be done, and the history of Christian Missions would come to a speedy and a glorious end. But, on the one side, 180 millions of Mohammedans and Jews, Abraham's children, have not been touched by the message of the one God through His Son; on the other, Christians, in virtue of a profession of the faith, enjoy the material advantages and power which it gives, but must trust to the divinely persuasive and leavening influence of the kingdom which is not of this world. If we confine ourselves to the 160 millions of Reformed Christians, then the mass to be influenced and won to pure Christianity is 1280 millions. But were these 160 millions in earnest, the task would not be more difficult, from the Lord's teaching. The most hopeful estimate cannot go further than this, that in the most evangelical churches not more than a third, and in the least active not more than a tenth, of the communicants pray, or give, or energize in any way for the nations whom the Lord charged every one of His members to disciple. If so few have in so short a time as a century brought $2\frac{3}{4}$ millions of native converts to the truth at this hour, and have pioneered and civilised far beyond these, what would not be the result if at least the two-thirds of all evangelical communicants, whom we are entitled to expect to pray and work, remembered the missionary charge and claimed fulfilment of the missionary promise?

The Future.—From the political side the new world seems to be at the beginning of its history. The English-speaking empires of Great Britain and the United States go on expanding. The Canadian and Australasian Dominions are in their infancy. The Indian Empire compels reluctant statesmen to lengthen the cords and strengthen the tent-pegs. From Scotland, by the Mediterranean and Red Sea to the Himalayas and the Pacific Ocean, is one missionary highway. Japan and China are bursting with the buds of promise, like the forests of an arctic spring-time. The great islands of Borneo and New Guinea are being dragged into the mighty march. Only Islam and Judaism remain, now sullen and now actively hostile, as anticipating the inevitable for them also. From the spiritual side we watch God's haste, the one day, as the uncultured races flock into the kingdom; God's leisure, the thousand years, as hoary Brahmanism and its Buddhist offspring slowly yield. Every year rebukes our little faith by the large and ever larger answer which God gives it. If the century has produced a new earth, such are the triumphs of science and civilisation, it has not the less revealed a new heaven to the churches, when we contrast the Christendom of 1784 with that of 1884.

Daily is Christ coming to the world and to every Christian. The development of Christian missions in the future depends on the faith and obedience with which the Church and its members apply the lesson of the past, as taught by Jewish seer (Zech. iv. 6) and Christian apostle (1 Tim. ii. 4: "Not by might, nor by power, but by my Spirit, saith the Lord of hosts;" "God our Saviour willeth that all men should be saved and come to the knowledge of the truth."

CHAPTER XVIII.

SHORT BIBLIOGRAPHY OF MISSIONS.

ON its scientific and even popular sides the literature of missions is meagre. Theologians have neglected the subject. Church historians have, with the splendid exception of Neander, written as if the Church still tarried at Jerusalem—existed only for Christendom. Missionaries have done most for the subject, but they are men of action and toil, though more distinguished also in letters in proportion to their number than ministers not in the front of the battle. Purely literary men and artists have not yet awoke to the wealth of materials to which the history of missions is adding every decade. Since Southey and Heber (1820) no one has given us even a missionary hymn that will live. Edinburgh has a statue of David Livingstone, and his dust rests in Westminster Abbey, because he was the explorer that he might be the missionary. Portraits of Wilson and Duff adorn the hall of the New College of Edinburgh, and the memory of Henry Martyn will be perpetuated in the new cathedral at Truro, and in Simeon's Church at Cambridge. But even such sectarian honours have not been paid by the Baptists to William Carey, whom it has been left to a purely scientific agricultural society in Calcutta to commemorate by a marble bust. The day is at hand when all that will be changed, and the nation may fitly recognise its noblest dead.

GENERAL.

A.D.

Isaiah, with Commentaries by Rev. T. C. Cheyne, D.D., and Dr. Plumptre.

63. **Luke**: The Gospel and the Acts of the Apostles, with Commentary by Dr. Plumptre, edited by Bishop Ellicott.

97. **Paul, Peter, John**: Epistles and Revelation, with Notes by Bishop Lightfoot, Bishop Ellicott, Canon Westcott, Bishop Barry.

A.D.
325. **The Fathers**, translated, in Ante-Nicene Christian Library, and Dods' Augustine. (Clark.)
180. **Dean Merivale**, History of the Romans under the Empire. 8 vols. 1865.
438. —— The Conversion of the Roman Empire. 1864.
1066. —— The Conversion of the Northern Nations. 1866.
Neander, Life of Christ.
1415. —— General History of the Christian Religion and Church. 9 vols. Translation. (Bohn.)
—— History of the Planting and Training of the Christian Church by the Apostles. 2 vols.
—— Memorials of Christian Life in the Early and Middle Ages.
1853. **Brown**, History of the Propagation of Christianity among the Heathen since the Reformation. 3rd edition. 3 vols.
1871. **Grundemann**, Allgemeiner Missions-Atlas. 1867–71. Gotha.
1881. **Warneck**, Article on Protestant Missions in Herzog's *Real-Encyklopädie*, translated, since this book was written, by Professor T. Smith, D.D. 1884.
1882. **Thompson**, Moravian Missions, with Map. Andover, U.S. 1883.
1884. —— Kleiner Missions-Atlas. (Coln and Stuttgart.)
1883. **R. Young**, Modern Missions and Light in Lands of Darkness. 2 vols.
1884. **W. Fleming Stevenson, D.D.**, Lectures on Missions. (In the press.)
—— Praying and Working.

INDIA.

1792. [1] **William Carey**, An Enquiry into the Obligations of Christians to use Means for the Conversion of the Heathen. (Leicester; reprinted there also in 1822—very rare.)
1794. **Melville Horne**, Letters on Missions addressed to the Protestant Ministers of the British Churches. (London; reprinted at Andover, Massachussets, in 1815—rare.)
1812. [1] **Henry Martyn**, The Letters and Sargent's Memoir.
1831. **James Hough**, History of Christianity in India from the Commencement of the Christian Era. (London; 5 vols. —3 and 4 are rare.)

[1] Of special interest and value.

A.D.
1837. John Marshman, **C.S.I.**, The Life and Times of Carey, Marshman, and Ward. 2 vols. (Also popular edition, Strahan. 1864.)
1839. [1] **Duff**, Missions the Chief End of the Christian Church. 1st edition.
1850. **Adoniram Judson**, Life, by his son. 1883.
1834. **William Carey, D.D.**, Life by George Smith, LL.D. (In preparation.)
1875. **John Wilson, D.D., F.R.S.**, of Bombay, Life by the same. 2nd edition. 1879.
1878. **Alexander Duff, D.D., LL.D.**, Life by the same. 2 vols. (New York edition in 1 vol. is the best.)
1874. **Dr. Robson**, Hinduism and its Relations to Christianity.
1883. **M. A. Sherring**, The History of Protestant Missions in India from their Commencement in 1706 to 1871, with Mission Map. (Mr. Storrow is preparing an edition to end of 1883.)
Church Missionary Atlas, 31 Maps. 1879.

CHINA AND JAPAN.

1271. **Colonel H. Yule, LL.D.**, "Marco Polo" and "Cathay."
1834. **Robert** Morrison, Memoirs by his Widow. 2 vols.
W. C. Burns, Life of, by Prof. Islay Burns.
Legge, Edkins, Williamson. (All that they have translated and written is of value.)
1878. Minutes of Japan Convention of Missionaries.
1880. **Gracey**, China, Outline Missionary Series. (Snow.)
Dixon, The Land of the Morning, Japan and its People.
Mrs. Bishop (Isabella Bird), Travels in Japan.
1883. **Gilmour**, Among the Mongols.
Dods, Mohammed, Buddha, and Christ. 1877.

AUSTRALASIA AND SOUTH SEAS.

1799. A Missionary Voyage in the Ship *Duff*.
1865. **Rufus Anderson**, The Hawaiian Islands, their Progress and Condition under Missionary Labours. (Boston.)
1843. **John Williams**, Memoirs of, by Prout.
—— Narrative of Missionary Enterprises.
1875. **A. W. Murray**, Forty Years' Mission Work in Polynesia and New Guinea.

[1] Of special interest and value.

1878. **Selwyn, G. A.**, Bishop, Memoir by Tucker. 2 vols. (See Mr. Gladstone's Review of Bishop Patteson, Selwyn's successor, in *Gleanings*, vol. ii.)
Geddie, Life of. (Toronto.)
Steel, Dr., The New Hebrides.
Whitmee, Polynesia, Outline Missionary Series. (Snow.)

AMERICA.

A.D.
John Eliot, Life by Dr. John Wilson. 1828.
David Brainerd, Life, by J. Edwards.
1853. **Allen F. Gardener**, Commander, R.N., Memoir.
1883. **Croil**, The Missionary Problem. (Toronto.)

AFRICA AND MADAGASCAR.

1871. **David Livingstone**, Blaikie's Personal Life of, and all his own Writings.
1881. **Robert Moffat**, A Life's Labours in South Africa.
1877. **E. D. Young**, Nyassa, a Journal of Adventure whilst establishing the Settlement of Livingstonia.
1876. **Major Malan**, South African Missions.
1878. **J. E. Carlyle**, South Africa and its Mission Fields.
1883. **R. N. Cust**, A Sketch of the Modern Languages of Africa, with Language Maps. 2 vols.
Sibree, South Africa, Outline Missionary Series. (Snow.)
———— Madagascar, ditto.
1881. **Matthews**, Nine Years' Mission Work, with Historical Introduction.
1880. Ten Years' Review of Mission Work in Madagascar, with Map.

GENERAL MISSIONARY CONFERENCES.

1855. **Bengal**, 284 pages. Calcutta. (Baptist Mission Press.)
1862-63. **Panjab**, 398 pages. Lahore. (Lodiana Press.)
1872-73.[1] **Allahabad**, First Decennial, with Map. (London, Seeley.)
1879. [1] **South India and Ceylon**, Bangalore. 2 vols. (Madras, Addison & Co. 1880.)
1882-83. **Calcutta**, Second Decennial, with Map.

[1] Of special interest and value.

1877. ¹ **China,** Shanghai, with Map. (Presbyterian Mission Press, 1878.)
1878. **Japan,** Tokiyo, Minutes of Convention.
1860. **Liverpool.** (James Nisbet, 1860.)
1878. **London,** Mildmay Park. (John F. Shaw, 1879.)

ENGLISH PERIODICALS.

Church Missionary Intelligencer, Monthly.

The Missionary Review published at Princeton, U.S., Two-Monthly.

The Gospel in all Lands, Weekly. Baltimore, U.S.

The Christian Express, Monthly. Lovedale.

Africa, Quarterly. (Partridge.)

Each Missionary Church and Society has its own periodical, generally a monthly, but not one of either the Protestant or Romish magazines is so written as to be of durable interest, except the first, which represents the Church Missionary Society. The second is an independent American critic of all missions and missionary administration at home. The one weak and unworthy feature of the administration of missions, both at home and abroad, is their relation to the press, to literature. Since the *Calcutta Review* (quarterly) ceased in 1862 to be conducted by evangelical editors, from Sir John Kaye and Dr. Duff to Sir Richard Temple, missions have found no adequate literary representation. Dr. Duff had organized a quarterly under Canon Tristram and an able staff for this purpose, when a publishing difficulty arrested a movement which ought to be delayed no longer. All that is wanted is the same co-operation among the home missionary agencies as that which gives tenfold power to their representatives who work as brothers in the face of the common foe. Meanwhile missionaries of ability are driven to the *Proceedings* of the Royal Geographical and other learned Societies for the statement of facts and even of principles which can be there treated only on the non-spiritual side. A good catholic or evangelical monthly or quarterly for the discussion of missionary questions, with a weekly for the diffusion of foreign gospel intelli-

¹ Of special interest and value.

gence, is the immediate need and pressing want of missions. Such periodicals would keep the missionaries, European, American and native, *en rapport* with the peoples and the churches of Christendom. No expenditure of money or time or literary ability could measure the results, in prayer and effort of all kinds for the realization of the Lord's own petition taught to every disciple—
Thy Kingdom come.

Christianity the Reason of History.—The latest conclusions of historical criticism are in harmony with the whole course of Christian missions from Abraham to the present hour. While the old historians chronicled only dynasties and wars, and the late Mr. Green sought for the reason of events and of progress in the people, the Cambridge Professor of Modern History finds the motive power in the expansion of the nation best fitted to civilise the world.[1] That is, God in history has been and is directly working out the evangelization of the race. History, in a high sense, is the record of missions as these appear to the spiritual as well as philosophical eye.

Taking our stand on the Creed given by our Lord Himself, as each of us seeks to carry out the Charge in which it is embodied, —*Go ye therefore and make disciples of all the nations, baptizing them in the name of the Father and of the Son and of the Holy Ghost*,—we joyfully and lovingly add, with all Christendom since the fourth century,—"I believe in the holy catholic church, the communion of saints, the forgiveness of sins, the resurrection of the body, and the life eternal."

[1] *The Expansion of England*, by Professor Seeley.

INDEX.

ABERCROMBIE, Dr. J., 176.
Abraham, 7, 13, 161.
Abyssinia, 122, 209.
Accadian deities, 10.
Adalbert, 97.
Adamnan, 67.
Aden, 185, 190, 207.
Æbba, 71.
Ælfred, 90.
Æthelbert, 72.
Afghanistan, 201.
Africa, 26, 104, 125, 153, 209.
Aidan, 70, 75.
Airthrey, 170.
Aitchison, Sir C., 140.
Akbar, 151.
Alaric, 49, 80.
Albanus, 61.
Alcuin, 62, 89.
Alexander, Bishop, 174.
Alexandria, 54.
Algeria, 153.
America, 111, 208; missions, 178; churches, 191.
Amharic, 122.
Anderson, Mrs., 177.
Andover College, 178.
Andrea, 123.
Angel of Jehovah, 17.
Angelology, 4.
Anselm, 109.
Anskar, 91.
Anthony, St., 145.
Antioch, the Pisidian, 39.
Antioch, the Syrian, 36, 39, 53.
Antonines, 49.
Apollos, 41.
Apostles, 1.
Arabia, 207.
Argyle, Marquis of, 177.

Arianism, 77; confession, 78.
Armagh, 65.
Armenian Church, 79.
Arndt, 123.
Asia, Missions, 197.
Asser, 91.
Associations, Missionary, 186.
Asturias, 109.
Athanasius, 78, 145.
Augsburg Confession, 144.
Augustin of Canterbury, 71.
Augustine of Hippo, 4.
Australia, 130, 190, 208.

BEDA, 89.
Baldæus, 122.
Barnabas the Apostle, 36.
Bartholomew, 55.
Bartolomeo, Fra, 151.
Basel Missionary Society, 181.
Beiroot, 206.
Belgian king, 153.
Bell, Benjamin, 176.
Bennie, J., 170.
Bereta, 72.
Berlin Academy of Sciences, 124.
Berlin Missionary Society, 18.
Bernard of Clairvaux, 109.
Beschi, 150.
Beyroot, 206.
Bible Societies, 172, 179.
Bible Society, British and Foreign, 172; National, 173.
Bibliography, 213.
Bihé, 178.
Bland, Mrs. 135.
Bobbio, 84.
Bœmish, 129.
Bogatzky, 126.
Bogue, Dr., 166.

Bogoris, 97.
Bohemia, 97.
Boniface, 86.
Bourne, 137.
Boyle, Robert, 135.
Braidwood, Mrs., 177.
Brainerd, 130, 137.
Bridget of Sweden, 148.
Brigid, 65.
Britain, 59.
British Church, 65; Society for Jews, 174
Brito, 150.
Buddhism, 56, 204.
Burmans, 179.
Burns, W. C., 189.
Butler, Dr., 179.

CÆDMON, 76.
Cæsarius of Arles, 83.
Cairns, Dr., 50.
Cairns, Lord, 172.
Calcutta, 160, 175.
Calcutta Review, 217.
Caldwell, Bishop, 175.
Calvin, 119, 147.
Calvinistic Methodists, 175.
Campbell, John, 168, 170.
Canaan, 10.
Canada, 190.
Canterbury, 72.
Captives as missionaries, 60.
Carey, William, 157, 213.
Catechumens' School, 55.
Cathay, 102.
Central Africa, 210.
Ceylon, 200.
Chalmers, Thomas, 184, 186.
Chambers, W., 142.
Charlemagne, 91.
Charters, East India Company's, 140.
Chartier, 119.
Chater of Olney, 158.
Chaucer, 38.
Chichester, Earl of, 171.
China, 53, 56, 152, 190, 202.
Chinese rites, 152.
Christian David, 128.
Christian Vernacular Society, 174.
Christians, The name, 57.
Chrysostom, 80.
Church Missionary Society, 171.
City of God, 13.
Clement of Alexandria, 55.
Clement of Rome, 59, 97.
Clement the Scot, 88.
Clotilda, 82.

Clovis, 82.
Code, Theodosian, 57, 58.
Codex Argenteus, 79.
Coke, Dr., 138.
Colbert, 152.
Coldstream, Dr. J., 176.
Coleridge, 5.
Coligny, 119.
Colman, 75.
Colonial Churches, 190.
Columba, 65.
Columbanus, 70, 84.
Columbus, 112.
Comenius, 123.
Communicants and Missions, 211.
Congo, 210.
Constantine, 57.
Constantinople, 53, 206.
Cook, Captain, 157, 167.
Cop, 147.
Copenhagen College, 125.
Coptic Church, 209.
Corbie, 91.
Corea, 203.
Cornwallis, Lord, 143.
Corporation for Propagation of the Gospel, 135.
Coryate, 140.
Cosmas, 56.
Council of Jerusalem, 40; of Nicæa, 58; of Constantinople, 58; of Trent, 113, 146.
Counter Reformation, 146.
Covenant, Missionary, 11.
Covenanters, 133.
Creed, The, 218.
Cromwell, 135.
Crowther, Bishop, 210.
Crusades, 100.
Culdees, 67.
Cullen, Rev. G. D., 176.
Cunobelinus, 60.
Cushman, 135.
Cust, Mr. R. N., 209.
Cuthbert, 76.
Cyrillus, 96.

DAMASCUS, 206.
Daniel, 20.
Danish-Halle Mission, 124; Missionary Society, 180.
Dante, 102.
Darien Expedition, 133.
David, 18.
Denmark, 92.
Dinajpore, 160.
Disraeli, 109.

INDEX.

Dober, 129.
Dominican Missions, 102.
Domitian, 49.
Domitilla, 49.
Douglas of Cavers, 176.
Douglas, Rev. Dr. Carstairs, 190.
Dubois, Abbe, 148.
Duff, Alexander, 4, 128, 142, 184, 213; Ship, 168.
Dundas, 170.
Dutch Missions, 122, 202.

EAST INDIA COMPANY, 138, 144.
Edinburgh, 75; Medical Missionary Society, 176.
Edward VI., 139.
Edwardes, Sir H., 140.
Edwards, Jonathan, 5, 137, 156.
Egede, 127.
Egypt, 209.
Eligius of Noyon, 83.
Eliot, John, 136.
England and Missions, 133; Presbyterian Church, 189.
Ephesus, 42.
Erasmus, 110, 114; his Ecclesiastes, 115.
Ernan, 66.
Erskine, Dr., 168.
Eskimos, 127.
Established Church of Scotland, 188.
Eurasians, 177.
Europe's First Missionary, 40.
Evangelical Eclectic Society, 170.
Evangelical Magazine, 166.
Evangelist, 2.
Ewing, Greville, 168.

FINNIAN, 65.
Fordyce, Rev. J., 187.
Fountain, Mr., 161.
Franciscan Missions, 102, 108.
Francis of Assisi, 101.
Franke, 123, 126.
Franks, 81.
Free Church of Scotland's Missions, 55, 170, 184.
French Missions, Romanist, 149, 152, 202, 210.
Frey, G. C., 174.
Fridigern, 77.
Fridolin, 70.
Friedrich IV. of Denmark, 124.
Friend of India newspaper, 163.
Friends, Society of, 176.
Froissart, 38.
Fulda, 88.

Fuller, Andrew, 156.
Fulness of the Time, 23.
Fursæus, 75.

Gall, St., 70, 84.
Gallican liberties, 83.
Gambier, Admiral, 171.
Gauzbert, 93.
General Assembly, the First, 41.
Gerhard, 123.
German Missionary Societies, 181.
Germanus of Auxerre, 83.
Gibbon, 50.
Gilbert, Sir H., 139.
Gildas, 60.
Gladstone, Mr. W. E., 24, 216.
Glasgow Missionary Society, 169.
Gnostic heresy, 43.
Goa, 147, 151.
Gobat, Bishop, 174.
Godthaab, 127.
Gordons of Eromanga, 190.
Gossner Missionary Society, 181.
Goths, 77.
Grant, Charles, 142, 171; his sons, 143.
Great Britain, 59.
Greek Church, 100, 154, 201.
Green, J. R., 86, 213.
Greenland, 127, 129.
Gregory, Thaumaturgus, 52.
Gregory the Great, 71.
Gregory of Utrecht, 89.
Greig, Peter, 168.
Grotius, 122.
Grundler, 125.
Gustavus Vasa, 119.
Gutzlaff, 130.

HACKLETON, 156.
Hadrian, 54.
Hakon, 93.
Haldane, James, 168.
Haldane, Robert, 170.
Hall (Bombay), 178.
Hall, Robert, 157.
Hallock, Dr., 179.
Hardcastle, J., 167.
Harold, Klak, 92.
Heathenism, 14, 16.
Heber, 35, 213.
Henrietta Home, 177.
Hepburn, Dr., 205.
Hermannsburg Missionary Society, 181.
Herrnhut, 128; New, 129.
Hexapla, The, 56.
Heyling, 122.
Hiacomes, 137.

Hilary of Arles, 83.
Hilda, 75.
History and Missions, 6, 217.
Hogg, Rev. Dr., 191.
Homoousion, 58.
Honoratus, 83.
Hoornbeek, 122.
Hottentots, 180.
Hovas, 210.
Hughes, R. Joseph, 172.
Huguenots, 119.
Hungary, 98.
Hunter, Rev. T., 188.
Huss, 113.
Hutten, Von, 145.
Hyde, 136.
Hymn, Columba's, 68.
Hymn, First Missionary, 34, 126.
Hymn, Patrick's, 64.
Hypatia, 54.

IGNATIUS, 53.
India, 111, 124, 138, 147, 150, 174, 185, 197.
Ingalls, Mrs., 179.
Inglis, Dr., 184.
Innes, Dr., 170.
Inquisition, 109.
International Association for Africa, 153.
Iona, 66.
Inverness, 66.
Ireland, Presbyterian Church, 189.
Irenæus, 81.
Irish Church, 62, 65.
Irish Romanist Missions, 151.
Isaac, 17.
Isaiah, 20.

JACOB, 18.
Jamaica, 169, 208.
James VI., 135; the Just, 34, 53.
Japan, 152, 203.
Jäschke, 130.
Jerome, 80; of Prag, 113.
Jerusalem, 47, 53, 206.
Jesuits, Order of, 146.
JESUS CHRIST, 25.
Jews, 109, 174.
John the Baptist, 30; the Divine, 30, 42.
Jonah, 16, 72.
Joshua, 18.
Judah, 18.
Judaism, 15, 22, 47.
Judson, 178.
Jugganath, 165.

Julius Cæsar, 81.
Junius, 122.
Justin Martyr, 53.

KAFIR MISSIONS, 170.
Karengs, 179, 200.
Kaye, Sir John, 217.
Kentigern, 61.
Kettering, 157, 159.
Kiernander, 142.
Kildare, 65.
Kilian, 70, 84.
Kilpatrick, 62.
Kingdom of Christ, 30.
Kingsley, C., 54.
Knox, John, 133.
Knut, 93.
Kublai Khan, 102.
Kyelang, 130.

LANGE, 125.
Languages of Africa, 209.
Lansing, Rev. Dr., 192.
Lapland, 93, 120.
Latrobe, 130.
Lawrence, Lord, 140.
Le Comte, 152.
Legge, Dr., 203.
Leibniz, 124.
Leicester, 157.
Leighton, 5.
Leipzig Missionary Society, 181.
Lerins Isles, 83.
Lery, 119.
Lightfoot, Dr., 52.
Lindisfarne, 70.
Lioba, 89.
Liudger, 91.
Livingstone, David, 176, 210, 213.
London, 61; Missionary Society, 166; Society for Jews, 174.
Lord, H., 139.
Loricæ, 70.
Love, Dr. John, 167.
Loyola, 113, 146.
Lullius, 102; *Ars*, 104; Mission, 106.
Lupus of Troyes, 83.
Luther, 110, 113.
Lütken, 124.
Luxeuil, 84.

MACAO, 153.
Macaulay, Z., 168.
Mack, 162.
Mackenzie, Colin, 140, 153.
Macleod, Norman, 188.
Madagascar, 210.

INDEX. 223

Madura Mission, 150; rites, 150.
Majorca, 105.
Maleach, Jehovah, 17.
Mankind and Missions, 194.
Maories, 208.
Marco Polo, 102.
Mark, 54.
Marshman, John, 162.
Marshman, Dr., 161.
Marshman, Mrs., 177.
Martin of Tours, 81.
Martyn, Henry, 106, 171, 213.
Mason, Dr., 179.
Masters, Streynsham, 140.
Mather, Cotton, 136.
Mauritius, 200.
Mayhews, 137.
Medical Missions, 176; Edinburgh Society, 176.
Melanchthon, 114.
Melchizedek, 10.
Melrose, 71.
Menezes, 151.
Messianic Psalms, 19.
Methodius, 96.
Michael Gustavus Adolphus, 120.
Michaelius, Jonas, 192.
Middleton, Bishop, 175.
Miesrob, 79.
Mills, S., 72, 178.
Milton, 4, 50, 136.
Missionaries, the first, 33; Scots, 85; Roman, 87, 146; Moravian, 130; woman, 177; medical, 177; total, 193; conferences, 216; literature, 213.
Missionary, the word, 1; the persons, 2; the call, 8, 212; the covenant, 11; the charge, 28; the prayer, 29; the Apocalypse, 43; the first triumph, 50; martyrs, 34, 107, 210; hymns, 34, 126; colleges, 55, 105, 125, 137; Institute, 55; sisterhoods, 65; doors, 132, 211; influence of East India Company, 144; agreement, 163; churches, 183; societies, 198; diagram, 195.
Missions, the subject, 1; the methods, 2, 148; the root, 16, 19; the history, 6, 27, 211; evidential value, 33; the statute book, 42; statistics, 52, 128, 193-199; to Mohammedans, 103; to Jews, 109, 174; in each country, 196.
Mitchell, Rev. D., 169.
Mitchell, Rev. James, 169.
Moffat, R., 168.

Mohammedanism, 56, 103.
Moheccans, 136.
Monachism, 145.
Moncreiff, Rev. Sir Henry, 170.
Monte Corvino, 108.
Moravian Missions, 97, 127, 130.
Moritz, 122.
Moses, 18.
Moulton, 156.
Muir, Sir W., 140.
Mungo, 61.
Murdoch, Dr., 174.
Museum of Alexandria, 54.

NATIONAL BIBLE SOCIETY, 173.
Nazareth, 206.
Neander, 73, 85, 212.
Nesbit, Rev. R., 169.
New Guinea, 208.
New Hebrides, 185.
New Zealand, 203.
Newell, S., 178.
Newton, Rev. J., 170.
Netherlands Missionary Society, 180.
Nicene Council, 58.
Nicene Creed, 58.
Nicobar Islands, 130.
Nile, 210.
Nilus, 98.
Ninian, 61.
Nitschmann, 129.
Niven, Rev. W., 188.
Nonconformists, 134.
Normans, 91.
North German Missionary Society, 181.
Northamptonshire, 155, 160.
Norway, 93.
Nott, S., 178.
Nottingham, 156.
Nuteschelle, 98.
Nyassa, Lake, 153, 176.

O'BECK, 142.
Ogilvie, Dr., 188.
Olaf the Saint, 94.
Olaf, Tryggvasson, 93.
Olga, 99.
Origen, 52.
Orissa, 165.
Ostrogoths, 77.
Otto of Bamberg, 98.
Owen, Rev. J., 172.
Oxenstierna, 120.

PAGANISM, 50, 58.
Pagell, 130.

Parables of the kingdom, 31.
Parker, Dr., 176.
Patagonia, 208.
Paterson, David, 177.
Paterson, Rev. J., 188.
Palestine, 9, 206.
Palladius, 62.
Pantænus, 55.
Patriarchates, The four, 53.
Patrick, 62.
Paraguay, 153.
Paul, 27, 35, 38.
Paulerspury, 157.
Paulinus, 74.
Pax Britannica, 23.
Pax Romana, 22.
Pearce, S., 157.
Peggs, Rev., 165.
Pentecost, 32.
Persecutions, 49.
Persia, 207.
Peter the Apostle, 34, 42.
Philip the Evangelist, 3.
Philippine Islands, 153.
Philo, 54.
Photius, 97.
Pietists, 123, 128.
Pike, Rev. G., 165.
Pilgrim Fathers, 134.
Pitt, 170.
Pittsburgh Synod, 191.
Pliny, 38.
Plütschau, 125.
Pococke, 122, 136.
Poland, 98.
Pomponia Græcina, 48.
Portugal, 151, 202.
Pothinus, 42, 81.
Prayer and Missions, 155, 203, 204.
Presbyterianism, 134, 184, 189.
Propaganda Institutions, 149.
Prophecy, 17, 18.
Primitive Methodists, 175.
Pratt, Josiah, 171.
Press, 180, 213.
Prideaux, 136.
Psalms, Messianic, 19.
Puritans, 134.

QUAKERS (*see* Friends).
Queen, 138.

RAHAB, 18.
Rajpootana, 188.
Raleigh, Sir W., 130.
Red Indians, 129, 134.
Reformation, 110, 121, 133.

Regensburg, 97.
Remigius, 82.
Revelation, Book of the, 43.
Rhenish Missionary Society, 181.
Ribaut, 119.
Ricci, 152.
Richier, 119.
Riedel, 180.
Ripa, 152.
Ritchie, Mr., 170.
Robert de Nobili, 148, 150.
Robinson, John, 134.
Roman Empire, 6, 21, 52; Missionaries, 87, 154.
Ross, Rev. J., 170.
Rubruquis, 102.
Rügen, 98.
Russia, 99, 201.
Ruth, 18.
Ryland, John, 156.

SAALBANK, 139.
Sandeman, Rev. D., 190.
Saracens, 100, 107.
Saxo Grammaticus, 99.
Schleswig-Holstein Missionary Society, 181.
Schmidt, Georg, 130.
Schotten klöster, 70.
Schultz, 141.
Schwarr, 180.
Schwartz, 141.
Scotland and Missions, 132, 167; Propagation Society, 133.
Scoto-Irish Church, 62, 85.
Scott, Thomas, 158, 171.
Scottish Missionary Society, 168.
Seeley, Prof., 218.
Seelye, Miss, M.D., 177.
Septuagint, 54.
Serampore, 162; Mission, 163.
Serapeum of Alexandria, 54, 58.
Sergeant, John, 137.
Severinus, 80.
Shaftesbury, Lord, 172.
Shoolbred, Dr., 189.
Shrubsole, W., 167.
Shweir, 206.
Siam, 205.
Sigtuna, 93.
Sisterhoods, 65.
Slavery, 127.
Slavs, 96.
Smith, Prof. T. 187.
Smith, Sydney, 184.
Societies for Woman's Missions, 177; American, 178; German, 181.

Society, Christian Knowledge, 125;
  Propagation, 125, 175; Baptist, 159,
  165; London, 166; Scottish and
  Glasgow, 168; Church Missionary,
  171; Bible and Tract, 172; Propaga-
  tion of Gospel among Jews, 174, 179;
  Wesleyan Methodist, 175; All, 198.
Solomon, 19.
Somerville, Rev. Dr., 169.
Sorbonne, 146.
South Seas, 208; America, 208.
Southey, 213.
Spangenberg, 129.
Spanish Missions, 153.
Spener, 123.
Spirit, Holy, 17, 32, 212, 218.
Stach, 129.
Star in the East, 26.
Statistics of Missions, 52, 128, 193-199.
Steere, Bishop, 176.
Steinkopff, 172.
Stephen the Martyr, 3, 34.
Stettin, 98.
Stevenson, Dr. Fleming, 189.
Straits Settlements, 200.
Sturm, 88.
Sutcliff, John, 156.
Swan, Mr., 169.
Sweden, 93.
Symeon, 53.
Synod of Cashel, 62; Whitby, 75.
Syria, 185.

Tacitus, 38.
Takawompbait, 137.
Tanganyika Lake, 153.
Tanjore, 125.
Teignmouth, Lord, 172.
Temple, Sir R., 217.
Tennyson, 35.
Terry, 140.
Tertullian, 61.
Thecla, 48.
Thekla, 89.
Theocracy, 15, 17.
Theodore of Canterbury, 76.
Theodosius, 58.
Theophilus, 53.
Tholuck, 129.
Thomas, 55.
Thomas, John, 160, 176.
Thomson, Rev. W. R., 170.
Tibetan Missions, 130, 200.
Timothy, 3.
Toleration, 33, 46, 57.
Tonsure, 75.

Torquemada, 109.
Tournon, Cardinal, 150, 152.
Tours, 82.
Tract Society, 172; American, 179.
Tradpert, 84.
Tranquebar, 125.
Tristram, Canon, 217.
Tryphæna, 48.
Tunis, 106.
Turks, 115, 205.
Tuticorin, 149.

UDNY, G., 142.
Ulfila, 78.
Unitas Fratrum, 127.
United Methodist Free Churches, 175.
United Original Secession Church, 190.
United Presbyterian Church, 169, 170, 188.
Universities Mission, 175.
Upsala, 79.
Ursinus, 124.
Uruguay, 208.

VALENTINUS, 80.
Vanderkemp, Dr., 180.
Venn, Henry, 171.
Verbeck, Dr., 204.
Vienne, Council of, 105.
Villegagnon, 119.
Virgilius, 70.
Visigoths, 77.
Vladimir's Baptism, 99.

WADDELL, H. M., 188.
Walæus, 122.
Wales, Presbyterian Church, 190.
Walpurga, 89.
Ward, 161.
Welz, 123.
Wellesley, Lord, 162.
Wenger, 172.
Wesleys, 138.
Wesleyan Missionary Society, 175.
West Indies, 208.
Western, 127.
Whitby Monastery, 76.
Whitby Synod, 75.
Whitefield, 138.
Wiclif, 112.
Wilberforce, 143.
Wilfrid of York, 75, 76.
Willehad, 91.
Willibrord, 70.

William the Conqueror, 94.
Williams College, 178.
Wilson, Captain James, 167.
Wilson, Dr. John, 76, 169, 213.
Wilson, Mrs. Margaret, 177.
Wilson, Mrs. (Miss Cooke), 177.
Winfrith, 86.
Wolff, Joseph, 174.
Wolsey, 146.
Women's Missions, 177.
Wood, Dr. John, 139.

XAVIER, F., 146.
Xavier, G., the nephew, 151.

YATES, 172.
York, 73.

ZAMBESI, 210.
Zanana agencies, 177, 187.
Zeisberger, 129.
Ziegenbalg, 125.
Zinzendorf, 127.

Just published, in crown 8vo, price 5s.,

EXEGETICAL STUDIES.

By PATON J. GLOAG, D.D.,

AUTHOR OF 'A COMMENTARY ON THE ACTS OF THE APOSTLES,' ETC.

CONTENTS.—I. Blasphemy against the Holy Ghost. II. Our Lord's Blessing to Peter. III. Salted with Fire. IV. The Women at the Cross. V. The Groaning Creation. VI. Saved as by Fire. VII. Women veiled because of the Angels. VIII. Baptism for the Dead. IX. Paul's Thorn in the Flesh. X. Duality of Mediation and Unity of God. XI. The Complement of Christ's Sufferings. XII. Exaltation of the Poor and Humiliation of the Rich. XIII. The Indwelling Spirit lusteth to Envy. XIV. The Spirits in Prison. XV. Christian Perfection. XVI. The Threefold Testimony.

BY THE SAME AUTHOR.

In crown 8vo, price 7s. 6d.,

THE MESSIANIC PROPHECIES

(Being the 'Baird Lecture' for 1879).

'We regard Dr. Gloag's book as a valuable contribution to theological literature. We have not space to give the extended notice which its intrinsic excellence demands, and must content ourselves with cordially recommending it.'—*Spectator.*

In demy 8vo, price 12s.,

INTRODUCTION TO THE PAULINE EPISTLES.

'This introduction to St. Paul's Epistles is a capital book, full, scholarly, and clear; ... no difficulty is shirked or overlooked,'but dealt with fairly and in an evangelical spirit. To ministers and theological students it will be of great value.'—*Evangelical Magazine.*

In Two Volumes, demy 8vo, price 21s.,

A CRITICAL AND EXEGETICAL COMMENTARY
ON THE
ACTS OF THE APOSTLES.

'The Commentary of Dr. Gloag I procured on its first appearance, and have examined it with special care. For my purposes I have found it unsurpassed by any similar work in the English language. It shows a thorough mastery of the material, philology, history, and literature pertaining to this range of study, and a skill in the use of this knowledge which (if I have any right to judge) place it in the first class of modern expositions.'—H. B. HACKETT, D.D.

In Two Volumes ex. 8vo, price 28s.,

THE DOCTRINE OF SACRED SCRIPTURE:

A CRITICAL, HISTORICAL, AND DOGMATIC INQUIRY INTO THE ORIGIN AND NATURE OF THE OLD AND NEW TESTAMENTS.

By GEORGE T. LADD, D.D.

'This work is one which will certainly be studied by all scientific theologians, and the general reader will probably find here a better summary of the whole subject than in any other work or series of works.'—*Church Bells.*

'This important work is pre-eminently adapted for students, and treats in an exhaustive manner nearly every important subject of Biblical criticism which is agitating the religious mind at the present day.'—*Contemporary Review.*

'These massive volumes give us the most extensive, elaborate, and thorough-going work upon this doctrine which has ever been produced. . . . The author had made years of preparation for his work. He was determined to accomplish it thoroughly. He has endeavoured to be exhaustive, and as complete as human work can be.'—*Presbyterian Review.*

In ex. crown 8vo, price 7s. 6d.,

BIBLICAL STUDY;

ITS PRINCIPLES, METHODS, AND HISTORY.

Together with a Catalogue of Books of Reference.

By C. A. BRIGGS, D.D.

With Introduction by A. B. BRUCE, D.D.

'Dr. Briggs is one of the ablest, most learned, and in the best sense most progressive of the younger Biblical scholars of America. . . . In an eminent degree he combines the historical spirit with its reverence and learning, and the scientific spirit with its freedom and candour. . . . We have great pleasure in recommending his work to the notice of all Biblical students.'—*Nonconformist.*

'Written by one who has made himself a master of the subject, and who is able to write upon it both with the learning of the scholar and the earnestness of sincere conviction. . . . Is deserving of a cordial reception from Biblical students in this country.'—*Scotsman.*

In demy 8vo, price 9s.,

A POPULAR INTRODUCTION
TO THE
HISTORY OF CHRISTIAN DOCTRINE.

By Rev. T. C. CRIPPEN.

'The present work provides for a large constituency, who, we hope, will avail themselves of the information here made available to them for the first time.'—*Methodist Recorder.*

'The essence of a whole library is included in Mr. Crippen's work. . . . It is a scholarly work, and must have entailed an incalculable amount of research and discrimination.'—*Clergyman's Magazine.*

'If this book can be made known widely, we feel satisfied that it will be as widely used and valued. It is easy for reference, and the Appendices contain most valuable summaries of exceedingly important matters. The whole scope of Christian doctrine is more or less covered by this compendious history.'—*Christian World.*

In crown 8vo, price 6s.,

STUDIES IN THE CHRISTIAN EVIDENCES.

By ALEXANDER MAIR, D.D.

'Dr. Mair writes as one who has fully assimilated the various elements which enter into the category of Christian Evidences; and he has presented them in these pages with an order and accuracy, and a clearness, rising at times into a sober and chastened eloquence, which will make the work one of the highest value to the student.'—*Literary Churchman.*

'An admirable popular introduction to the study of the evidences.'—*Baptist.*

'Dr. Mair's work is one of the most useful for its purpose of any we have seen.'—*Church Bells.*

'One of the very best works we have perused on the subjects therein treated.'—*Evangelical Magazine.*

In demy 8vo, price 10s. 6d.,

THE LORD'S PRAYER:
A PRACTICAL MEDITATION.

By NEWMAN HALL, LL.B.

'A new volume of theological literature by the Rev. Newman Hall is sure to be eagerly welcomed, and we can promise its readers that they will not be disappointed. . . . A very able and suggestive volume.'—*Nonconformist.*

'This work will prove a help to many. Its devotional element is robust and practical.'—*Churchman.*

'Mr. Hall's thoughts are sharply cut, and are like crystals in their clearness. . . . Short, crisp sentences, absolute in form and lucid in thought, convey the author's meaning and carry on his exposition.'—*British Quarterly Review.*

'We heartily commend this able as well as earnest, exegetical as well as spiritual, volume to all our readers.'—*Evangelical Magazine.*

In crown 8vo, price 6s.,

CHRISTIAN CHARITY IN THE ANCIENT CHURCH.

By G. UHLHORN, D.D.

Translated with the Author's sanction.

'A very excellent translation of a very valuable book.'—*Guardian.*

'This book is a careful and learned monograph on a subject which is always interesting.'—*Academy.*

'It is without hesitation that we recommend this admirable treatise, which will amply repay perusal. Its intention is excellent, its subject momentous, its arguments are solid, its style winning, and its learning beyond dispute.'—*Tablet.*

In demy 8vo, price 10s. 6d.,

LECTURES,
CHIEFLY EXPOSITORY,
ON
ST. PAUL'S EPISTLES TO THE THESSALONIANS.

With Notes and Illustrations.

By JOHN HUTCHISON, D.D.

'We have read this book with real interest, and we are sure that it will furnish much help to clergymen who may undertake the work of expository preaching, and that both clergymen and laymen will find it helpful and edifying.'—*Church Bells.*

'Models of pulpit exposition.... Would that we had many expositions as thoughtful and scholarly as Dr. Hutchison's.'—*Methodist Recorder.*

'To the working minister this work supplies an admirable model, and to the unprofessional reader it will be pleasant and profitable for instruction.'—*Outlook.*

In crown 8vo, price 5s.,

MODERN PHYSICS:
STUDIES HISTORICAL AND PHILOSOPHICAL.

By ERNEST NAVILLE.

'A work so remarkably able is sure to be heartily welcomed by scientific students... Christian scientists should at once procure this learned and able volume.'—*Evangelical Magazine.*

'We have M. Naville in this present work at his very best.... He is peculiarly clear and cogent in his treatment.'—*Presbyterian Churchman.*

HERZOG'S
BIBLICAL ENCYCLOPÆDIA.

'A well designed, meritorious work, on which neither industry nor expense has been spared.'—*Guardian.*

'This certainly is a remarkable work. . . . It will be one without which no general or theological or biographical library will be complete.'—*Freeman.*

'The need of such a work as this must be very often felt, and it ought to find its way into all college libraries, and into many private studies.'—*Christian World.*

Now complete, in Three Vols. imp. 8vo, price 24s. each,

ENCYCLOPÆDIA OR DICTIONARY
OF
BIBLICAL, HISTORICAL, AND PRACTICAL THEOLOGY.

Based on the Real Encyklopadie of Herzog, Plitt, and Hauck.

EDITED BY PHILIP SCHAFF, D.D., LL.D.

Now complete, in Four Vols. imp. 8vo, price 18s. each,

COMMENTARY ON THE NEW TESTAMENT.
With Illustrations and Maps.

EDITED BY PHILIP SCHAFF, D.D., LL.D.

Volume I.	*Volume II.*
THE SYNOPTICAL GOSPELS.	ST. JOHN'S GOSPEL AND THE ACTS OF THE APOSTLES.
Volume III.	*Volume IV.*
ROMANS to PHILEMON.	HEBREWS to REVELATION.

In ex. demy 8vo, price 12s.,

THE PHILOSOPHICAL BASIS OF THEISM:
AN EXAMINATION OF THE PERSONALITY OF MAN TO ASCERTAIN HIS CAPACITY TO KNOW AND SERVE GOD, AND THE VALIDITY OF THE PRINCIPLES UNDERLYING THE DEFENCE OF THEISM.

By SAMUEL HARRIS, D.D., LL.D.

'The whole volume will be found, by all who are interested in its subject full of suggestive thought, and of real assistance in unfolding to the mind the true account and justification of its religious knowledge.'—*Spectator.*

'The course pursued by the author of this book is a very exhaustive and satisfactory one. . . . His book is a singularly able treatise on the subject and a kind of cyclopædia of reference to its literature.'—*Courant.*

Just published, in demy 8vo, price 10s. 6d.,

THE THEORY OF MORALS.

By PAUL JANET,
MEMBER OF THE INSTITUTE, PARIS.

TRANSLATED FROM THE LATEST FRENCH EDITION.

CONTENTS.—*Book First*—1. Pleasure and Good. 2. Good and Law. 3. The Principle of Excellence, or of Perfection. 4. The Principle of Happiness. 5. Impersonal Goods. 6. The True, the Good, and the Beautiful. 7. Absolute Good. *Book Second*—1. Nature and Basis of the Moral Law. 2. Good and Duty. 3. Definite and Indefinite Duties. 4. Right and Duty. 5. Division of Duties. 6. Conflict of Duties. *Book Third*—1. The Moral Consciousness. 2. Moral Intention. 3. Moral Probabilism. 4. Universality of Moral Principles. 5. The Moral Sentiment. 6. Liberty. 7. Kant's Theory of Liberty. 8. Virtue. 9. Moral Progress. 10. Sin. 11. Merit and Demerit—The Sanctions of the Moral Law. 12. Religion.

BY THE SAME AUTHOR.

In demy 8vo, Second Edition, price 12s.,

FINAL CAUSES.

TRANSLATED FROM THE FRENCH BY WILLIAM AFFLECK, B.D.

'This very learned, accurate, and, within its prescribed limits, exhaustive work. . . . The book as a whole abounds in matter of the highest interest, and is a model of learning and judicious treatment.'—*Guardian.*

'Illustrated and defended with an ability and learning which must command the reader's admiration.'—*Dublin Review.*

'A great contribution to the literature of this subject. M. Janet has mastered the conditions of the problem, is at home in the literature of science and philosophy; . . . in clearness, vigour, and depth it has been seldom equalled, and more seldom excelled, in philosophical literature.'—*Spectator.*

'A wealth of scientific knowledge and a logical acumen which will win the admiration of every reader.'—*Church Quarterly Review.*

In demy 8vo, price 10s. 6d.,

THE BIBLE DOCTRINE OF MAN.

(SEVENTH SERIES OF CUNNINGHAM LECTURES.)

By JOHN LAIDLAW, D.D.

'An important and valuable contribution to the discussion of the anthropology of the sacred writings; perhaps the most considerable that has appeared in our own language.'—*Literary Churchman.*

'The work is a thoughtful contribution to a subject which must always have deep interest for the devout student of the Bible.'—*British Quarterly Review.*

'Dr. Laidlaw's work is scholarly, able, interesting, and valuable. . . . Thoughtful and devout minds will find much to stimulate, and not a little to assist, their meditations in this learned and, let us add, charmingly printed volume.'—*Record.*

Professor LUTHARDT'S WORKS.

In Three handsome crown 8vo Volumes, price 6s. each.

'We do not know any volumes so suitable in these times for young men entering on life, or, let us say, even for the library of a pastor called to deal with such, than the three volumes of this series. We commend the whole of them with the utmost cordial satisfaction. They are altogether quite a specialty in our literature.'—*Weekly Review.*

Apologetic Lectures on the Fundamental Truths of Christianity. *Sixth Edition.* By C. E. LUTHARDT, D.D., Leipzig.

Apologetic Lectures on the Saving Truths of Christianity. *Fourth Edition.*

Apologetic Lectures on the Moral Truths of Christianity. *Third Edition.*

In demy 8vo, price 9s.,

St. John the Author of the Fourth Gospel. Translated and the Literature enlarged by C. R. GREGORY, Leipzig.

'A work of thoroughness and value. The translator has added a lengthy Appendix, containing a very complete account of the literature bearing on the controversy respecting this Gospel. The Indices which close the volume are well ordered, and add greatly to its value.'—*Guardian.*

Crown 8vo, 5s.,

Luthardt, Kahnis, and Brückner.
The Church: Its Origin, its History, and its Present Position.

'A comprehensive review of this sort, done by able hands, is both instructive and suggestive.'—*Record.*

HISTORY OF THE CHRISTIAN CHURCH.

By PHILIP SCHAFF, D.D., LL.D.

A New Edition thoroughly Revised and Enlarged.

Now Ready,

Section First—APOSTOLIC CHRISTIANITY, A.D. 1-100. In Two Vols. ex. demy 8vo, price 21s.

Section Second—ANTE-NICENE CHRISTIANITY, A.D. 100-311. In Two Vols. ex. demy 8vo, price 21s.

Section Third—NICENE AND POST-NICENE CHRISTIANITY, A.D. 311-600. In Two Vols. ex. demy 8vo, price 21s.

'For a genuine healthy Christian criticism, which boldly faces difficulties, and examines them with equal candour and learning, we commend this work to all who are interested in investigating the early growth of the Christian Church.'—*Church Quarterly Review.*

'These volumes cannot fail to prove welcome to all students.'—*Freeman.*

'No student, and indeed no critic, can with fairness overlook a work like the present, written with such evident candour, and, at the same time, with so thorough a knowledge of the sources of early Christian history.'—*Scotsman.*

In Three Volumes, demy 8vo, price 12s. each,

A HISTORY OF THE COUNCILS OF THE CHURCH.

FROM THE ORIGINAL DOCUMENTS.

TRANSLATED FROM THE GERMAN OF
C. J. HEFELE, D.D., BISHOP OF ROTTENBURG.

VOL. I. (*Second Edition*) TO A.D. 325.
By REV. PREBENDARY CLARK.

VOL. II. A.D. 326 TO 429.
By H. N. OXENHAM, M.A.

VOL. III. A.D. 429 TO THE CLOSE OF THE COUNCIL OF CHALCEDON.

'This careful translation of Hefele's Councils.'—Dr. PUSEY.

'A thorough and fair compendium, put in a most accessible and intelligent orm.'—*Guardian.*

'A work of profound erudition, and written in a most candid spirit. The book will be a standard work on the subject.'—*Spectator.*

'The most learned historian of the Councils.'—*Père Gratry.*

'We cordially commend Hefele's Councils to the English student.'—*John Bull.*

In demy 8vo, Third Edition, price 10s. 6d.,

THE TRAINING OF THE TWELVE;

OR,

EXPOSITION OF PASSAGES IN THE GOSPELS EXHIBITING THE TWELVE DISCIPLES OF JESUS UNDER DISCIPLINE FOR THE APOSTLESHIP.

BY

A. B. BRUCE, D.D.,

PROFESSOR OF DIVINITY, FREE CHURCH COLLEGE, GLASGOW.

'Here we have a really great book on an important, large, and attractive subject—a book full of loving, wholesome, profound thoughts about the fundamentals of Christian faith and practice.'—*British and Foreign Evangelical Review.*

'It is some five or six years since this work first made its appearance, and now that a second edition has been called for, the author has taken the opportunity to make some alterations which are likely to render it still more acceptable. Substantially, however, the book remains the same, and the hearty commendation with which we noted its first issue applies to it at least as much now.'—*Rock.*

BY THE SAME AUTHOR.

In demy 8vo, Second Edition, price 10s. 6d.,

THE HUMILIATION OF CHRIST,

IN ITS PHYSICAL, ETHICAL, AND OFFICIAL ASPECTS.

SIXTH SERIES OF CUNNINGHAM LECTURES.

'These lectures are able and deep-reaching to a degree not often found in the religious literature of the day; withal, they are fresh and suggestive. . . . The learning and the deep and sweet spirituality of this discussion will commend it to many faithful students of the truth as it is in Jesus.'—*Congregationalist.*

'We have not for a long time met with a work so fresh and suggestive as this of Professor Bruce. . . . We do not know where to look at our English Universities for a treatise so calm, logical, and scholarly.'—*English Independent.*

In Three Vols. 8vo, price £1, 11s. 6d.,

A HISTORY OF CHRISTIAN DOCTRINES.

TRANSLATED FROM THE FIFTH AND LAST GERMAN EDITION OF
DR. K. R. HAGENBACH
(*With Additions from other Sources*).

'It possesses an almost unique value as a history of Christian dogma. We have no English work that can be compared with it.'—*British Quarterly Review.*

'It is superfluous to commend a work which has been of such great service.'—*English Churchman.*

BY THE SAME AUTHOR.
In Two Volumes, demy 8vo., price 21s.,

HISTORY OF THE REFORMATION
IN
GERMANY AND SWITZERLAND CHIEFLY.

Translated from the Fourth Revised Edition of the German.

'We highly appreciate for the most part the skill and the proportion, the vivid portraiture and fine discrimination, and the careful philosophic development of ideas by which this most readable and instructive work is characterised.'—*Evangelical Magazine.*

'Dr. Hagenbach undoubtedly has in an eminent degree many of the higher qualifications of a historian. He is accurate, candid, and impartial; and his insight into the higher springs of the Reformation is only equalled by his thorough knowledge of the outward progress of that movement.'—*Scotsman.*

BY THE SAME AUTHOR.
In demy 8vo, price 9s.,

GERMAN RATIONALISM

IN ITS RISE, PROGRESS, AND DECLINE. A CONTRIBUTION TO THE CHURCH HISTORY OF THE 18th AND 19th CENTURIES.

'This is a volume we have long wished to see in our language. Hagenbach is a veteran in this field, and this volume is the ablest, and is likely to be the most useful of his works.'—*British Quarterly Review.*

In Two Volumes, demy 8vo, price 21s.,

COMMENTARY ON ST. PAUL'S EPISTLE TO THE ROMANS.

BY FRIEDRICH ADOLPH PHILIPPI.
Translated from the Third Improved and Enlarged Edition.

'A serviceable addition to the Foreign Theological Library.'—*Academy.*

'A commentary not only ample for its critical stores, but also valuable for its sober exegesis.'—*John Bull.*

'If the writer is inferior to Meyer in critical acumen, he is at least equal to him in theological learning and religious insight; and his commentary has independent worth—it is no mere repetition of other men's labours.'—*Church Bells.*

In One large 8vo Volume, Ninth English Edition, price 15s.,

A TREATISE ON THE GRAMMAR OF NEW TESTAMENT GREEK,

REGARDED AS THE BASIS OF NEW TESTAMENT EXEGESIS.

TRANSLATED FROM THE GERMAN OF DR. B. G. WINER.

With large additions and full Indices. Third Edition, Edited by Rev. W. F. MOULTON, D.D., one of the New Testament Translation Revisers.

'We need not say it is *the* Grammar of the New Testament. It is not only superior to all others, but *so* superior as to be by common consent the one work of reference on the subject. No other could be mentioned with it.'—*Literary Churchman.*

In demy 8vo, price 8s. 6d.,

SYNTAX OF THE HEBREW LANGUAGE OF THE OLD TESTAMENT.

BY HEINRICH EWALD.

TRANSLATED FROM THE EIGHTH GERMAN EDITION BY JAMES KENNEDY, B.D.

'The work stands unique as regards a patient investigation of facts, written with a profound analysis of the laws of thought, of which language is the reflection. Another striking feature of the work is the regularly progressive order which pervades the whole. The author proceeds by a natural gradation from the simplest elements to the most complex forms.'—*British Quarterly Review.*

'It is well known that Ewald was the first to exhibit the Hebrew Syntax in a philosophical form, and his Grammar is the most important of his numerous works.'—*Athenæum.*

In demy 8vo, Sixth Edition, price 7s. 6d.,

AN INTRODUCTORY HEBREW GRAMMAR;

WITH PROGRESSIVE EXERCISES IN READING AND WRITING.

BY A. B. DAVIDSON, M.A., LL.D.,
Professor of Hebrew, etc., in the New College, Edinburgh.

In Twenty handsome 8vo Volumes, Subscription price £5, 5s.,

MEYER'S
COMMENTARY ON THE NEW TESTAMENT.

'Meyer has been long and well known to scholars as one of the very ablest of the German expositors of the New Testament. We are not sure whether we ought not to say that he is unrivalled as an interpreter of the grammatical and historical meaning of the sacred writers. The Publishers have now rendered another seasonable and important service to English students in producing this translation.'—*Guardian.*

(Yearly Issue of Four Volumes, 21s.)
Each Volume will be sold separately at 10s. 6d. to Non-Subscribers.

CRITICAL AND EXEGETICAL
COMMENTARY ON THE NEW TESTAMENT.
ST. MATTHEW'S GOSPEL TO JUDE.

By Dr. H. A. W. MEYER,
OBERCONSISTORIALRATH, HANNOVER.

First Year.—Romans, Two Volumes; Galatians, One Volume; St. John's Gospel, Vol. I. **Second Year.**—St. John's Gospel, Vol. II.; Philippians and Colossians, One Volume; Acts of the Apostles, Vol. I.; Corinthians, Vol. I. **Third Year.**—Acts of the Apostles, Vol. II.; St. Matthew's Gospel, Two Volumes; Corinthians, Vol. II. **Fourth Year.**—Mark and Luke, Two Volumes; Ephesians and Philemon, One Volume; Thessalonians, One Volume (*Dr. Lünemann*). **Fifth Year.**—Timothy and Titus, One Volume (*Dr. Huther*); Peter and Jude, One Volume (*Dr. Huther*); Hebrews, One Volume (*Dr. Lünemann*); James and John, One Volume (*Dr. Huther*).

The series, as written by Meyer himself, is completed by the publication of Ephesians with Philemon in one volume. But to this the Publishers have thought it right to add Thessalonians and Hebrews, by Dr. Lünemann, and the Pastoral and Catholic Epistles, by Dr. Huther.

'I need hardly add that the last edition of the accurate, perspicuous, and learned commentary of Dr. Meyer has been most carefully consulted throughout; and I must again, as in the preface to the Galatians, avow my great obligations to the acumen and scholarship of the learned editor.'—BISHOP ELLICOTT *in Preface to his* 'Commentary on Ephesians.'

'The ablest grammatical exegete of the age.'—PHILIP SCHAFF, D.D.

'In accuracy of scholarship and freedom from prejudice, he is equalled by few.'—*Literary Churchman.*

'We have only to repeat that it remains, of its own kind, the very best commentary of the New Testament which we possess.'—*Church Bells.*

'No exegetical work is on the whole more valuable, or stands in higher public esteem. As a critic he is candid and cautious; exact to minuteness in philology; a master of the grammatical and historical method of interpretation.'—*Princeton Review.*

WORKS BY DR. I. A. DORNER.

In Three Volumes, 8vo, price 10s. 6d. each,

A SYSTEM OF CHRISTIAN DOCTRINE.

'A monument of thoughtfulness and labour.'—*Literary Churchman.*

'Dorner's "System of Christian Doctrine" is likely to prove, when completed, his most masterly and profound work. . . . Great thanks are due to Mr. Cave for the pains and the skill he has so conscientiously expended on this magnificent work.'—*Baptist Magazine.*

In Five Volumes, 8vo, price £2, 12s. 6d.,

HISTORY OF THE DEVELOPMENT OF THE DOCTRINE OF THE PERSON OF CHRIST.

'So great a mass of learning and thought so ably set forth has never before been presented to English readers, at least on this subject.'—*Journal of Sacred Literature.*

In Two Volumes, 8vo, price 21s.,

HISTORY OF PROTESTANT THEOLOGY,
PARTICULARLY IN GERMANY,
VIEWED ACCORDING TO ITS FUNDAMENTAL MOVEMENT, AND IN CONNECTION WITH THE RELIGIOUS, MORAL, AND INTELLECTUAL LIFE.

With a Preface to the Translation by the Author.

'This masterly work of Dr. Dorner, so successfully rendered into English by the present translators, will more than sustain the reputation he has already achieved by his exhaustive and, as it seems to us, conclusive *History of the Development of Doctrine respecting the Person of Christ.*'—*Spectator.*

PROFESSOR GODET'S WORKS.

In Three Volumes, 8vo, price 31s. 6d.,

A COMMENTARY ON THE GOSPEL OF ST. JOHN.

By F. GODET, D.D.,
PROFESSOR OF THEOLOGY, NEUCHATEL.

'This work forms one of the battle-fields of modern inquiry, and is itself so rich in spiritual truth, that it is impossible to examine it too closely; and we welcome this treatise from the pen of Dr. Godet. We have no more competent exegete; and this new volume shows all the learning and vivacity for which the author is distinguished.'—*Freeman.*

In Two Volumes, 8vo, price 21s.,

A COMMENTARY ON THE GOSPEL OF ST. LUKE.

TRANSLATED FROM THE SECOND FRENCH EDITION.

'Marked by clearness and good sense, it will be found to possess value and interest as one of the most recent and copious works specially designed to illustrate this Gospel.'—*Guardian.*

In Two Volumes, 8vo, price 21s.,

A COMMENTARY ON ST. PAUL'S EPISTLE TO THE ROMANS.

'We prefer this commentary to any other we have seen on the subject. ... We have great pleasure in recommending it as not only rendering invaluable aid in the critical study of the text, but affording practical and deeply suggestive assistance in the exposition of the doctrine.'—*British and Foreign Evangelical Review.*

'Here indeed we have rare spiritual insight and sanctified scholarship.'—*Weekly Review.*

Just published, Second Edition, in crown 8vo, price 6s.,

DEFENCE OF THE CHRISTIAN FAITH.

TRANSLATED BY THE HON. AND REV. W. H. LYTTELTON.

'Will at once take rank with the ablest works on Christian evidences. ... The work, wherever known, must be appreciated.'—*Baptist Magazine.*

www.ingramcontent.com/pod-product-compliance
Lightning Source LLC
Chambersburg PA
CBHW032222230426
43666CB00033B/591